Education, Psychoanalysis, and Social Transformation

Series Editors:

jan jagodzinski, University of Alberta
Mark Bracher, Kent State University

The purpose of this series is to develop and disseminate psychoanalytic knowledge that can help educators in their pursuit of three core functions of education:
1. facilitating student learning,
2. fostering students' personal development, and
3. promoting prosocial attitudes, habits, and behaviors in students (i.e., those opposed to violence, substance abuse, racism, sexism, homophobia, etc.).

Psychoanalysis can help educators realize these aims of education by providing them with important insights into:
1. the emotional and cognitive capacities that are necessary for students to be able to learn, develop, and engage in prosocial behavior,
2. the motivations that drive such learning, development, and behaviors, and
3. the motivations that produce antisocial behaviors as well as resistance to learning and development.

Such understanding can enable educators to develop pedagogical strategies and techniques to help students overcome psychological impediments to learning and development, either by identifying and removing the impediments or by helping students develop the ability to overcome them. Moreover, by offering an understanding of the motivations that cause some of our most severe social problems—including crime, violence, substance abuse, prejudice, and inequality—together with knowledge of how such motivations can be altered, books in this series will contribute to the reduction and prevention of such problems, a task that education is increasingly being called upon to assume.

Radical Pedagogy: Identity, Generativity, and Social Transformation
By Mark Bracher

Teaching the Rhetoric of Resistance: The Popular Holocaust and Social Change in a Post 9/11 World
By Robert Samuels

Television and Youth Culture: Televised Paranoia
By jan jagodzinski

Psychopedagogy: Freud, Lacan, and the Psychoanalytic Theory of Education
By K. Daniel Cho

New Media, Cultural Studies, and Critical Theory after Postmodernism: Automodernity from Zizek to Laclau
By Robert Samuels

Visual Art and Education in an Era of Designer Capitalism: Deconstructing the Oral Eye
By jan jagodzinski

A Deleuzian Approach to Curriculum: Essays on a Pedagogical Life
By Jason J. Wallin

A Therapeutic Approach to Teaching Poetry: Individual Development, Psychology, and Social Reparation
By Todd O. Williams

A Therapeutic Approach to Teaching Poetry

Individual Development, Psychology, and Social Reparation

Todd O. Williams

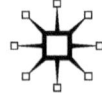

A THERAPEUTIC APPROACH TO TEACHING POETRY
Copyright © Todd O. Williams, 2012.
Softcover reprint of the hardcover 1st edition 2012 978-0-230-34040-4
All rights reserved.

First published in 2012 by
PALGRAVE MACMILLAN®
in the United States—a division of St. Martin's Press LLC,
175 Fifth Avenue, New York, NY 10010.

Where this book is distributed in the UK, Europe and the rest of the world, this is by Palgrave Macmillan, a division of Macmillan Publishers Limited, registered in England, company number 785998, of Houndmills, Basingstoke, Hampshire RG21 6XS.

Palgrave Macmillan is the global academic imprint of the above companies and has companies and representatives throughout the world.

Palgrave® and Macmillan® are registered trademarks in the United States, the United Kingdom, Europe and other countries.

ISBN 978-1-349-34298-3   ISBN 978-1-137-10203-4 (eBook)
DOI 10.1057/9781137102034

Library of Congress Cataloging-in-Publication Data

Williams, Todd O.
   A therapeutic approach to teaching poetry : individual development, psychology, and social reparation / by Todd O. Williams.
      p. cm.—(Psychoanalysis, education, and social transformation)
   Includes bibliographical references.

   1. Poetry—Study and teaching. 2. Poetry—Authorship. 3. Poetry—Therapeutic use. I. Title.

PN1101.W47 2012
808.1071'2—dc23   2011049930

A catalogue record of the book is available from the British Library.

Design by Newgen Imaging Systems (P) Ltd., Chennai, India.

First edition: June 2012

To Amber

CONTENTS

Acknowledgments ix

Introduction: The Therapeutic Value of Poetry xi

One	Gaining Awareness and Overcoming Defenses	1
Two	(Neuro) Psychoanalytic Regression and Integration	17
Three	The Teacher as (Whole, Useful, and Permanent) Object	37
Four	The Poem as (Self-, Transformational, Transitional, and Reparative) Object	55
Five	A Poetry Therapy Model for the Classroom	75
Six	Cultivating Empathy: Wordsworth's *Lyrical Ballads*	93
Seven	A Reparative Text: Tennyson's *In Memoriam*	107
Eight	Integrating Experience: Morris's *The Defence of Guenevere and Other Poems*	123
Nine	Desire and Reparation: Rossetti's *Goblin Market and Other Poems*	137

Notes 151

Works Cited 159

Index 169

Acknowledgments

Thank you to Mark Bracher for your advice, support, and inspiration. I also want to thank everyone at Palgrave Macmillan who worked to bring this project about. I want to thank all of the teachers over the years who have shaped me as a teacher, writer, and scholar. Thanks to Amber for proofreading, editing, and indexing. A big thanks to Lou Rivera for fixing my computer twice during this process and saving me from disaster. Thank you to the Kent State and Kutztown libraries, especially the ILL departments.

Thank you to Patricia Donahue at *Reader*; my introduction is a revised version of "The Therapeutic Value of Poetry for Students and Readers." *Reader: Essays in Reader-Oriented Theory, Criticism, and Pedagogy* 58/59 (Winter 2010): 78–96.

Thank you to Nick Mazza at the *Journal of Poetry Therapy* published by the Taylor and Francis Group; chapter five is a revision of "A Poetry Therapy Model for the Literature Classroom." *Journal of Poetry Therapy* 24.1 (March 2011): 17–33.

Finally, thank you to Florence Boos, Patrick O'Sullivan, and Rosie Miles of the William Morris Society; chapter eight builds on "Teaching Morris's Early Dream Poems through the Three Registers." *Journal of William Morris Studies* 17.2 (Summer 2007): 99–114.

Introduction: The Therapeutic Value of Poetry

Teachers of literature often encourage intellectual development and affective maturation in students. However, the potential of an approach to literary studies that is grounded in therapeutic practice remains largely untapped.[1] The goal of *A Therapeutic Approach to Teaching Poetry* is to make the study of poetry more valuable both for students and for society. Students and readers of literature already experience personal and social benefits from texts, but this book seeks to maximize the developmental potential of poetry in the classroom by enacting classroom practices that help students develop a greater awareness of themselves and others. Though the therapeutic value of poetry has long been recognized, this book offers strategies to maximize its benefits in the classroom.

Poetry offers students the opportunity to increase their self-awareness by helping them examine their experiences in terms of affects and images as well as language. Reading poetry enables students to have new thoughts, perceptions, and affective experiences that can benefit them greatly. The study of poetry can also validate affective experiences, particularly painful ones that are often repressed. This can help students to realistically cope with negative aspects of reality. Poems can be used to cultivate empathy as they bring readers into the experiences of various others. Poems can serve as loving external objects that help students repair negative attitudes toward the world that stifle their potential for effecting social change. And, poems stimulate imagination and creativity in students, which they can apply to other aspects of their lives. If we encourage students to relate to poems affectively, imaginatively, empathetically, and creatively, we can help them achieve the goals of experiencing personal renewal and developing a more positive, proactive relationship to the world. These positive personal changes that studying poetry can bring about are also all prerequisites for social transformation on a larger scale.

I use the concepts of renewal and reparation to describe my ultimate goals for this pedagogical approach. Renewal refers to the development of an open sense of self that is both strong and flexible. It involves a deepening self-awareness within the three registers of experience: affective, imagistic, and linguistic. The affective register refers to emotions and visceral, bodily experiences; the imagistic refers to images and image sequences (fantasies) formed in the mind; the linguistic refers to language and culturally agreed-upon symbols used to communicate and think.[2] Students are typically taught to read and experience poetry strictly in terms of linguistic meaning, but when students learn to pay attention to their experience of poetry through all three registers and begin to analyze their experiences, they become better integrated and more self-aware. They become more open to the way new experiences enable them to develop. With a clear understanding of one's identity in place, the renewed and renewing self is better able to avoid political and social manipulations, and is in tune with creative potentials that allow for new and better possibilities for the self and for the world.

Reparation refers to the ongoing ability to locate good, supportive objects in the world that enable one to maintain hope without becoming unrealistic. These objects may be other people whom we form important relationships with, or they may be other kinds of external objects, for example, a poem or a work of art. Reparation also necessarily involves developing empathy and a deeper awareness of one's relationships with others. Poems can serve students as good objects when they reflect familiar experiences back to them. When students find understanding and recognition of their own painful emotions in a text, they feel support and a sense of normalcy. The support that poems offer can give one hope in a chaotic and violent world. Only when we repair our relationship to the external world will we then be prepared to take action to make things better. Not only do poems make us more aware of who we are, but they also make us more comfortable with that awareness. Poems also make us more aware of others.[3] When we read the experiences of others in a poetic text, we feel empathy with them. The empathy that poems offer proves imperative to social justice. We must become aware of ourselves as socially dependent beings, and learn to feel compassion for others in their suffering if we will ever be able to improve material reality.

A Therapeutic Approach to Teaching Poetry explains how the study of poetry, by providing experiences similar to those produced by poetry therapy, can help students discover themselves and develop their potentials to effect change in the world. This pedagogy draws on a number of theoretical and therapeutic models including poetry therapy, psychoanalysis, experiential therapy, metaphor therapy, cognitive science, and neuroscience. This approach to teaching poetry is founded on the belief that education should not only develop students' skills in analysis and communication but also promote self-awareness and social responsibility. This book provides an innovative pedagogical strategy for promoting the development of individuals who can live more personally fulfilling, productive, and socially responsible lives.

From poetry therapy's emergence as a field in the late 1960s, its practitioners have applied poetry to psychotherapy and used it in therapeutic practice.[4] *A Therapeutic Approach to Teaching Poetry* proposes the application of therapy to the way we understand and teach poetry. This book explores the interface between poetry, therapy, and pedagogy for the purpose of aiding in student development and in positive social transformation. I use the term "therapy" in a very broad sense here. Psychoanalyzing students or doing specific problem-focused, individualized therapy with students would not be feasible or practical in the classroom and would bring with it a number of ethical concerns. Yet, reading poems and works of literature, or experiencing various art forms in general, and responding to them, does have therapeutic value that teachers can more effectively maximize in the classroom. While our goals in academia will not coincide completely with those of poetry therapists, and while we can only rarely, if ever, offer the kind of individual attention that therapists can offer their clients, we do share a belief in the value of literary works for people and for society as a whole.

The work of poetry therapists, along with that of psychoanalytic theorists, offers important insights into the power of poetic language for the reader, which could prove useful to teachers and scholars of literature. Therapy has different goals than literary studies, but if we can integrate these goals of therapy with our goals as writers and teachers, we can make literary studies more beneficial to our students. The insights of poetry therapists can help us maximize the potentially beneficial dynamics of the relationship between reader and text. Reading poetry allows us to explore affective states more deeply, which helps us to become more self-aware and more in tune with our experiences. Reading poetry also allows us to get outside of ourselves and empathize with others, which is especially valuable for us as social beings. At times, poetry can help us cope with problems or negative emotions by offering us recognition and allowing for transcendence. Poetry can also stimulate our imaginations and lead us to become more creative, proactive people.

This approach to poetry necessarily involves a shift from the traditional focus on the meaning of a text toward a focus on the experience of a text. This shift in focus offers us a way to make the most of poetry and its potential benefits. The difficulty and frequent ambiguity of poetry often becomes a major source of frustration and anxiety, particularly when students have been taught to focus on the goal of locating a specific meaning for a text. This will often lead students to implement defense mechanisms that attack or dismiss the text. We must learn to put meaning aside as secondary, and focus instead on the immediate experience of a poem. This, after all, is where we can locate the unique power of a poetic text. Of course, this does not give one a license to find absolutely any meaning whatsoever in any given text. Our experience of a poem must always remain grounded in its language. But the psychological states this language gives rise to provide our primary focus.

As we come to understand how poems push against the limitations of language, our experience of poetry is enhanced. This experience can even develop or alter as we gain a deeper understanding of authors or contexts, or as we continue to have new experiences. What keeps a poem alive, so that we return to it again and again, is our ability to experience it differently, perhaps more deeply, at different moments. As fluid subjects, our experience of everything continually changes. Because of its relative ambiguity, poetic language can change with us, show us how we change, and, most importantly, help to bring about change. Norman Holland and Murray Schwartz write of "[a] criticism in possibility," which "implies not just an end-product, the discovery of a 'meaning' assumed to be 'in' the text, but a growing, changing, living relation to the literary work as we change and as diverse other readings become available" (85). We are not rigid subjects, and poems are not rigid texts. We should not treat ourselves or our texts as such. We should emphasize the exploration of the experience of a poetic text on a more individual level, since this will prove valuable in aiding students in personal development and mental well-being with all of their social benefits.

A consideration of poetry in terms of its therapeutic value brings with it a variety of implications for the profession of literary studies, both in the classroom and for scholarship, particularly in terms of value judgments. The basis of value judgments of literary works necessarily shifts when one focuses on psychological benefits for readers and students. We would have to consider literature for its potential value for students in terms of personal development rather than in terms of traditional canonical criteria. In a clinical context, as Kathleen Adams and Stephen Rojcewicz tell us, "the selection of poems to be used is itself one of the most critical points in the practice of poetry therapy" (7).[5] But even poetry therapists disagree on what kinds of poems work best for their patients. Arleen Hynes and Mary Hynes-Berry lay out criteria for bibliotherapists to choose poems that will prove most useful for therapeutic purposes. Thematically, poems should reflect universal experience or emotion, and should not be overly personalized; they should not be trite, but should have a power that makes the reader feel instead of just know the experience portrayed; they should be comprehensible and not overly obscure so as to alienate the reader; and they should be positive, offering hope while dealing realistically with suffering. Stylistically, poems should have a compelling rhythm; they should use striking, concrete imagery; they should use clear, precise language; and they should be fairly succinct in the treatment of their theme (65–76). Kenneth Gorelick writes that "effective literature is not abstruse, is culturally sensitive, finds hope in the human condition, is life-affirming, and presents possible solutions without being prescriptive" (127). Jack Leedy favors "poems that are close in feeling to the mood of the patient," offering recognition first, while ultimately offering hope to those experiencing negative emotions. Therapeutically useful poems, according to Leedy, should not encourage guilt or silence; rather, they should give meaning to experience and bring optimism for renewal (67–68).

Other therapists, however, have warned of the danger that overly hopeful poems may present. Nicholas Mazza warns that such poems may actually increase one's sense of despair by invalidating the depth of the reader's emotional experience (19). Allan Cole also favors poems that offer accurate recognition of grief and sadness over those that compensate the reader and offer false hope. In his specific dealing with elegiac poetry, Cole finds the elegy to be "a valuable resource for helping to experience the magnitude of loss precisely by affirming it" (200). Exploring a poem should allow readers to deal realistically with emotions; it should not invalidate emotions by offering false hope. However, readers can, at times, incorporate positive images or expressions found in poems that help them better cope once the poem has dealt with and validated their negative emotions. Productive coping can only occur after readers have become aware of their emotions, accepted their validity, and taken responsibility for them.

Locating the effect that a specific poem will have on a specific reader, of course, is an inexact practice. What one reader finds validating, another may find alienating. What affects one reader very profoundly may leave another cold. The purpose of introducing poetry into therapy, Charles Crootof insists, is to find personal meaning for the patient (44). We cannot expect, and even less insist on, a particular experience that a reader should have. We must focus on each individual's process of exploring the self through exploring poems. Thus, Crootof finds nondidactic poetry most valuable, since didactic poetry limits possibilities for personal renewal and almost always raises hostility from readers (47–48). Charles Rossiter et al. come to a similar conclusion in their qualitative study. They found that poems themselves or facilitators of poems (like teachers) that "make explicit requests or directly suggest particular responses" tend to create resistance in readers (10). Mazza, similarly, favors open-ended poetry, since it may operate as a catalyst for self-exploration (19). Poetry that demands response and interpretation is of specific value for the classroom. While scholarship in this area can and should speculate on the value of specific poems for specific or even general readers, introducing poetry into the classroom will elicit a variety of responses and serve a variety of purposes for individuals.

In terms of what we hope to achieve with this approach, Hynes and Hynes-Berry give an overview of the goals of poetry therapy, which provide a foundation for our goals in the classroom: improve individuals' capacity to respond to texts through images, concepts, and feelings about them; increase self-awareness; increase awareness of interpersonal relationships; and improve reality orientation (24). In relation to these goals, I focus on the concepts of personal renewal through heightened awareness and reparation of relationship schemas as the ultimate goals for what we can hope to help students achieve through the study of poetry.

Seeking renewal refers to helping students to develop strong but flexible egos, so that they become more self-aware and more open to their creative potentials. One of the primary goals of literary studies, like psychoanalytic therapy and poetry therapy, should be to increase self-awareness and awareness of others by encouraging a more honest approach to life. The benefits of greater awareness to people and to society as a whole are immeasurable. Deeper awareness would expose faulty motives and actions that cause suffering to both the self and others.

In poetry, we find a particularly powerful literary tool for enhancing awareness on various levels. Poetry offers mental and imaginative stimulation in a condensed form requiring concentrated focus, and demanding emotional, mental, and even verbal, response. As readers, we become open to the details of experiences and their implications. We learn to become more alert to the details of our environment, as well as our inner being, and we learn to carefully contemplate these details in terms of what they mean to ourselves and to others. As we explore the complex elements of a poetic text, analyzing them so that the text reveals itself, we also reveal our own selves in all of our complexity and contradiction. This deep, intense focus that poetic works demand makes poetry the ideal literary genre for raising general awareness of both internal and external realities. Students can use poetry both to increase self-awareness so that a new self emerges, and to open up the self so that they may always continue to renew and discover new elements of themselves.

One important aspect of this engagement with poetry is to aid one in integrating one's self and one's experiences within affective, imagistic, and linguistic registers of experience. While poetry functions through an established system of language, it also challenges this system by operating through more primal modes of expression. Poets create images through language that operate as metaphors for what is beyond adequate expression through traditional language. Images in poetry evoke personal images in the minds of readers. Musical and formal elements of poetry evoke affective responses beyond what traditional language can. Students may explore these levels of response to poetry including, but also going beyond, traditional linguistic meaning. This approach offers students a thorough understanding of how poetry functions through the three registers while allowing them to explore their personal responses to poetic texts. Poems become objects that students relate to, explore their relationships with, integrate into themselves, and make use of in their personal development.

Students tend to approach poems by asking, "What does this poem mean?" because that has typically been the focus of their previous literature classes. We might instead ask "What does this poem evoke in the reader?" and "Why might this poem be important, valuable, or beneficial to the reader?"[6] Poetic texts, more than other literary forms, operate across the three registers of mental experience. Poems function through language in order to capture and evoke sensory images in the mind that capture or evoke affective states. An approach to teaching poetry through the three registers would avoid simply interpreting a poem at the linguistic level of meaning and would instead focus on the poem's effect on imagination and affects. The key to this methodology is essentially to approach and discuss poetic texts with a consideration of each register. The goal is to come to understand poetic texts in terms of how we, as unique individuals, experience them through these three registers. This approach leads students toward deeper mental integration. It raises their awareness of themselves and their views of the world since readers experience not only poetic texts, but everything in the world through these three registers.

By reading poets' expressions of intense emotions, and by having students express emotions themselves in response to poems, students become connected with affective experiences that they are frequently cut off from in their day-to-day lives. Jan L. Hitchcock and Sally Bowden-Schaible write, "[H]ow very much needed now these integrative capacities of poetry are in the larger context of a world where emotions, given such free rein, yet encouraged with minimal consciousness, are also so easily manipulated" (138). Emotional awareness allows us to recognize when we are being emotionally manipulated to adapt or accept views that could have negative personal or social consequences. Emotional awareness becomes socially beneficial, in particular, when one learns to empathize with others and experience compassion.

As with emotions, students rarely pay attention to their personal mental images—the images they form in their minds when thinking. Poets frequently make use of such images in their figurative language, especially metaphors and similes, and in their rich linguistic descriptions. Since in poetry these images are linguistically expressed, as opposed to in painting or in film where the image is presented visually, students must use their imaginations to fill in their own unique versions of these images in their minds. These personal images often arise through memories or associations that are affectively charged themselves. When students respond to poetry by discussing their own images and affects in language, they are essentially doing the work of the poet and becoming more integrated in these three registers of experience.

When they respond to poetic images through their own mental images, their creativity and imagination are engaged and stimulated. Students can begin to discover creative potentials for themselves that are often lost in a consumer-driven society where commercialism and political ideologies seek to create passive consumers. Hitchcock and Bowden-Schaible see the social value of poetry for our times in similar terms. They write,

> [W]hat greater revolution to truly imagine a different reality on the level of the collective also, to be able to simultaneously experience and see beyond in different ways how daily economic inequity, racism, and just being a member of any given society socialized us into a reality beyond which we are not encouraged to consider... [O]nce, through poetry, as with any other catalyst to consciousness of other realities, we are moved into those new levels of experience and awareness, the potential for all varieties of new integration and change—therapeutic and/or "revolutionary," individual as well as collective—is laid open. (137)

Poetry encourages students to become active creators as they relate to texts and to the world in general. As their minds open to new possibilities for themselves and for the world, they become more predisposed to take the kind of socially beneficial action that can bring about positive change.

In order to move toward a more honest, fulfilling, and productive life, one must overcome one's self-restricting immature or neurotic defense mechanisms while maintaining a strong but realistic sense of self. We all have the potential to become more aware and to change based on that awareness, but we also tend to resist change. Many personal defense mechanisms, serving fragile and rigid ego structures, can create major obstacles for the attainment of awareness and the achievement of a renewed self. These same mechanisms may cause one to ignore or deemphasize social issues in order to decrease anxiety. Jacques Lacan sees the self as conflicted and the ego as imaginary. We create and protect a view of ourselves that does not necessarily reflect our true desires and that often restricts our potential for prosocial activity. The subject must recognize this unavoidable internal division in order to open the self up to creative potential, otherwise the subject becomes trapped by an imaginary ego with various defenses designed to keep itself intact. Our goal is to lead the subject to realize a fluid and relative self, what Julia Kristeva calls the "unsettled, questionable subject-in-process of poetic language" (*Desire* 140).[7] This subject has a deep connection with the inner, visceral self and a deep understanding of external reality that certain defense mechanisms can only block. "By approaching life as a process and becoming aware of how one tampers with the flow of that process," Hirsch Silverman writes, "we take a major step toward unifying our split with life" (22). This approach to life creates a confident self with a strong identity, but also one that is open to constant renewal. The subject-in-process avoids rigid ego structures, allowing new possibilities for the self as posited within the field of language.

A strong sense of self is important, but a sense of self as fluid offers a more realistic and valuable conception, since we must continue to grow and change throughout life as we learn and mature. As teachers, we want to use poetry as confrontation and challenge to self, not as diversion and not as a substitute ego. Leedy writes, "Poetry encourages patients to explore their feelings, to feel more deeply, to extend their emotional range yet to discover patterns, also, of control and fulfillment" (70). We want students to relinquish rigid control of their emotions, fantasies, and other repressed elements of self. We want them to explore and experience their inner selves—not to deny their selves in order to avoid anxiety, but to confront the reality of anxiety, and put that anxiety toward creativity and activities aimed at confronting and solving personal and social issues.

While dealing with defenses in a large class remains important, it often proves difficult because of their uniqueness to each individual. We could take a somewhat aggressive approach by refusing to recognize immature defensive behavior or even to call students out on it, but we must also take care not to further damage fragile egos and bring about a deeper retreat. What we can reasonably do is discuss the nature of defenses and anxiety honestly, and try to offer a supportive environment that allows and encourages students to deal with strong negative reactions in a productive way. A therapeutic approach to poetry offers this type of environment by putting less stress on the text's or the instructor's authority. We can, instead, approach texts for their possibilities and levels of meaning, rather than seeking one master reading. Downplaying the teacher's authority over a text empowers students and enables them to engage in the text actively and creatively rather than simply passively consuming a text or a class. Ideally, this approach will carry on into students' lives on a broader scale so that they become free of master narratives put forth by politics, commercial capitalism, and the media.

Of course, some readers and students will not welcome this potential of poetry, and will enact defenses to avoid any possible personal benefits such as heightened awareness and recognition of emotion. Fortunately, by its very nature, poetry in itself is an effective means of overcoming defenses. One major cause of anxiety that may arise in readers occurs when a text evokes shameful or painful emotions or memories. Poetry's ability to remove shame and guilt through recognition and validation of emotional states proves valuable in breaking down defenses that are mainly manifested in the classroom and in general readers by a rejection of the text. Sharon Hymer points out that repression of certain negative thoughts and emotions comes from shame; works of art can break down this shame, allowing for honest personal realizations and the ability to express them (62–65). Geri Giebel Chavis writes, "Poetry's characteristically metaphorical language forges unusual links, often catapulting us into new awareness and bypassing the logical, walled-up self...Without thinking, we experience how renewal is possible" (29). The aesthetic beauty of poetic language is a powerful factor in breaking down ego defenses and raising awareness of feelings, images, and ideas. Poetry and other modes of art put form to fragmented and abstract emotions. Norman Holland discusses how form itself can act as a positive defense—one that enables coping without distorting reality (*Dynamics* 132). This sublimation applies to both the reader and the writer of a work.

While putting us in the moment of a feeling, poetry also offers an assuring separation from our pain. A poem offers a safe distance from painful emotions and helps to reduce resistance (Akhtar 233–234; Mazza 25). This distance offered by an imaginative work reduces the need for initial defensive rejection. While this distance may at first serve as an externalization and avoidance of one's own interior state, it can provide a stepping-stone in acknowledging something that the reader may integrate and accept when ready. "The poem is able to produce liberating and creative psychologic action without necessitating movement in the real world," writes Edward Stainbrook (8). Likewise, Holland explains, "our model tells us that the introjection necessary for full experience of a work depends on two conscious expectations: first, that the work will please us; second, that we will not have to act on it" (*Dynamics* 98). Reading poetry, however, is an active process in its own way, liberating one from repression and other defenses, and allowing one to explore and discover unconscious thoughts, affects, and processes.

Our second major classroom goal, reparation, comes from the psychoanalytic theory of Melanie Klein, who sees our identities as relational where the personal and the social are never far apart.[8] Poetry can help us to repair our view of the social world by offering the kind of hope that can lead us to prosocial actions and attitudes. As we go through life, we inevitably have negative experiences and witness negative aspects of humanity, especially violence, which can lead us to feel angry or depressed and apathetic. We repair this negative view of the world when we have positive experiences and witness positive aspects of humanity, especially love and compassion. Reparation does not involve a loss of realism, but maintains hope in the face of an imperfect world. Poetry that is overtly hopeful can aid us in reparation, but poetry that offers a realistic view of pain and suffering proves even more beneficial because it offers recognition of our negative experiences and emotions and links us to a common humanity. Poetry offers readers recognition of affective states and invasive thoughts that they may find uncomfortable or shameful. In poetry, we may discover a connection to another human being who understands and validates what we are going through. Poems, then, become good objects for us that offer support in the face of suffering and frustration.

Klein's concept of reparation essentially refers to the process through which one replaces negative, aggressive feelings toward one's significant others, and others in general, with more loving feelings. Poetry can assist the reader in making reparation in a number of ways. For one, a poem can stand in as a loving, supportive object for the reader by providing images of strong loving objects. Poems can also function as reparative objects for the reader by offering recognition and validation of emotional states, providing a sense of normalcy and wellness, and also offering support to help one cope with negative emotions. Poetry therapists often treat, or use, poems as potential loving objects for their patients, since poetry offers recognition of familiar emotions that are often experienced as shameful or illegitimate. Morris Morrison explains, "The reader...quickly finds that he is no outsider. Though the poet speaks for himself, the reader discovers his own psyche, his own thoughts and feelings, being expressed. He is not so alone as he had imagined himself" (88–89). Feelings that were once shameful are now "legitimate rather than a sign of weakness or frivolity" (Hynes and Hynes-Berry 28). One finds in poetry a common emotional unity in human kind. The recognition the reader finds in a text offers real human understanding, which strengthens self-confidence. Anxiety related to negative emotions becomes tolerable, and one can now probe more deeply into one's psyche. Gilbert Shloss explains that in poetry therapy "powerfully rendered poetic expression often stimulates in the client a sense of permissiveness to explore his own fantasies or emotions" (7). Recognition of what is already conscious leads to a recognition of formerly unacknowledged thoughts and feelings as well, moving one toward enhanced self-awareness and the kind of development that we strive for in education.

Poetry also posits subjects in relation to the object world, that is, the world of human beings, linking us to others by evoking empathy, and showing us our dependence on others for love and growth. As supportive loving objects, poems encourage exploration of and interaction with other people. Because our identities are so tied-up to our relationships, repairing the self essentially means repairing the other, or our view of the other. If we experience other people as nonhuman or as threatening, we can never feel repaired ourselves. We will fall victim to paranoia and fear, and will become vulnerable to various sorts of demagoguery and propaganda with all of their negative social consequences. But if we can first come to understand ourselves as relational and dependent on others, and then come to empathize with others, we will learn to factor human suffering and consequences into social and political issues. In poetry, we find voices that offer us recognition for things we are familiar with, but also voices that we can empathize with. In both cases, poetry links us to others in positive ways that predispose individuals to prosocial attitudes and behaviors.

We can use poetry to enhance our capacity to empathize with others, an essential element in positive human relationships and in social justice on a broader scale. Along with the important realization of self comes the realization of the other. Poetry can increase awareness of others, leading one to realize one's dependence on other people and the importance of interpersonal relations. Poetry therapy works by "allowing the patient to identify with other human beings, who have experienced similar conflicts, anxieties, and feelings, and who have been able to state, for all humanity, a universal theme or dilemma" (Berger 75). The reader comes to have a relationship with the text that provides recognition of the self, but also recognition of and empathy for the other. Hynes and Hynes-Berry explain: "The recognition that one can be heard is the most elementary stage in developing awareness of others. The awareness increases significantly at the point where the participant sees that listening is also possible" (34). Poetry can make us feel deeply for others, but it also allows us to gain understanding of the cognitive processes of others. Furthermore, it encourages a broader understanding of material circumstances that affect others. We can use poetry not only to get students to recognize and sympathize with human suffering, but we can also get them to consider some of the broader social and psychological forces behind it. The relationship that arises between reader and text can encourage one to relinquish narcissistic structures, explore the social world, and seek real, beneficial human relations.

Empathy provides the foundation for all meaningful relationships. And, along with the personal benefits of strengthening interpersonal relations, the development of empathy is imperative for the functioning of a just society. "To be fully human we cannot just be aware of others. We must also feel for them... The way we feel about interdependence and sharing clearly has an effect on how we live and respond" (Hynes and Hynes-Berry 35). Since we cannot function outside of the external world, we must learn to develop mutually nourishing relationships. Some poems deal specifically with the power of the interpersonal. Other poems give recognition of a common humanity and offer the reader a kind of prototypical relationship, which can foster recognition of the need for and the value of real human relationships.

Poems can both perform reparation and encourage exploration of the external world where reparation may occur. They encourage creativity by integrating our experience and offering a rewarding relationship with language. I propose a classroom approach that treats the poem as an object in the psychoanalytic sense, by which I mean something that students may relate to or have a relationship with, internalize and project themselves into, and use for positive development, rather than stand in material opposition to. As Holland and Schwartz write, "We cannot even talk or think about a text without establishing a relation to it" (29). As objects, poems bring about heightened awareness of others and a heightened sense of reality in general. They transcend norms of experience to offer new self-awareness and insights. They offer us a space between subject and object, and between fantasy and reality, that opens up the potential for transformation, change, and renewal. Poetry also stimulates individual creativity—the foundation for reparative acts. Poetry assists in the achievement of—and can even bring about—reparation for the reader, especially when we encourage personal and creative responses to poems. When we treat poems as objects rather than subjects, in the classroom or in general, we allow and encourage them to have these profound effects on us.

Our ultimate goal for a renewed self with repaired interpersonal relations must be achieved through a creative engagement with language. Shloss cites a major goal of poetry therapy as "to use poetry as a means of encouraging the development of the client's self-actualized creativeness" (6). Silverman explains, "The purpose of poetry therapy is to help a maladjusted person to learn, by various ways and in time, new ways of dealing with and thinking about himself and other people, and new responses to his life situations" (25). In poetry therapy, this renewal often occurs by getting clients to express themselves through poetry, but the relationship to the work of art itself has an element of creativity for the reader. The poem stands as a work of art by itself, but the reader's interpretation of and relationship to the poem make the reader into an artist, "making an original relationship between two elements, neither of which is necessarily original in itself" (Hynes and Hynes-Berry 55). Where the poem goes, so goes the reader—toward renewal and reparation of the self. Stainbrook explains that poetry brings with it the "potential for formulating statements of existence and for structuring experiences out of which a revitalized and remoralized self may emerge" (5). Through active analysis and response to a text, Gorelick tells us, "All persons are potentially capable of responding to the creativity of others with their own creativity" (126). These insights from poetry therapists give us some guidance as to how we can approach literary texts in the classroom to encourage the emergence of a renewed and repaired self.

The increased reality orientation that poetry offers teaches readers that many things are beyond their control, but poetry also teaches that one does have the ability to alter processes, perceptions, and even affective reactions. By offering a variety of words and images, poetry shows the many possibilities of being. As it encourages readers to evaluate new modes of thought and image schemas, some will arise as preferable—as more positive or pragmatic. Poets are essentially meaning makers. As they create meaning for themselves, they offer various perspectives to readers who may apply these new modes of meaning making to their own lives. As readers begin to reassess, revise, and renew their own perceptions and cognitive processes, they will become artists themselves. Poetry has the ability to stimulate the reader's own creative potential. Active reading itself functions as a kind of personal creative process. Crootof explains, "The poem may touch off a series of psychic events that contribute to the patient's feeling of well-being in a way similar to what is experienced after having been involved in a creative act" (47). This experience of the creative act, even if achieved vicariously, gives the reader a sense of mastery over emotions and personal thought processes. Irving Leon explains, "The structure of the creative product promotes a sense of unity, thereby maintaining cohesion, against centrifugal fragmentation" (389). The reader becomes able to integrate various components of self so that renewal and reparation may take place. Ideally, a new self will emerge—one that is more aware, relativistic, hopeful, confident, and one with more positive and mutually beneficial relations with others.

Poetry offers heightened awareness of one's self and one's interpersonal relations, enabling more positive and efficient functioning within one's environment. It can bring about productive change by challenging various existing mental schemas and offering alternatives. And, poetry provides a vehicle to move one toward the ultimate goal of transcending negative and debilitating emotions, thoughts, and schemas by offering one possibilities for renewal of self and reparation of personal relationships. Gorelick explains that poetry helps people to "discover the truth of their own existence, enhance their creative and problem solving abilities, communicate and relate better to others, and experience the healing properties of beauty"

(117–118). Poetic beauty can be very subjective and difficult to pin down, but I hold that an individual experiences beauty when personal renewal and reparation occur with a poetic text or another work of art. The best thing we can give our students as teachers of literature is an opportunity to encounter and explore this kind of individual experience of poetic beauty.

We in the field of literary studies should focus on the potential benefits of poetry, as well as other literary forms, for encouraging students and readers toward positive personal and social development. When approaching poems, we should ask what value they can have for readers in these terms. Poetry therapy provides us with a useful model for pursuing this goal. This approach must consider what emotional states or thought processes a particular poem gives recognition to. It must ask how a poem can lead toward greater internal and external awareness through intense observation and disarming beauty. It should consider how poems elicit reflection and response that will help one to integrate experience. It should look at what possibilities or alternative perspectives are offered by a poem that could aid one in reassessment of negative or faulty thought processes. Such an approach must also look at how poems can either lead toward or provide personal symbolic expression that will serve one in achieving the goals of renewal and reparation. This approach must necessarily deal in uncertainty, while embracing the possibility and potential of poetic language to provide important psychological benefits to individuals that could ultimately have a positive effect on our society at large.

The remainder of this book might be divided into four sections. Chapters one and two deal with achieving renewal through poetic language mainly through the concepts of Freud, Lacan, Kristeva, and various poetry therapists. Chapter one focuses on using poetry to overcome defenses, while chapter two focuses on integrating the three registers of experience through reading poetry. Chapters three and four shift to a Kleinian/object relations approach as they deal with relational aspects of the teacher, student, reader, and text. Chapter three considers the role of the teacher in this therapeutic pedagogy. Chapter four considers in detail how poetry can be used to achieve social reparation. Chapter five is the central chapter of this book as it provides a detailed yet flexible classroom model for this approach that is grounded in poetry therapy, experiential therapy, and metaphor therapy. The remaining four chapters consider specific texts by William Wordsworth, Alfred Tennyson, William Morris, and Christina Rossetti. While any poetry or literary text can be used with this approach, I have found that these poets coming out of the Romantic tradition work particularly well. In the introduction to her recent book on poetry therapy, Giebel Chavis includes a section on Romantic poetry where she writes that it "affirmed poetry's power to guide, illuminate and heal" (22). I spend some time discussing the aesthetics of these authors in terms of their therapeutic value, but I also use the authors' works as vehicles to discuss specific themes and issues relevant to the potential of this pedagogical approach to literature. I use Wordsworth to discuss emotional motivation and empathy. Tennyson's elegy *In Memoriam* allows for a discussion of mourning and reparation. The Morris chapter illustrates the way that responding to art can stimulate individual creativity. Finally, I use Rossetti to show the value of figurative language and ambiguity for achieving renewal and reparation.

Chapter One

Gaining Awareness and Overcoming Defenses

Awareness and Renewal through Poetry

Poetic language provides a powerful tool for opening the self to new possibilities. Lacanian psychoanalysis offers us an understanding of how this renewal can occur through language. "In poetry, as in psychoanalysis," Bice Benvenuto and Roger Kennedy explain in their book on Lacan, "language is pushed to its limits, and becomes a struggle with the inexpressible" (199). Poetry functions much like the speech of the analytic process, in which speech is loosened so that desire may make itself manifest. Desire manifested in language subverts the rigid, imaginary ego with all of its defenses that limit truth and subjectivity. Through poetry, we can escape the code of normal speech and discover a new definition of being for ourselves. "There is poetry," according to Lacan, "whenever writing introduces us to a world other than our own and also makes it become our own" (*Seminar III* 78). In essence, poetry imposes upon us the otherness of language—what Lacan calls the symbolic order—but also allows us to find our unique place within that otherness. The systems of language that our culture uses predate our birth, but also provide us with the potential to explore, realize, and create our identities and our world. Lacan places poetry in the dual roles of both the analyst—introducing the true nature of our subjectivity by effecting desire—and the fully realized analysand—realizing our own capacity for creative subjectivity. Though, for our purposes, these roles are essentially the same. Ideally, analysis prepares the analysand to accept the role of interpreter, just as teachers prepare students to become strong, independent analytical readers and writers. Bruce Fink explains, "Once patients begin to wonder about the why and wherefore of their words, thoughts, and fantasies, begin to formulate questions about them, their desire is engaged in the analysis" (25). Lacan refers to the "true termination of an analysis" as "the kind that prepares you to become an analyst." The goal for both the analyst and analysand is to confront "the reality of the human condition" (*Seminar VII* 303). Poetry forces such a confrontation—a confrontation with human lack and desire through language.

The first step toward this ultimate goal of becoming our own interpreter and creator is to abandon the imaginary ego created during the mirror stage, and to recognize one's position as subject in the symbolic order—the order of language. Lacan's mirror stage refers to a stage in infancy in which the infant sees its reflection in the mirror and "assumes an image" of a whole self as the true self. This provides the infant with an organized image of self that defends against its fragmented experience and motor incompetence. At the same time, the infant looks to the image of the adult parent (the other) and anticipates attaining the other's perceived wholeness. This image "situates the agency known as the ego" (*Écrits* 4). The ego forms, then, based on a *méconnaissance*, or misrecognition, of the self that takes place in order to maintain an imaginary notion of wholeness and control. This *méconnaissance* becomes the foundation for the imaginary ego, which gains support in the symbolic through certain master signifiers that we form attachments to in order to maintain our sense of identity. Lacan explains the imaginary nature of the ego:

> There's no doubt that the real I is not the ego...the ego isn't the I, isn't a mistake, in the sense in which classical doctrine makes of it a partial truth. It is something else—a particular object within the experience of the subject. Literally, the ego is an object—an object which fills a certain function which we here call the imaginary function." (*Seminar II* 44)

The ego provides us with a false notion of ourselves, rooted in the image of the other, as a whole being.

Lacan differentiates between *moi* (the imaginary ego) and *je* (the subject in the symbolic order). The ego is a rigid, false self. The subject is a more genuine realization of self, though determined by the otherness of the symbolic. But the subject is not rigid because the symbolic allows for play within its confines. Lacan explains,

> All I need do is think about myself [*moi*]—I am eternal. From the moment I think about myself [*moi*], no destruction of me is possible. But when I say I [*je*], not only is destruction possible, but at every instant there is creation. Naturally, it isn't absolute, but for us, if a future is possible, it is because there is this possibility of creation. And if this future isn't, likewise, purely imaginary, it is because our I is carried forward by the entire discourse which came before. (*Seminar II* 292)

Lacan calls poetry "the creation of a subject adopting a new order of symbolic relations to the world" (*Seminar III* 78). Poetry moves us away from the complaisant, imaginary *moi* concept of ourselves—the ego, where our desire is bounded in a false image and a misunderstanding of self, and displaced onto ideologies and material objects—toward the "creative subjectivity" of *je*, where the subject, freed from the desire of the other, may locate desire through the loosening of speech. "[C]reative subjectivity," Lacan insists, "has not ceased in its struggle to renew the never-exhausted power of symbols in the human exchange that brings them to the light of day" (*Écrits* 71). Language defines us, and imposes its own limitations, but only through language can we be freed from a false, imaginary concept of ourselves. In the symbolic, we can escape the oppressive identity established during the mirror stage. In poetry, we subvert the law that imprisons our experience in cliché, where we fall victim to the master signifiers imposed on us through social and parental expectations. Where the *moi* self accepts master narratives and adapts the kind of personal complaisance and apathy that allow for injustice and violence, or forms attachments to ideologies that cause suffering, *je* is free and proactive, recognizing and analyzing problems, and seeking solutions on both a personal and social level.

Poetic language can serve as an initiation into the kind of analytic discourse that allows *je* to emerge. Lacan implies, accurately, that the text itself can take on the role of the analyst—that poetry can function to bring about the kind of awareness and renewal that takes place in the analytic process. Here, we recall Robert Penn Warren's statement, "[I]n one sense... the reader does not interpret the poem but the poem interprets the reader" (212). With this in mind, we must be careful not to let the authority of the text overwhelm our identities as readers. Certainly, Lacan would not want the kind of transference—which is more like introjection—that takes place within ego psychology to take place with a literary text. Lacan says that when commenting on a text "[o]ne of the things we must guard most against is to understand too much, to understand more than what is in the discourse of the subject,... I would go as far as to say that it is on the basis of a kind of refusal of understanding that we push open the door to analytic understanding" (*Seminar I* 73). Here, he is warning about a kind of ego transference where "the subject reconcentrates his own imaginary ego essentially in the form of the analyst's ego" (*Seminar II* 245), or in the ego of the poet or poem. "Any conception of analysis," Lacan explains, "that is articulated...to defining the end of the analysis as identification with the analyst, by that very fact makes an admission of its limits" (*Seminar XI* 271). We do not want students to simply become the poem, but to find themselves and an empathetic other through the poem. Lacanian analysis seeks to defy limitations and open up possibilities for the subject. The analyst does not want to become the other of the mirror stage for the analysand. The analyst, instead, should be positioned as the "cause" while the analysand moves along in analysis. Fink explains, "When the analyst is viewed as the cause of the analysand's unconscious formations, the analyst can be considered a 'real' object for the analysand (which is denoted by the expression 'object a')" (38–39). As "object a," the analyst is located within the analysand while maintaining otherness. The analyst does not want to stand as an ideal ego. The analyst, instead, seeks to bring about or cause a new psychoanalytical perspective that is attuned to the unconscious and to desire. K. Daniel Cho provides a useful overview of analytic strategies that a teacher might use when approaching poetry.

> The simplest way to use the tool of the analyst's desire is to ask questions: "What does this mean?" "Can you tell me?" "What do you think?" and so on. Or, to make brief leading statements: "Tell me more," "Very interesting," "You're on to something," and so on. Or, even, to express a lack of knowledge: "I have never thought of it that way," "I want to know more," and so on. Rather than showing incompetence, the analyst's desire signals that the analyst is not a master, not all knowing. (59)

Poetry can stir desire in these ways by presenting unusual language, images, and thought processes that the reader must struggle with. Teachers, likewise, should remember to keep the desire of the text-as-analyst in play, so that it may help in raising awareness, and not close it off by offering authoritative readings.

Poetry sets desire in motion by drawing attention to its own lack. It is a failure of sorts, because, as poets and other creative writers often point out, language ultimately proves inadequate to capturing meaning. Warren explains that "the poet fails, as fail he must in some degree, in the exercise of his creative control and second, in so far as each reader must, as a result of his own history and nature, bring to the poem a different mass of experience, strength of intellect, and intensity of feeling" (212). Poetry should serve as a cause of desire that the reader uses to open up possibilities within the symbolic code. The reader should use poetry not to define the self, but to recognize the artifice of a certain type of clichéd definition of self. Poetry destroys this clichéd self without creating a new self in its own image. Instead it allows for the possibility of renewal in the reader. This renewed self will be one with the capacity to recognize the truth of desire. As we locate desire in a text, a desire that is metonymic, endless, and essentially objectless, we move closer to our own desire. Lacan explains,

> Psychoanalytic experience...exploits the poetic function of language to give [one's] desire its symbolic mediation. May this experience finally enable you to understand that the whole reality of its effects lies in the gift of speech; for it is through this gift that all reality has come to man and through its ongoing action that he sustains reality. (*Écrits* 103)

We are of the symbolic, but we can operate creatively in the symbolic. This is the poetic function. Here, we escape the constraints that keep us from realizing our potential as individuals and as a society. If speech, the act of language, is a gift, as Lacan insists, then poetry makes the most of this gift. We receive this gift in its fullest sense every time we read, interpret, and create poetry—every time we engage in poetic language. The poem, as analyst, moves the analysand toward the position of the interpreter— the analyst of poetic language who can realize desire in the text and in the self. Just as the analyst molds the analysand into an analyst, poetry can operate to create poets—people who recognize the clichéd language of the master signifiers that seek to define and confine them. The poet seeks to transcend the confinement of language through creativity. The poet, in this sense, refers not strictly to one who writes poetry, but to a renewed, and ever renewing, approach to life.

One might correctly say that reading a poetic text is like being analyzed insofar as it can put desire in play and lead one to discover one's own desire. I am not proposing that browsing works of poetry over a period of time might serve as a substitute for the analytic process, but we can see the parallels when we examine how poetry illustrates a struggle with desire through language and, in doing so, operates on the reader to encourage a genuine recognition of the subject in relation to the world. With its element of surprise, poetry escapes the clichéd master signifiers that determine one as a generic being. Poetry helps destroy this false or illusory self through creativity. For creative destruction to come about, we must look for alternatives to the master discourse that stifles personal creativity and encourages complacency or compliance in the face of social problems. Since language, to a large degree, determines our subjectivity, this reconstitution of our identity can only come about through a creative and poetic use of language. First, we must recognize that we are determined by the other—language, parents, authority, ideology—in order to recognize how our identity is falsely created. Poets, as Lacan points out, already recognize how the language through which we define ourselves does not belong to us (*Seminar II* 7). Poets recognize the inadequacy of language—the lack in the other. But poets also recognize the need for creativity and the need for language to create subjectivity. Mark Bracher explains that poetic language moves us closer to filling the innate lack of being that we sense in the other and in ourselves. This will ultimately lead to a fragmentation of the self because there is no absolute, transcendental signifier. "We approach the recognition that the absolute truth about being is that there is no absolute truth, and that the absolute signifier of being is that which signifies the lack of such a signifier" ("Rouzing" 195). This recognition is part of the goal of Lacanian analysis, and an important first step in discovering our potentials as social beings.

Julia Kristeva specifically discusses poetic language as a means of regressing to the core self. To Kristeva, this regression becomes revolutionary, challenging the self and the culture in order to bring about change. Her concept of the "semiotic chora" refers to a realm of the subject's interconnectedness with the maternal body, which includes the womb as well as stages of infancy before separation is established. Kristeva explains:

> Discrete quantities of energy move through the body of the subject who is not yet constituted as such and, in the course of his development, they are arranged according to the various constraints imposed on this body—always already involved in a semiotic process—by family and social structures. In this way drives, which are "energy" charges as well as "psychical" marks, articulate what we call a chora: a nonexpressive totality formed by the drives and their stases in a motility that is as full of movement as it is regulated. (*Revolution* 25)

The poet seeks to attain a link with the instinctual body through language and form. Instinctual drives provide the motivation for poetic expression, while poetic expression makes these drives manifest in the symbolic. Thus, poetry brings us back to the long-forgotten core of our inner being, getting us in touch with the unconscious and with our primary interdependence. Kristeva calls poetic language "a resumption of the functioning characteristic of the semiotic chora within the signifying device of language" (50).

Poetic language offers a challenge to formal symbolic structures—to meaning in general—and offers a regressive return to the chora and to the maternal, the realm of our most primal desires. Kristeva stresses the destructive, violent nature of this semiotic return. "In 'artistic' practices," she writes, "the semiotic... is revealed as that which also destroys the symbolic" (*Revolution* 50). As the bodily drives invade language in poetry, the system of language and meaning begins to breakdown. For Kristeva, as for Lacan, any discussion of the subject must involve a discussion of the linguistic function. With its regressive elements, poetic language is subversive as a challenge to master signifiers and clichéd language that are designed to define and confine us. The self-awareness and awareness of desire that we can attain through poetry is subversive because commercial and political culture seeks to define our desires for us and offers us an endless supply of false fulfillments, including objects and ideologies that provide displacements for desire. By linking us to our core self, poetry transgresses the social norms that are imposed upon us, opening up the self and ultimately the world we exist in by getting us in touch with our primal desires.

Though subversive to symbolic law, the semiotic can only be realized in language. Kristeva's "thetic" refers to the differentiation that allows for one to move from the semiotic to the symbolic in order to posit a separate identity. The breach of the thetic, however, occurs in the semiotic return to the maternal chora through poetic language. Kristeva explains, "[T]he signifying economy of poetic language is specific in that the semiotic is not only a constraint as is the symbolic, but it tends to gain the upper hand at the expense of the thetic and predicative constraints of the ego's judging consciousness" (*Desire* 134). Poetic language operates across this thetic boundary as it returns to the maternal semiotic through the symbolic, getting one in touch with the instinctual body that society forces one to repress. The semiotic in poetic language reveals the subject's "oceanic longing" as it pushes toward an annihilation of being by challenging symbolic and social structures. Only through the thetic phase and the entrance into the social world can the subject locate itself as independent of the maternal.[1] This thetic separation from the maternal, introducing the concepts of presence and absence, as well as subject and object, provides the structure for language. The entrance into the symbolic creates the division between the symbolic and the prior, maternal semiotic that brings the subject back to "'instinctual drive' activity relative to the first structurations (constitution of the body as self) and identifications (with the mother)" (137). The subject in the symbolic cannot simply abandon the maternal, however. The separation from the chora remains incomplete. The maternal constantly returns, especially in poetic language, but this return offers us a deeper awareness of the inner self and of desire.

"Language as symbolic function constitutes itself at the cost of repressing instinctual drive and continuous relation to the mother," Kristeva explains. "On the contrary, the unsettled and questionable subject of poetic language...maintains itself at the cost of reactivating this repressed instinctual, maternal element...poetic language would be for its questionable subject-in-process the equivalent of incest" (*Desire* 136). Poetic language, in this sense, transgresses the ultimate taboo of the paternal social structure. Kristeva says, "The very practice of art necessitates reinvesting the maternal chora so that it transgresses the symbolic order" (*Revolution* 65). "The artist introduces into the symbolic order an asocial drive, one not yet harnessed by the thetic" (70–71). Through art and literature, the social code is destroyed—but this comes about as a creative destruction. Where the social code begins to crumble, the primal psychic space of the subject reemerges. Literature to Kristeva represents "the very place where social code is destroyed and renewed" (*Desire* 132). Literature challenges the symbolic in order to put something more essential to the subject in its place. "The artist sketches out a kind of second birth. Subject to death but also to rebirth," Kristeva explains (*Revolution* 70). The confining structures of language, and of identity, crumble in poetry and this gives it its revolutionary power.

Defenses as Obstacles versus Coping Mechanisms

Defense mechanisms often stand as obstacles to our efforts to help students gain awareness and achieve renewal through poetry. Students will often limit themselves by rejecting texts that challenge the ego and induce anxiety. We need to approach poems in such a way that attempts to thwart this rejection based on ego defenses, and use the challenge to the ego for positive, prosocial growth. One important step is to understand how and why students and readers enact various defenses. As Phebe Cramer writes of attaining necessary therapeutic compliance, "[I]t is highly beneficial to know something about the patient's defenses" ("Defense Mechanisms" 641). While the French theorists, specifically Lacan, launch often vehement attacks on the school of ego psychology, Anna Freud's classic and still-influential book *The Ego and the Mechanisms of Defense* offers valuable insight into defense mechanisms. Anna Freud lists "three powerful motives for the defense against instinct:" superego anxiety (based on internalized guilt from parental censure), objective anxiety (being restraints from the outside world), and anxiety due to the strength of the instincts (where the ego fears being overwhelmed by their strength) (60). She refers to the superego, with all of its guilt and social censure, as "the mischief-maker which prevents the ego's coming to a friendly understanding with the instincts" (55). While we seek to control and contain our instincts, we must first come to an understanding of our inner world. Understanding allows our higher mental functions to deal with primal negative instincts in ways that avoid neurotic defenses or stifling anxiety. Thus we should pass on to our students an understanding and an honest assessment of human nature, so that they learn to devalue the social constructs that cause them to experience instincts and emotions with fear or shame. Poetry can help with this as it often deals with human instincts and emotions as its subject.

Anna Freud examines a number of specific defense mechanisms that we may consider in terms of their relevance in the classroom. Each of these mechanisms involves the avoidance of one's genuine self and/or a retreat from external reality. When a text invokes anxiety, students have a number of defense mechanisms in place to repress or avoid that anxiety rather than face it and use it as a catalyst for personal development. One common mechanism is the denial of affect or experience. Another, closely related, is reaction formation, which turns an experience into its opposite. Many students will treat a text that is deeply moving or relevant to them dismissively as if it is actually ineffective and irrelevant. Other times, a text that a student understands too deeply is treated as if it is not understood or is incomprehensible—particularly when the poetic text, as is often the case, is difficult or somewhat ambiguous. In such cases, texts that offer a potentially positive regression to the primal self that could lead to increased awareness instead bring about an intellectual regression where the reader becomes unable to process the material. These defense mechanisms can turn the positive potential effects of a poetry class for the reader into a strong negative rejection of a work, a poet, a class, or a teacher. Students can fall into defenses of isolation, avoidance, and inhibition where they cut themselves off from the class or any material that evokes shame or other anxious feelings. One thing we can do as teachers is express to our students the profound effects that texts have on us. We can also acknowledge in the classroom that certain emotional responses or realizations about our nature as humans do bring feelings of shame with them. We should be careful not to encourage students to share our specific reactions to texts, but showing them how we relate to texts emotionally can help students feel more comfortable expressing their own emotions or self-realizations.

Another major theorist who can help us in our understanding of defenses is Harry Stack Sullivan with his concept of the self-system. In Sullivan's interpersonal model, defenses find their roots in early infantile interaction with the primary caregiver. From early infancy, he says, "grades of anxiety first become of great importance in learning... Behavior of a certain unsatisfactory type provokes increasing anxiety, and the infant learns to keep a distance from, or to veer away from, activities which are attended by increasing anxiety" (159). Children initially learn from the parent through a system of rewards and anxiety-inducing punishments. From this early learning, the subject constructs a basic good-me concept of self along with a bad-me concept of self. "The essential desirability of being good-me," Sullivan says, "is just another way of commenting on the essential undesirability of being anxious" (165). Guilt and other forms of anxiety come about when the good-me concept of self is violated. More recently, Roy Baumeister et al. have taken a similar view that humans struggle to sustain "favorable views of self," and defenses arise in order to "protect self-esteem" when something "violates the preferred view of self" (1082). The avoidance of such anxiety stifles development by closing off the subject into a preset self-system. Sullivan explains, "The self-system is...an organization of educative experience called into being by the necessity to avoid or to minimize incidents of anxiety" (165). Therefore, "it is anxiety which is responsible for a great part of the inadequate, inefficient, unduly rigid, or otherwise unfortunate performances of people" (160). We become detached from our true inner selves by the constraints of parents and society in general. When we do not integrate our emotions and learn to deal with our anxieties over them, it becomes difficult to accept and appreciate what poetry can offer us. "The origin of the self-system can be said to rest on the irrational character of culture or, more specifically, society," writes Sullivan (168). Although the self-system serves a valuable purpose in preventing unfavorable changes that would involve the unlearning of important lessons in childhood and throughout life, Sullivan maintains that "the self-system is the principle stumbling block to favorable changes in personality" as well (169). While we must create some concept of ourselves, we must avoid closing ourselves off and limiting our possibilities and potentials. Sullivan discusses the denial of human desires with his concept of "selective inattention" (170). We want to avoid this kind of denial by using poetry as a means to honestly explore our emotions and desires. We can minimize the anxiety that comes with this exploration by setting up a classroom environment where the expression of emotions and desires is supported and encouraged.

Many will argue, however, that defenses are not necessarily bad things. Typically, this becomes a matter of definition. Anna Freud concludes her book on defenses by arguing that

> the ego is victorious when its defensive measures effect their purpose, i.e. when they enable it to restrict the development of anxiety and "pain" and so to transform the instincts that, even in difficult circumstances, some measure of gratification is secured, thereby establishing the most harmonious relations possible between the id, the super-ego and the forces of the outside world. (175–176)

Salman Akhtar, likewise, insists that some defenses can prove valuable in dealing with pain, and that poetry can sometimes aid in certain defenses such as offering a manic type of diversion (233–234). But manic defenses impede real awareness, and only offer distraction from negative emotions. Instincts must be controlled for social purposes, but must not be denied. One of our goals in studying poetry, which is also a good goal in life, is to face and learn to effectively cope with—rather than avoid or react with hostility toward—anxiety-inducing internal and external reality.

More recent theorists have explored the differences between what we might refer to as positive and negative defenses. George Vaillant follows Anna Freud in praising the ego for its adaptability to the external world through defenses. He relates the mind's defenses to the body's immune system as it protects us "by providing a variety of illusions to filter pain and to allow self-soothing." Rather than disavowing the "emotional and intellectual dishonesty" of the mind's defenses, Vaillant sees them as often "mature and creative" (1). He differentiates between four levels of defense mechanisms: "psychotic defenses" that can "profoundly alter perception of external reality" (40); "immature defenses" that, according to Vaillant, "represent the building blocks of personality disorder" (45); "neurotic defenses," which are "more private" and "less intrusive to others" (59), and where self-deception is less overt and "the user feels responsible for his or her conflicts" (60); and, finally, the mature defenses, which tend to face, rather than avoid, both internal and external reality in some productive way. Mature defenses are adaptive, while the lower-level defenses are maladaptive in various degrees and cause suffering both to the subjects enacting them and to others. The mature defenses (altruism, sublimation, suppression, anticipation, and humor) alter reality in their own way, but not in a way that we would describe as pathological. While an individual's perception of reality, obviously, remains subjective to an extent, we should seek an honest and realistic assessment of our conflicts with ourselves (id and superego), with our objects or others, and with reality. Vaillant's mature defenses may, to use his terminology, "minimize" reality, but they do not "ignore," "exaggerate," or otherwise "distort" it (36–37). In this sense, we may question whether mature defenses should be referred to as defense mechanisms at all.

Cramer has set out to provide a useful differentiation between "coping" and "defense" to be "understood as two different types of mechanisms that may serve as means for adaptation" ("Coping" 920). While both serve the same purpose—to deal with anxiety—they follow different psychological processes. Essentially, Cramer explains, coping mechanisms are conscious and intentional processes, while defenses are not:

> [C]oping mechanisms involve a conscious, purposeful effort, while defense mechanisms are processes that occur without conscious effort and without conscious awareness (i.e., they are unconscious). Also, coping strategies are carried out with the intent of managing or solving a problem situation, while defense mechanisms occur without conscious intentionality; the latter function to change an internal psychological state but may have no effect on external reality, and so may result in nonveridical perception, that is, in reality distortion. (921)[2]

Defenses restrict positive insight or activity on both a personal and social level, while coping requires conscious, purposeful action.

While not everyone agrees with Cramer's distinction (see Newman; Erdelyi), it provides a useful terminology through which we may distinguish these two different processes. Maria Miceli and Cristiano Castelfranchi agree with Cramer's two criteria for distinguishing coping from defenses, but add a significant third one. "In the case of the defense mechanisms," they write, "we suggest that their intervention involves a manipulation of mental representations, whereas coping involves only a revision" (288–289). While coping, like defense, has the goal of reducing stress, it also comes with the goal of "epistemic accuracy"—that is, believing what is true (290). Coping strategies adhere to what one at least believes to be reality, but defense mechanisms do not. "Acceptance," Miceli and Castelfranchi write, "is strictly linked to adherence to reality in that one realizes the problem and the distress it involves...Recognition of the problem makes it possible to tackle and, potentially, to solve or at least to limit its negative consequences" (293–294). Uwe Hentschel et al. also use the term coping as an alternative to defense. They write that the concept of coping should be "understood as a process of adaptation that permits the person to work toward the attainment of his or her goals." They continue, "[C]oping involves the organization and integration of the person's accumulated experience and available resources; it is attuned to the characteristics and requirements of the outside world" (15). Ideally, we seek to use poetry for positive coping, which does not distort reality, but can actually increase realism. Defense mechanisms can thwart our goal of achieving complete honesty and deep awareness. This awareness is important in achieving positive strategies for coping with negative emotions and representations on a personal level, as well as developing proactive, positive strategies for dealing with and solving social problems rather than ignoring them because they are, as is often the case, unpleasant.

One of the most noted positive mechanisms of defense—or, let us say, strategies for coping—that is particularly relevant to artists is sublimation. Anna Freud defines sublimation as conforming your identity with social values through creative activities such as writing or reading poetry (52).[3] But sublimation only maintains its value when it avoids manic denial or escape into fantasy. It may serve as a valuable tool in gaining awareness only if the sublimation is analyzed in order to unveil deeper truths about its creator or its appreciator. We want to engage our students in poetry in ways that specifically require the exploration, not the avoidance, of self and of other.

Sigmund Freud sees creative writing as an avoidance of reality while implying that it might also allow us to confront reality through fantasy.

While artistic form may have a unity that does not exist in real life, it does evoke and confront real emotions and realistic circumstances, and it allows for a connection to the internal world of fantasy and imagination that we tend to lose touch with in adulthood. Poetry and other creative works can link us back to our inner fantasy world and our primal desires. We must give up fantasy for reality in adult life, but creative writing operates through fantasy in a way deemed socially acceptable. As adults, we become ashamed of our fantasy life, but the realm of creative writing still allows an important connection with fantasy (*IX* 145). This is not to imply a loss of reality, but a capacity for one to experience the inner self through the separation offered by a work of art. Freud explains that "many things which, if they were real, could give no enjoyment, can do so in the play of phantasy, and excitements which, in themselves, are actually distressing, can become a source of pleasure for the hearers and spectators at the performance of a writer's work" (144). While this separation may appear to be manic and a defense mechanism in itself, it may offer an important opening into the inner realms of both affect and imagination that readers can then integrate into consciousness.

Poetry also eases defenses by removing the shame that we experience with certain affects, fantasies, or invasive thoughts. Sigmund Freud discusses the value of literary works in these terms when he explains, "[A]ll aesthetic pleasure which a creative writer affords us...[,] our actual enjoyment of an imaginative work[,] proceeds from the liberation of tensions in our mind. It may even be that not a little of this effect is due to the writer's enabling us thenceforward to enjoy our own day-dreams without self-reproach or shame" (*IX* 153). In this way, the authority of a published text can actually work as a positive for conquering defenses. Holland explains, "The thought of others reading or seeing [a text] as we do licenses our response. They take over some of the functions of a superego, and, because they constitute so relaxed a superego, my own ego need not be so self-conscious, so oriented to action as if they were not there" (*Dynamics* 98). Poetry allows us to face our fantasies, our desires, our pain—all very human—without self-reproach or social stigmatism. Again, we should be careful not to encourage students to take on poetic voices as substitute egos. We want them to own their unique responses to texts. Once students and readers become aware of and honest about their inner beings, then positive change may begin.

Poetry can also aid in enlarging reality orientation, which defense mechanisms inhibit. Developmentally, one must establish a realistic relationship with one's self and one's environment. This process begins in early infancy, but, because of various defenses, adults often lose touch with the reality of their self and their relationship to the external world. Indeed, as Hynes and Hynes-Berry point out, "it is not always easy to keep the different facets of one's world in perspective" (36). Poetry can assist in establishing a more accurate assessment of reality as it encourages one to relate coherently to various images and concepts. Readers are encouraged to "examine the more complex—and potentially more troubling—realities of their emotional, social, and psychological lives" (37). Examination of a text may reveal that one has unrealistic expectations for the future, for example, or that one has rewritten the past to make it less troubling (37). Poetry gives us universal truths without tying us down with absolutes for our identity or for the world we live in. Drawing on the work of existential therapist Irvin Yalom, Hynes and Hynes-Berry show how poetry and other forms of literature not only force us to recognize certain essentials of reality such as the unfairness of life, the inevitability of suffering and death, and our ultimate aloneness; but they also show us our responsibility for our own actions, and the importance of leading an honest and noble life in relation to others (38). Through poetry we not only confront reality, but we also see possibilities as to how we might change our world through creativity and action.

In order to gain deeper self-awareness, one must overcome debilitating or maladaptive personal defenses. By delving deeply into the unconscious, poetry offers a challenge to the existing ego, but it can also offer one new possibilities for a more genuine self to emerge. As Susan Vaughan puts it, "After learning the rules your [neurological] networks contain in psychotherapy, the next step is to begin to challenge your character's closely held values, question their operation modes" (74). This challenge to the existing ego does not come without a destructive element. "Clearly, getting in touch with the inner self will not always be a pleasant experience. Sadness and pain are frequently part of the growth process," write Hynes and Hynes-Berry (30). New revelations and realizations can lead to an experience of fragmentation, but this fragmentation is a necessary step for ultimate renewal. Stephen Levine writes,

> [A] major theme of my thinking is the necessity of fragmentation, the refusal to find premature solutions that would only cover over differences in a façade of unity. At the same time, I find myself striving always towards integration, motivated by a hope for wholeness and reconciliation. It is this activity of working through disintegration that I consider to be at the core of the creative and therapeutic processes. (xvi)

The relativism that comes with the destruction of the rigid ego may initially lead to a sense of despair. Stainbrook explains, "[A] most fundamental and growing threat to many persons is a sense of the loss of control of the purpose of life." However, he continues, "only by losing these absolutes of traditional meaning can one be free and hopeful in the creation of new relative alternatives. Sustaining relative truths cannot be created confidently until the 'Absolute Truth' is relinquished" (4). This initial despair or anxiety that comes with the challenge to the ego will prove only temporary provided that the reader continues along the path toward renewal achievable through the creative potential of the poetic function. The engaged reader and expressive responder will, ideally, come to discover a new and ever-renewing outlook on life, one that is proactive in the face of personal despair and social problems. Finding the self means realizing that you have virtually endless possibilities for your identity. Finding the self essentially means losing the self, or losing the rigid image of self that limits experience. Defenses protect this rigid self, but they cannot free one from anxiety. Only an honest appraisal of self can allow for such freedom, and in poetry, we have a great tool for achieving this honesty.

Chapter Two
(Neuro) Psychoanalytic Regression and Integration

Regression

Renewal begins with a loss of a rigid self and a regression to a more primal state, before the dominance of the imaginary ego, where experience is pure and possibilities are endless. However, this regression can also bring about a sense of fragmentation and a frightening loss of identity. Poetry operates not only through language, but also through the more primal registers of image and affect. Poetry provides an invaluable tool for pressing into unconscious states specifically because of its minute attention to internal and external details and its condensed mode of expression. Experiencing poetry can bring about a kind of regression, getting one in touch with these primal elements of self while allowing one to reorder them. Renewal is achieved when we can locate and then integrate primary, often unconscious, elements of our experience and identity with linguistic expression and consciousness. Integration and increased self-awareness are major goals of psychoanalysis and poetry therapy.[1] Poetry provides a valuable aid in integrating experience and identity by focusing close attention on all of the moments and details of experience and then putting them in linguistic form. By tapping into our unconscious, poetry helps lead us toward a deeper and more honest understanding of our selves.

Poetry has a unique value among literary forms. Perhaps the most unique function of poetry is its ability to affect us, through language, at this uncanny, primal level.[2] Poetry transcends ordinary experience and operates at a heightened level of consciousness. The allowance for and recognition of this kind of experience that poetry offers can create a profound feeling of pleasure or even transcendence in readers.[3] This uncanny ability of poetry comes from its engagement with what Freud calls the primary processes, which offer a regression to the core of one's being, giving rise to pleasure and ecstasy even when dealing with negative emotions. These primary processes include the capacities for metaphoric and metonymic association, the primitive energies and emotions of the body, and visual orientation (*V* 601–606).

In *Interpretation of Dreams*, Freud describes dreams as regressive to the pre-linguistic, unconscious primary processes. Much of Freud's concept of the dream work also applies to poetic expression. Lacan relates Freud's dreamwork concepts of condensation and displacement to the literary devices of metaphor and metonymy (*Écrits* 152). Dreams function primarily through imagistic representations, much in the same way that poems use symbolic or metaphoric images in an attempt to reflect the inner state of the poet. As in the final stage of Freud's dream work, poets must translate their inner experience into an intelligible linguistic form. A recent statistical analysis by Sophie Schwartz revealed that the language patterns of dream reports resemble those of literary works (28). If we consider Freud's concepts of the primary and secondary processes, we see that the primary processes involving elements such as emotion, image, metaphor, and rhythm contain many of the same elements found in poetry, but like the final re-creation of the dream work, poetry must ultimately operate at the level of the secondary processes of language and thought, since it is a conscious craft. In poetry, we find, perhaps, the closest manifestation of primary processes in the secondary process of language. Through poetic language, we can begin to make the unconscious primal self manifest in conscious thought. This is the major goal of Freudian psychotherapy, and a crucial step in attaining a renewed self.

Like Freud's dream work, poetic language contains regressive elements that return us to our primal inner selves. Freud describes three types of regression occurring in dreams that we may also apply to writing and reading poetry: topical, temporal, and formal.[4] These concepts offer theoretical insights into how poetic expression functions and how we experience it.

Topical regression explains how we build from our experiences and use our imaginative capability to create new experiences in the dream world. In our real-world experience during waking life, we experience the world through sensory perceptions that are stored as memories. These memories become the foundation of our character with its conscious and unconscious elements. In dream life, these elements of our character—thoughts, motivations, actions, opinions, desires, etcetera—build from stored memories that become fragmented or otherwise altered by the dream work to create a new sensory experience in dreams. In the same way, a poet regresses into a more sensory-oriented state when creating poetry by paying careful attention to internal personal images and emotions. This regressive looking inward through which poetry functions also stimulates the reader's own personal images and evokes emotional reactions.

Mark Solms and Oliver Turnbull explain, through neuroscience, the nature of the visual aspects of the dreaming mind, which relate to Freud's concept of topical regression. If we accept the strong correlation between dreaming and the imagination—which neuroscientific evidence would appear to support—this research can only teach us more about the imaginative mind and the poetic function. "The visual regions of the brain," Solms and Turnbull explain, "can be regarded as involving three hierarchically organized zones" (209). The primary visual area simply takes in visual input. Damage to this zone causes blindness, but has no effect on dreaming. The second zone is dedicated to specialized tasks such as recognition of color, motion, and objects. Damage to this zone gives rise to complex visual disorders in both dreams and waking life. The third, and highest, zone deals with abstract aspects of visualization involved in arithmetic, writing, construction, and other higher spatial-oriented functions. Damage to this zone effects visual cognition, but has no effect on basic perception. However, damage to this zone produces a total cessation of dreaming (210). This implies that our visual input systems are reversed in dreaming. Just as in Freud's topical regression, our perception input focuses internally in dreams, rather than externally as in waking life. This may offer us some insight into the biological functioning of the imaginative mind, which involves a similar type of regressive looking inward.

Temporal regression, essentially a regression to an earlier age, deals with issues of desire, motivation, and development. In earliest pre-infancy, the child developing in the womb lives in a state of pure pleasure and security where the maternal body satisfies all needs. As Sandor Ferenczi explains, "[T]here is a stage in human development that realizes this ideal of a being subservient only to pleasure...I mean the period of human life passed in the womb. In this state the human being lives as a parasite of the mother's body" (218). The infant has the omnipotent feeling "that one has all that one wants, and that one has nothing left to wish for" (219). The infant in the womb lives free of anxiety. Upon birth, "[t]he first wish-impulse of the child, therefore, cannot be any other than to regain this situation" (221). After birth, infantile sexuality develops as motivated primarily by seeking a return to this state of pleasure. As one matures, the primary pleasure principle must reconcile itself to external reality. In this important step, one must realize the need for inhibition and control of infantile desires in order to function socially and to attain a realistic optimal amount of pleasure. In regression, we lose this inhibition and control and return to a state of pure pleasure seeking. While neither poetry nor dreams simply represent the wish fulfillments that Freud saw dreams as, the practice of creating and reading poetry does involve a seeking of gratification on numerous levels, as well as potentially getting us in touch with our primal desires in all of their complexity.

Freud makes the connection between works of art and primary and secondary mental processes explicit in his essay "Formulations on the Two Principles of Mental Functioning." He refers to the "unconscious mental processes" as "the older, primary processes, the residues of a phase of development in which they were the only kind of mental process" (*XII* 219). Fantasizing is a primary process free from the restraints of the secondary processes. This activity "begins already in children's play, and later, [is] continued as day-dreaming" in adult life (222). In "Creative Writers and Day-Dreaming," Freud makes this connection between the play of early childhood and the regressive creative writing of adulthood explicit saying that "every child at play behaves like a creative writer, in that he creates a world of his own" (*IX* 143). Freud also makes the link between creative writing and dreaming explicit in this essay saying that "our dreams at night are nothing else than phantasies"—the type that creative artists make use of (148). Of course, with the regression to fantasy and poetic form comes conflict and contradiction.

The primary and secondary processes conflict on multiple levels: emotion versus thought, poetic versus more straightforward modes of expression, and motivations of pleasure seeking versus the reality principle. Freud sees art, in all of its forms, as the place where these conflicting mental processes can find some common ground. In terms of the pleasure/reality conflict, Freud says that "art brings about a reconciliation between the two principles in a peculiar way. An artist is originally a man who turns away from reality because he cannot come to terms with the renunciation of instinctual satisfaction" (*IX* 224). Artists express the dissatisfaction with the external world of the reality principle—a dissatisfaction with the renunciation of primal urges. Art reaches people, according to Freud, because this dissatisfaction is universal to all humans. In this sense, art offers recognition and potentially greater awareness of the human condition, but also allows for a gratification of primal instincts that we typically repress.

Formal regression, which takes place in dreams as well as in poetry, deals specifically with primary and secondary processes of expression. Like dreams, poetry contains images, but poetry also has a musical quality that separates it further from ordinary language. Alice Jones writes, "Music summons feeling, and in a poem, so much more can be said, especially in the white spaces around the lines" (693). In order to better comprehend poetry's ability to express primal emotions, we may relate the musical, extra-verbal aspects of poetry to what Daniel Stern calls vitality affects in his classic book *The Interpersonal World of the Infant*.[5] Vitality affects make up the earliest pre-linguistic modes of communication between parent and child. They are communicated through physical gestures, which infants take in visually, as well as musical qualities of expression like tone and rhythm, which can express visceral states without a formal signifying system. Like visceral experience, however, vitality affects do not necessarily fall into specific categories of emotion. Stern describes them through examples such as "a 'rush' of anger or of joy, a perceived flooding of light, an accelerating sequence of thoughts, an unmeasurable wave of feeling evoked by music" (*Interpersonal* 55). We witness vitality affects in the nonsensical sounds infants make that imitate the rhythms and tones of adult language. Sounds of this type, along with other common infantile modes of verbal expression such as crying or laughter, provide the foundation of the earliest social interactions. What is important for development is that adults respond to the sounds or expressions of infants with exaggerated vocal and physical responses that reflect the infant's own vitality affects. These provide a foundational prototype for social interactions. The rewards of these earliest, primal interactions are essential for providing children the motivation to develop language, with its promises of greater and deeper social interactions. The promised rewards of greater and more meaningful social interactions, along with the frustrations that come with inadequate social functioning, drive one to develop formal language. The achievement of language enables one to function socially and offers one the sense of both a social and cultural identity.

Poetry combines the characteristics of both formal language and the more tonal and rhythmic elements of primal expression. Stern relates vitality affects to artistic expression, or what he calls "artistic style" (*Interpersonal* 159). When experiencing art, Stern says, "you can experience the level of intensity and quality of feeling that is occurring in the other and that may be elicited in yourself" (160). We find the expression of vitality affects in poetic language rewarding beyond what we find in ordinary prose. Vaughan finds vitality affects invaluable for communicating with her patients in therapeutic practice. Tonal elements of communication that hearken back to infantile expression modes provide the therapist with important personal connections with her adult patients (94). Jones writes, "Those earliest forms of language, the infant's coos and babbles, are not very far in the background of every poem" (690). This regressive, tonal quality of poetry makes it better able to capture emotions and convey them to the reader. "What poetry can do," writes Jones, "that nothing else can is this: swallow the reader, enter us, take us backstage of everyday reality into the realm of what we feel and experience and can never say" (696–697).

Rhythm is the regressive formal element most unique to poetry over other literary forms. Joost Meerloo writes that "the rhyme and rhythm of poetry often have a much more compelling force than the actual meaning of the words" (59). In the rhythm of poetic language, we find the necessary road to regression.[6] Regression allows us to break with our habitual self. The vehicle of rhythm brings us back to the primal self, the original source of life, from which a new self may emerge. Paul Christensen describes how rhythm reflects the movement of our own bodies, as well as the interior of the maternal body from which we came (90; 97). Poetry also lends itself to oration, giving us the sounds of our own voices and the emotional tones they carry (92–93). Meerloo expands on the primal and ubiquitous characteristics of rhythm even further. In relation to the body, Meerloo explains, "Breathing, of course, has its distinct rhythms, as do the intestines, the heart and the muscles, the molecules and even the intra-atomic particles" (55). He also attempts to explain the infant's receptiveness within the uterus to the sounds of the maternal body: "[T]he knowledge that amniotic fluid is a better sound conductor than air makes the existence of a prenatal syncopated rhythmic sound world more than likely" (55). We may relate these ideas to Kristeva's concept of the semiotic chora. As the subject returns to the chora, the rhythmic nature of the semiotic in poetry parallels the maternal interior. It contains, writes Kristeva, "'musical' but also nonsense effects that destroy not only accepted beliefs and significations, but, in radical experiment, syntax itself, that guarantee of thetic consciousness" (*Desire* 133). The rhythmic nature of poetry that links it to the maternal subverts the patriarchal, authoritative master signifiers that limit identity. Poetic regression not only offers us deeper self-awareness, but also liberates us from the limits our culture places upon us.

The ability of poetry, through rhythm, to return us to this joyous state of omnipotence in the womb gives it a soothing aspect, which makes it particularly adept at helping one to cope with negative emotions. Meerloo explains, "[R]hythm means recognition and responding to something familiar. Such preoccupation with familiar messages can be used as a defense against feelings of pain" (63). Rhythm reflects the familiar in the body and the voice, but poetic rhythm also reflects our external experience of time, seasons, and various functions of the natural world like winds and tides (54). The rhythms and tones of poetic language draw us into a comfortable, pleasurable realm of primary processes, while offering intellectual and rational reflection on human experience. Poetry can deal with painful, or otherwise emotionally charged, subjects through musical language experienced as beautiful by the reader. This quality of poetry allows one to recognize, accept, and ultimately transcend various negative thought processes and emotional states. Poetic rhythm connects us more deeply with ourselves and with our environment.

Metaphor, as a formally regressive primary process and as the central literary device in poetry, provides another significant therapeutic tool for readers. Lacan relates metaphor to Freud's concept of condensation, which, Lacan says, "envelopes poetry's own properly traditional function" (*Écrits* 152). To Freud, a dream as a whole is a condensing of thoughts and feelings into an imaginary scenario. Likewise, a poem attempts to capture human emotions and images in order to express them in a more or less cohesive and coherent whole. Metaphor is particularly adept at dealing with the pre-symbolic, primal elements of self because it functions mainly through the image to make meaning inexact. Metaphors open themselves up to multiple meanings when read, just as condensations in dreams branch out when interpreted. For example, a metaphor such as "my heart is a ball of fire" could mean that the speaker is a passionate being, in love, angry, in pain, perhaps experiencing acid reflux, or all of the above. Following such a branch of associations opens up a text and allows for more personal interpretations that in turn offer insights into the reader as much as they do into the poem.

In order to show that meaning, or a signifier, is always inexact, Lacan describes metaphor as a substitution of one signifier for another (*Écrits* 155–156). To Lacan, every signifier is a metaphor in a sense because meaning operates through a system of symbols that cannot accurately capture human experience such as the affects of the body or the images of the mind. Metaphors used in poetry embrace the inadequacy of language. Lacan says that "a definition of poetic style could be to say that it begins with metaphor, and that where metaphor ceases poetry ceases also" (*Seminar III* 218). Lacan uses metaphor to discuss the disconnect between human experience and expression due to the limits in the symbolic. Metaphor, he says, rips "the signifier from its lexical connections" (218). In Lacan, however, this acceptance of inner conflict that comes from an acknowledgment of the nature of the symbolic is the very thing that opens up the subject and allows for renewal. Poetry gives us the best linguistic form through which to explore our inner selves because it opens the self up to new and multiple possibilities of meaning.

Lacan uses metaphor in part to discuss the fragmentation of experience, but others have found the concept useful for its potential to find wholeness and cohesion. Akhtar refers to the primary processes of poetry as "libidinally gratifying." He writes, "Common to all these literary devices is the aim at fusion, linkage and bringing things together" (235). Metaphor defragments by condensing the multiplicities of the self. As in Freud's conceptualization of condensation in the dream work, poetry uses metaphor to bring together various disjointed thoughts, emotions, images, words, and experiences into a single image or episode (*V* 279–284). Charles Ansell explains, "The poem and the unconscious share a major feature: both are represented in compressed form" (13). Metaphor works to integrate the various registers and offers a pathway to the unconscious. Metaphor, Gorelick writes, "enlarges, it connects, it shatters old frameworks" (123). Locating a meaningful metaphor in poetry gives a reader a means to express emotional states. The unspeakable, pre-symbolic finds its symbolic expression in poetry through metaphor, and this achievement brings with it the possibility of renewal. Jones writes, "[W]hat is most important about poetry is how it approaches the unsayable" (684). Mazza discusses metaphor within the symbolic/ceremonial component of his theoretical framework for poetry therapy. When subjects attempt to deal with difficult emotions, such as depression suffered from a loss, metaphor can help them to connect their inexplicable, interior reality with a symbolic exterior reality (40–41). Thus, the reading of an elegiac poem may offer a subject dealing with loss a variety of benefits by providing recognition or newfound awareness to difficult emotional states through a condensed image or narrative. Metaphor in poetry gives the reader a concrete means of expression for what had hitherto remained unexpressed. While the regression to metaphoric expression in poetry draws attention to the limitations of language, it also offers the best mode within the symbolic to express and understand human experience.

Integration

While reading poetry allows us to regress to our primary processes, it also provides us an opportunity to progressively analyze our experience of poems on various levels. Regression only serves a purpose when it leads one toward awareness and renewal. One useful strategy for raising self-awareness in the classroom involves teaching poetry through the three registers of affect, image, and language. Poetic texts are both created by writers and processed by readers in these three registers. What cognitive scientist Wilma Bucci calls the referential process connects nonverbal systems (emotions and images) to each other and ultimately to words. Bucci explains the importance of the referential process for the integration of self:

> To account for the overall organization of the human information-processing system, connections among all representational systems are required. Nonverbal representations, including subsymbolic components that are processed continuously, synchronously, and in parallel, must be connected to one another and to the discrete symbols of language processed in single-channel, sequential format. (178)

In poetry, the inner self and the emotions must be brought into the register of language through the register of imagination or mental images. This referential process permits the "activation of dissociated emotion structures in a context where they can be tolerated, examined, and reconstructed" (13). Bucci points out that the referential process that links emotional experience to verbal expression is the domain of poets. The poet contrives "the construction of a symbolic context into which emotional experience may be embedded... In the expression of emotion... metaphors may be understood precisely as concrete and discrete symbols for unnamed, subsymbolic feeling states" (216). If we teach poetry through the three registers, students will learn to focus not just on language and ideas, but also on the mental images and affects that occur when reading poetry.

The linguistic register refers to language and other symbols or images that carry meaning and the use of these in our thought processes. If I draw a red octagon on the board in my classroom, for example, everyone will know that means "stop." If I ask why it means "stop," no one can offer me a good reason. These units of meaning, whether language or some other kind of symbol, only carry meaning because they are culturally agreed upon. They are generally arbitrary so that they do not belong uniquely to us.[7] They predate us and we are, to an extent, confined by them. The linguistic/symbolic being functions in the social world by taking part in the culture, but often experiences a disconnection from the subsymbolic, pre-linguistic inner world that is more personal, unique, and genuine. Psychoanalytic therapy seeks the emergence of this more genuine self. Poetry provides an important tool for bringing about this emergence via its challenge to clichéd language and master signifiers.

But language and symbols are also extremely important. When I ask my students what the benefits of language and symbols are—what they allow for and what would we miss out on without them—they typically come up with a number of things including communication, which is important in forming relationships and in education. Language is also important for the function of a society, providing the possibility of laws and social order. You cannot ignore the red octagon in the road or you will eventually cause an accident. Language also gives humans a higher and more complex capacity for thought. In many ways, it represents the highest register of experience. It is what separates humans from other forms of life on the planet. It is also generally the area that we, at least consciously, operate on in a classroom or as academic readers where we tend to ask only what a text means. Language clearly has value, but as we look at the other registers of experience, we come to see its limitations.

The imagistic register refers to the visual images that we form in our minds and the episodic fantasies that the mind creates, which, of course, are also largely visual. To illustrate this, I tell my students to try to bring up a concrete visual image in their minds of a table.[8] Then I ask if everyone is picturing a table. Yes, of course. Because of our shared cultural understanding of the word, we can assume that everyone is picturing some kind of surface with legs or some kind of base attached to it. Then I ask my students if they are all picturing the same thing. No. Why? Because one's images are personal and never adequately captured in language. Our images are all unique, because, in this example, we all have different experiences of tables that lead to different prototypes of table, and our brains, for whatever specific reason, went to a specific image of a specific table that was different from the other tables that other minds in the classroom went to. One may also apply this concept to poetry. A poet attempts to convey his or her personal images to a reader, but in doing so evokes images in the reader's mind that will be similar to but also different from those in the poet's mind, or in the minds of other readers. This explains in part why we each experience a particular poem differently.

The affective register refers to our emotions and the other bodily experiences that go with them (like a flutter in the stomach when we are nervous, or a rush of adrenaline when we are angry). We hear or read language, then we form mental images in our minds based on that language, and we also feel affects or bodily sensations. This register of experience is the most primal, and, paradoxically, both the most universal and the least expressible. The affective or visceral level of experience is, like the imagistic, unique to each individual and beyond adequate expression in language. We can explain emotions with words like "happy" or "sad" and, because we all have some universal experience of these feelings, we can communicate them to a certain extent. However, one can never fully convey one's inner affective state to another. Poetry, through its use of metaphor and images, attempts to express affects in a much deeper way than conventional language. When Tennyson writes "my light is low," for example, we get a deeper, though perhaps also more ambiguous, sense of his depression or his thoughts of mortality than we would through simple expressions like "I am sad" or "death troubles me." Poetic metaphors express affects by evoking correlate images in the minds of readers. Readers will tend to respond with affects similar to what the poet is trying to express. However, a reader's affective reaction to a certain image can never be wholly predictable, since we will all have different mental associations with specific images.

One way I get my students to better understand the three registers in relation to poetry is to have them consider how dreams work. In Freud's model of dreams, our desires or wishes—the latent content—are disguised by the dream work, which turns them into sensory images in dreams—the manifest content—that we must then turn into language in order not only to communicate the dream to others but also to understand it ourselves.[9] Poetry functions in a similar way: a poet finds an image or analogy that expresses his or her inner state and then translates this image or analogy into language. Bucci makes a useful revision of Freud's model of dreams through her multiple code theory. Bucci takes issue with Freud in two important ways. First, she sees dreams' latent contents, their activation, as emotion schemas rather than limiting them to wish fulfillments. Bucci writes, "The activated emotion schemas may include an unconscious wish seeking fulfillment, but may equally well be some other emotion structure—such as fear, worry, or conflict, or a problem the individual is trying to solve" (249). Second, Bucci sees the manifest content of sensory dream images as a direct, rather than censored, expression of the latent contents. "The images," she explains, "serve as objective correlatives of the feeling states, precisely as images do in creative art forms" (249). "Images," Bucci explains, "may be characterized as transitional in format, combining some features of both subsymbolic representations and verbal symbols" (175). They provide a transition from emotions and other implicit, purely subsymbolic registers to their expression in language. Bucci describes dreams as following a progression through the three registers from affect to image to a final re-creation in language. Poetic creation follows this same progression, which we reverse when reading.

After describing and discussing the three registers with my students, I ask them which register dreams primarily occur in. While there may be language or emotions experienced in dreams, we recognize that they primarily occur in the imagistic register. Following Freud and Bucci, I explain that if we accept that our dreams have meaning then there is some kind of affective force or desire behind them that our mind is trying to express.[10] When we dream, our mind converts these affects into mental images that make up the content of the dream. After we awaken from the dream, we might tell a friend or family member, or our analyst, about it, and then we are operating in the linguistic register. Poetry works exactly like this. A poet has some state of being to express. The poet explores mental images to express it. Then we see these in the figurative or metaphoric language of poetry. To analyze a dream, we work backward from language to get to the emotion behind it, and we can analyze poetry the same way. But we can also use these concepts to analyze our own experience of a poem. We read the language of the poem and come to some kind of linguistic, cognitive understanding of its meaning. But we can also look at the unique images that the poem brings up in our minds. Then, we can consider what affects the poem brings up in us. As we approach poems this way, our experience of a poem becomes integrated across the three registers. We can learn a great deal about ourselves when we gain this deeper and more complete awareness of our experience.

Integration and the Brain

While students have little trouble grasping the three registers as abstract concepts, I find it useful to approach them in biological terms as well. Along with introducing students to a more contemporary understanding of the mind/brain connection, this approach also gives them a more concrete understanding of how integration takes place in the brain when exploring literary works. Envisioning the brain as a network of interconnected cells and systems that give rise to thoughts, affects, functions, and perceptions—literally all human experiences—offers students a biological perspective on these psychological phenomena. They come to understand the brain and all that it does as a highly complex and highly active web of communications. While psychoanalysis has provided us with useful metaphors for describing mental experience, our contemporary understanding of the brain through neurobiology has taught us that making connections in the brain and achieving psychic change is not a metaphorical, but a physical phenomenon. Here, I will discuss the two models of mental integration that are recognized by the emergent field of neuropsychoanalysis—a left/right and a top/down model—and discuss their relevance to the teaching of literature.[11] Ultimately, what I am proposing is a different model or paradigm of integration for the literature classroom based on the three registers of experience, but reframing them in neuropsychoanalytic terms.

I begin by establishing a basic understanding of the biology of the brain with my students.[12] The human brain operates through a complex network of nerve cells called neurons. It is estimated that the brain contains 100 billion total neurons. Each neuron has multiple extensions called dendrites and one extending structure called an axon. Neurons communicate with each other through connections between an axon terminal of one cell and a dendrite of another. The area where two cells connect is called a synapse. Here, they communicate electrochemically when an electrical signal from an axon fires and leads to the release of chemicals called neurotransmitters. These neurotransmitters send signals to the postsynaptic cell that will either inhibit or stimulate its potential to fire and communicate with the next cell in the neural pathway. Each neuron in the brain can make up to around one thousand synaptic connections so that there are an estimated 100 trillion synapses in the brain.

Neurons tend to collect into areas and form structures called nuclei that serve unique brain functions; we refer to these areas as grey matter. Neurons within a nucleus are connected with each other through inter- or short-axon neurons. Nuclei also communicate with, or project to, other nuclei in other parts of the brain through bundles of long-axons called white matter. These axon pathways occur within each brain hemisphere, across left and right hemispheres, and across systems in different areas of the brain. Needless to say, this all becomes very complicated, and even with all of the huge advances in neuroscience over the past two decades, our understanding of the brain remains less than completely adequate. What is important to consider here, however, is that every human function from the simplest instinctual movement to the most complex thought and act of self-reflection involves the firing of neurons along a specific network of neural connections. As Joseph LeDoux says, "[T]he self is synaptic" (2). When we talk about integration in neuroscience, we mean linking systems and strengthening synaptic connections within and between systems.

The most important concept for neuropsychoanalysis in relation to integration is neuroplasticity. Up until fairly recently, neurologists thought of the brain as a hardwired organ, but they now understand that the brain is incredibly plastic: when we learn and have experiences and change as people, the synaptic connections in our brains literally change. Synapses between specific neurons can alter in a few different ways, either strengthening or weakening their connection and their capability for stimulation or inhibition. The axon can increase the amount of neurotransmitter it releases in order to increase its influence on the postsynaptic cell. The dendrites of the postsynaptic cell can change shape to either increase or decrease the effectiveness of a synapse. Or, new synapses can form when axons sprout new terminals to make new connections. The formation of new synapses primarily occurs with interneurons, neurons within a nuclei, so that, for example, people who play the violin have an increased brain area for the system influencing the motor functions of their fingers, and blind people will often have larger areas for auditory input systems.

The concept of brain plasticity has created a new paradigm for our understanding of psychoanalytic therapy. Neuropsychoanalysts now widely believe that when therapy brings about change in patients, the connections between the neurons that structure the brain also change. Susan Vaughan explains that "[w]e now have solid scientific evidence to suggest that the so-called 'talking cure,' originally devised by Freud, literally alters the way in which the neurons in the brain are connected to one another. This rewiring leads to changes in how you process, integrate, experience, and understand information and emotion" (4). Eric Kandel sees a major principle of the mind/brain connection as follows: "Insofar as psychotherapy or counseling is effective and produces long-term changes in behavior, it presumably does so through learning, by producing changes in gene expression that alter the strength of synaptic connections and structural changes that alter the anatomical pattern of interconnections between nerve cells of the brain" (39). Vaughn, thus, uses the metaphor of the therapist as "a microsurgeon of the mind" (3) and Norman Doidge refers to psychoanalysis as a "neuroplastic therapy" (215–244). So we can think of our brains as not only a complex web, but also an ever-changing complex web. As educators, we might consider the implications of what we do in terms of neuroplasticity. When we pass on knowledge or get students to think in new ways, we are changing their brains biologically. If nothing else, this should tell us that there is a lot at stake in education. When we teach literature in such a way as to increase awareness and integration, we are using literary texts to achieve nothing less than a neural restructuring of the brains of our students.

Neuropsychoanalysis recognizes two general models of integration that take place in the brain: a left/right model, where connections are strengthened between the two hemispheres of our brain across a large area of white matter called the corpus callosum, and a top/down model, where the more primitive parts of our brain (the hind brain and the limbic system) are brought under the influence of the higher-order, executive brain in the cerebral cortex of the forebrain. Language, particularly as it functions as a vehicle of higher-order thought processes, most notably self-reflection and regulation, is central to both types of integration. However, as I will explain, both of these neuropsychoanalytic models are based on an ego psychology model that may be problematic for the kind of literature classroom I envision.

For several decades now, pop-psychology has generalized the dominant functions of the left and right hemispheres of the brain, even proposing that some people are more dominated by one side or the other. Left-brained people are supposedly more logical and rational, and less creative, whereas, right-brained people are more intuitive and creative. In 1974, David Galin proposed a neuropsychoanalytical hypothesis that the left brain was the seat of consciousness—the ego—dominated by Freud's secondary processes, and the right brain was the seat of the unconscious dominated by primary processes. More recently, Louis Cozolino has adopted this theory stressing the importance of left-right integration in therapy. He explains the differences between the two hemispheres of the brain: "The right hemisphere is more highly connected with the body and the more primitive and emotional aspects of functioning. The left hemisphere is more closely identified with cortical functioning, whereas the right is more densely connected with limbic and brain stem functions" (30). In Cozolino's view, the right brain is the more primitive brain that we must connect with the higher functions of the left brain—including, most importantly, language. He writes, "[A]dequate language production requires an integration of the grammatical functions of the left and the emotional functions of the right. Left-right integration allows us to put feelings into words, consider feelings in conscious awareness, and balance the positive and negative affective biases of the left and right hemispheres" (29).

Mark Solms and Oliver Turnbull, however, remain wary of strict divisions in terms of left and right brain. While they acknowledge some functional dichotomies—the left brain being related to the verbal, logical, and analytic aspects of mental functioning, and the right being related to visuospatial, imagistic, and holistic processing—they maintain that "all of the attempts to dichotomize the basic mental functions of the left and right hemispheres have proved futile, and it is likely that there is no single fundamental factor that distinguishes the functions of the two hemispheres" (244–245). In order to disprove Galin's theory, Solms and Turnbull turn to clinical cases where after suffering damage to areas in the left brain, patients lose major aspects of their linguistic and even cognitive functions, yet their ego functions remain intact. They continue to act rationally and do not fall into the delusive state that would come with complete dominance of the primary processes. While the left brain is clearly the dominant sphere of language production, it is doubtful that it has any regulatory or executive function.

There are two connected areas of the left brain that have been specifically identified with higher-order linguistic functions. Broca's area, located in the frontal lobe of the left hemisphere, is essential for our ability to produce language. Wernicke's area, located in the temporal lobe of the left hemisphere, is essential for our ability to understand language.[13] Patients suffering from Broca's aphasia due to damage to Broca's area will eventually become mute, while those with Wernicke's aphasia will only speak nonsense. These two areas of the left hemisphere are essential for our capacity to map words to meaning so that we may both understand and produce them. However, the parallel areas of the right hemisphere, we now know, also play an important role in language. They are involved in the tonal or musical elements of speech. Appropriately, damage to the area parallel to Broca's in the right hemisphere causes patients to speak only in flat tones. And, likewise, patients with damage to the area parallel to Wernicke's in the right hemisphere cannot understand inflection in language. Those of us interested in poetic language should find this fascinating; the right hemisphere is involved in prosody. Even if the left brain lacks an executive function, the Freudian primary-/secondary-process parallel is accurate to some extent. The left brain is central to the secondary, formal aspects of language, while the right brain is important for the emotional, tonal, and somatic elements of communication. Norman Holland proposes that a major reason that literary language provides such a source of pleasure is because the brain makes sense of it by "applying right-hemisphere language systems that, with ordinary language, are less used" (*Literature* 7).[14] We may also relate this to Julia Kristeva's semiotic (which would be right brain) and symbolic (left brain) elements of poetic language. Poetic language represents, at least on a linguistic level, the integration of the two hemispheres. Those interested in *écriture féminine* will also find it significant that the female brain is thought by neurologists to have less strict hemispheric lateralization than the male brain. Female brains are more integrated between the two hemispheres.[15] A recent study has also revealed that musicians' brains are more bilaterally active than those of nonmusicians (Patston et al.). I suspect that the same would be true of poets.

Solms and Turnbull focus on a top/down model of integration, looking at the neurological separation of the brain into an older, inner brain involved in more primal functions, and a more recently evolved, outer, executive brain, with its unique regulatory prefrontal lobe. Cozolino also describes this form of top/down integration, which "includes the ability of the cortex [the outer brain] to process, inhibit, and organize the reflexes, impulses, and emotions generated by the brain stem and limbic system [the inner brain]" (29). Basically, this means getting in touch with the contents of the inner brain and our more primal elements, including emotions, desires, and unconscious memories, so that we may apply our higher, outer brain capacities for thought, reflection, and control to them. Solms and Turnbull see the external, executive brain, particularly the prefrontal lobes, as acting as judge and inhibitor and giving us consciousness and control over emotion in particular. The prefrontal lobes form a superstructure over the rest of the brain that "gives them the capacity to integrate all the information streaming into the brain (from its current visceral and environmental situation) with all the information derived from previous experience stored elsewhere in the brain—and then to calculate the best course of action before executing a motor response" (287). As Freud theorized, consciousness enables one to regulate primitive drives.

The prefrontal lobes are unique to human beings, while our basic inner brain structures are similar, in varying degrees, to those of animals. Solms and Turnbull relate the executive function to Freud's concept of the ego, and essentially offer an ego psychology model that favors a strengthening of the ego as it extends its influence over the id (the primal brain). "The aim of the talking cure, then, from the neurobiological point of view" they argue, "must be to extend the functional sphere of influence of the prefrontal lobes" (287–288). A strong ego reverses the effects of repression, bringing conscious inhibitory restraints on unconscious urges by making them conscious. Therapy or the talking cure, Solms and Turnbull argue, uses language to restructure neurological functions that make connections in the brain and regulate behavior. Solms and Turnbull call language "an extremely powerful tool for establishing supraordinate, reflexive, and abstract connections between the concrete elements of perception and memory, and for thereby subordinating behavior to selective programs of activity" (288). Likewise, literary language has the potential to serve as a tool in the classroom for helping students attain greater awareness that could help them to regulate behavior in positive and productive ways. We can potentially use literature to get students to express and become more conscious of their inner experiences—particularly their emotions—and, in this ego psychology model, they can reflect on their emotions, opinions, and behaviors in order to control or correct them through the function of the ego.

One problem with an ego psychology model, however, is that it is guilty of what neurologist Antonio Damasio has famously called "Descartes' Error." That is, it assumes that reason is entirely separate from emotion, and that emotion necessarily clouds reason. Damasio bases his hypothesis that reason and emotion are interrelated in highly significant ways on his studies of "neurological patients who had defects of decision-making and a disorder of emotion" (x). For example, one patient called Elliot suffered damage to the prefrontal cortex and some of its connecting axons after removal of a brain tumor. The result was a total loss of emotional experience. Elliot appeared almost normal in many ways and retained a reasonable intellectual capacity, but without the use of emotions to guide him, he lost the capability to make rational decisions. The truth of this Cartisian dualism between reason and emotion has been popularly assumed since the Enlightenment, but has recently come under severe scrutiny from contemporary neuroscience as well as psychology.[16]

Another important criticism of an ego psychology model comes from Lacan who was a harsh critic of ego psychology as well as of Descartes' cogito, which, he argues, gave rise to the imaginary concept of the ego in Western thought. The ego, to Lacan, is an artificial construct and the danger of ego psychology is that it essentially involves patients taking on the egos of their analysts, rather than locating their own desire through language. The danger in the literature classroom is in having the student simply take on the ego of the writer who is expressing the emotion or thought, or of the teacher who is guiding the student's experience of a text.

If we want to use literature psychoanalytically to help students raise genuine self-awareness, then this dynamic will always be a concern. To try to avoid this ego introjection, we must to some extent downplay the authority of texts and our authority as teachers. The most positive kind of learning occurs when we keep desire in play for our students, rather than close it off by authoritatively insisting on a certain meaning, experience, or political view of a text.

Neuroscience also teaches us about the nature of desire and the jouissance (or profound pleasure) of keeping that desire in play. These are issues that literary theory has concerned itself with for several decades now. Here, we can consider our contemporary understanding of the limbic system in the brain, and particularly the reward system within it that regulates pleasure and motivates behavior. The limbic system is a large, complicated, and heavily integrative system of nuclei with many subsystems. In fact, we might think of it as more of an expanding concept than a proper neurobiological system. The functions of the limbic system determine the way we engage with the world—our personality, mood, and temperament. Jeanette Norden explains that it is the system that "adds emotional texture to our lives." It is involved not only in emotions but in motivation, learning, memory, emotional memory, pleasure, and even executive functions. Within the limbic system is the endogenous reward system. This system involves a projection from the ventral tegmental area (VTA) in the midbrain to the nucleus accumben septi (a structure implicit in addiction) and to the higher-order cortex. This projection from the VTA gives rise to feelings of pleasure and well-being, and can be stimulated by any kind of behavior or outside influence that gives us joy—including feeling love, enjoying a good meal, or potentially, reading and learning. Holland cites this system as central to our enjoyment of literature and art (*Literature* 168–170).[17] The endemic reward system is the system that motivates us to seek pleasure and allows us to enjoy it. Damage to this system can lead one to lose all capacity for joy and fall into a deep depression. Essentially, it is the seat of desire in our brains. Imagining and anticipating pleasure also activates this system and motivates us to seek it. It is with this system in mind that I call for keeping desire in play in the literature classroom and not closing off desire by insisting on an authoritative meaning of a text, which would lead students to adapt the ego of the teacher or the author.

I propose a neuropsychoanalytically integrative model for the classroom based on the goal of integrating the three registers of experience in order to seek the truth of one's desire. If we think about integration of the three registers through an understanding of the biology of the brain, we find a useful model for thinking about how integration occurs in the literature classroom. We know we have linguistic systems in the brain, we have systems involving visual and other forms of sensory perception, and we have systems in the brain involved in experiencing affect.[18] I am proposing that we get students talking and writing about their subjective emotional responses to literary language and to the mental images that this language brings up in their minds. A biological understanding of the brain allows them to better visualize or conceptualize how this integration occurs through the alteration of synaptic connections between and within systems in the brain. Literature teachers tend to focus exclusively on linguistic meaning in the classroom, which is important, but which activates a more limited number of brain systems and does less to promote self- or social awareness. Many of us focus on historical or cultural contexts of the literary works that we teach, also important, and many of us even relate these contexts to contemporary social issues, but without helping students to attain an understanding of their responses to such issues through the three registers, that is, across different areas of the brain, it is less likely that they will resonate with students or significantly change their ways of thinking.

CHAPTER THREE

THE TEACHER AS (WHOLE, USEFUL,
AND PERMANENT) OBJECT

Melanie Klein's concept of projective identification provides an important theoretical basis through which we may consider the dynamics of the classroom. Students will often use projective identification with their teachers as a defense in order to avoid or short-circuit the frustrating process of learning and developing while concurrently creating a poor environment for education. However, projective identification also provides a useful means of communication between teacher and student that can help teachers empathize better with students, so that teachers can respond better to their educational needs. Projective identification can be a defense that disrupts education, or a tool that potentially enhances it. Projective identification refers to a process of projection where in fantasy one puts, or projects, parts of one's self into an other in such a way that seeks to create a response or alter the other. In the classroom, students will expel and project anxiety-causing parts of themselves into teachers who will then experience their own anxiety; or, students may project their interest and genuine excitement about a class into a teacher, causing the teacher to feel gratified and encouraged. Projective identification can have positive or negative consequences in the classroom depending on the nature of the projections and the way they are responded to.

The roots of projective identification occur in early infanthood. Klein discusses how, in the infant, "split-off parts of the ego are...projected... *into* the mother. These...bad parts of self are meant not only to injure but also to control and take possession of the object. In so far as the mother comes to contain the bad parts of self, she is felt to be not a separate individual but rather *the* bad self." Klein explains that this "leads to the prototype of an aggressive object relation" (*Selected* 183). This negative aspect of projective identification forms "the basis of many anxiety situations"—paranoia in particular (186). When students project bad parts of themselves into their teacher, it will increase anxiety and prove severely detrimental to education. However, Klein writes, it is "not only the bad parts of the self which are expelled and projected, but also good parts of the self." These parts of the ego that "are expelled and projected into the other person represent the good, i.e. the loving parts of self" (183). In this positive projective identification, the prototype of a loving object is formed so long as this projection is not so excessive as to give one the sense of losing the good parts of self to an idealized other. A teacher experienced as a good object can provide education that students experience with gratitude, but a teacher who is overly idealized, particularly as an absolute authority over texts, may prevent students from taking the necessary responsibility for their own education. "The processes of splitting off parts of the self and projecting them into objects," Klein writes, "are thus of vital importance for normal development as well as for abnormal object relations" (184). Irving Solomon writes, "The therapist has to distinguish between projective identification as a form of communication and projective identification as a means of expulsion of unwanted parts of the self into the external object" (26). Projective identification may enable deeper understanding for the mother with her infant, for the analyst with the patient, or, I propose, for teachers with their students, but it can also act as a major impediment to education when students use it as a defense. However, even in its negative or aggressive application, it can potentially be used as a means of better understanding students and their needs.

Projective identification is the key primal defense mechanism of what Klein calls the paranoid/schizoid position where objects are not experienced as whole, but divided into strict categories of good and bad. Bad objects then become threatening and must be attacked in return in fantasy. The prototype of the infant's early object experience is the mother's breast, but in the paranoid/schizoid position, the breast is not a whole object but is split between the good breast, which provides nourishment and life, and the bad breast, which, in its absence, withholds these things and threatens survival. Klein is primarily concerned with the conflicts between negative emotions of hatred and fear and positive loving emotions that the individual must balance. Klein links the development of these instincts to primary object relations. In early infantile fantasy, the good breast must be protected and restored; this motivates the infant to split it off from the bad breast. The bad breast becomes the object of hatred and fantasy attacks. In these attacks, the infant seeks to possess and/or destroy the valuable contents of the maternal body that it imagines as being withheld, robbing one of nourishment and pleasure. Infants project internal impulses onto their objects—love onto good objects, and sadistic impulses onto bad objects that then become objects of fear insofar as they withhold or potentially retaliate in response to the infant's fantasy attacks. Infants also introject their objects. The early introjection of a strong, loving object—a good mother—ultimately proves crucial for later positive development. In maturity, the good object must become a whole object that is ultimately good, but not purely good, not ideal or perfect but still loved and loving.

Klein conceives of two positions of early infantile experience that provide a base structure for the adult subject, the aforementioned paranoid/schizoid position and the depressive position. The paranoid/schizoid position begins at birth and remains dominant until around three to four months of age. "Paranoid" refers to the infant's fears of retaliation from objects attacked in fantasy. As the infant projects its own hatred and aggression onto these objects, it fears annihilation at their hands. The schizoid aspect of the position refers to the infant's splitting of good and bad objects as a defense mechanism in order to protect good objects from attacks and aggression. This splitting offers an unrealistic defense against sadism until the child grows capable of loving whole objects. Klein sees the rise of anxiety due to aggressive instincts as primary and immediate in the child's life. "I hold," she writes, "that anxiety arises from the operation of the death instinct within the organism, is felt as fear of annihilation (death) and takes the form of fear of persecution" (*Selected* 179). The defenses against aggressive instincts that arise in the paranoid/schizoid position are necessarily employed for the survival of the underdeveloped ego. Klein writes, "The vital need to deal with anxiety forces the early ego to develop fundamental mechanisms and defenses. The destructive impulse is partly projected outward and...attaches itself to the first external object, the mother's breast" (180).

In later infancy, one achieves the depressive position. Here, the infant moves "from a partial object relation to the relation to a complete object" and must cope with the realization that the good mother and the bad mother are one and the same (*Selected* 118). This leads to anxiety over the loss of, or damage done to, the primary good object through earlier sadistic fantasies. The infant realizes that prior attacks on the bad mother were also endured by the good mother. This gives rise to guilt and the fear of abandonment due to one's own destructive tendencies. As Klein explains, "[F]eelings both of a destructive and of a loving nature are experiences towards one and the same object and this gives rise to deep and disturbing conflicts in the child's mind" (141). This depressive anxiety necessarily leads one to make loving reparation to the maternal object as a whole object if mental health is to be attained. This gives rise to symbolization as a means of coping. Both symbolization and the creation of new object relationships provide tools for repairing the primary relationship with the mother. "The ego feels impelled," Klein states, " to make restitution for all the sadistic attacks it has launched on [the good] object" (120). The subject must resolve and maintain the depressive position through this ongoing process of reparation where the object is made whole—imperfect, but ultimately loving. Klein explains, "The drive to make reparation, which comes to the fore at this stage, can be regarded as a consequence of greater insight into psychic reality... [I]t shows a more realistic response to the feelings of grief, guilt and fear of loss resulting from the aggression against the loved object" (189). The subject must heal the damage done to the mother in fantasy, and maintain the mother as a whole object. Through this process, the subject maintains a realistic view of the world, love overcomes hatred, and personal development may continue. This drive to repair, Klein writes, "paves the way for more satisfactory object relations and sublimations" (189). The Kleinian subject, however, remains fluid and prone to employing negative defenses against the anxiety inducing guilt of the depressive position, which typically involve a regression to paranoid/schizoid thinking where objects are partial and the debilitating fear of annihilation dominates. As the primary object in the child's life, this relationship to the breast, and eventually to the whole mother, plays a central role in development. A successful passage through the paranoid/schizoid position, where the ego remains intact, becomes essential for successful integration in the depressive position, and throughout adult life. In the classroom, students will often defend against anxiety by splitting their teachers in ways that turn them into representations of students' own authoritative superegos through both overly positive and negative projective identification. Teachers then come to represent either the ideal ego (the purely good mother) or the harsh superego (the purely bad mother)—both of which impede education.

As a defense, like any other defense, projective identification seeks to decrease anxiety. Students will often project positive, good elements of themselves, the parts of themselves that could master classroom material through the frustrating process of learning, into an ideal object/teacher who has already mastered the material and can simply pass it on to them in a stress-free environment. The idealized teacher is not a whole object, but a purely good one who does not bring about the anxiety required in learning. When the teacher is coaxed, through projective identification, into taking this idealized role, it may make for a comfortable classroom, but it will not provide the optimal environment for learning and student development. However, students may experience not just the normal anxiety involved with learning in the classroom; they may also experience anxiety due to their envy of the teacher on whom they feel dependent in order to achieve their educational goals. In these cases, students project negative elements of self, in particular their harsh superegos that make them feel inadequate, into teachers whom they experience as inadequate. Such teachers have nothing to offer, and therefore will not bring about envy and the anxiety that goes with it. But such teachers also cannot provide education. Students expel their own fears of inadequacy into the teacher in order to make the teacher feel inadequate. Vulnerable teachers will feel attacked not only by students, but also by their internal superegos that make them feel "not good enough." Teachers may make the situation worse by reacting to students' attacks with counterattacks where they experience students as uncaring, lazy, stupid, or otherwise unworthy of their effort as teachers, and, in some cases, where they will verbally reprimand students in the classroom. In such cases, an educational environment will quickly decline in a way that is difficult to recover from.

One major problem with projective identification in the classroom is that by expelling parts of self, positive or negative, students lose self-awareness and cannot realize their potential. We want our students to move beyond unrealistic paranoid/schizoid defenses into the depressive position where realistic awareness can occur. In the depressive position, objects are not strictly split between good and bad, but are experienced as whole. A teacher thus will not be overly idealized or harshly attacked through projective identification. In the depressive position, students are able to take back the elements of self that they have expelled so that they can take responsibility for them. Not only is the teacher then experienced as a whole object, neither ideal nor bad, but the student becomes whole as well. When defensive projective identification is relinquished, the students' egos grow stronger and more integrated. They become subjects separate from the teacher, and the teacher becomes an object separate from them rather than simply an object of their projections. The student can then take on the role of one who can achieve mastery instead of projecting that role into an idealized teacher, and students can tolerate frustration instead of attacking its perceived external source. Betty Joseph explains that real understanding occurs in the depressive position, where one is able to "use" understanding "in the sense of discussing, standing aside from a problem, seeking, but even more, considering explanations." This level of understanding involves "the capacity to take responsibility for one's impulses" (140). Only in the depressive position does one have the capacity for self-reflection and the mature object relations necessary to gain deeper awareness and to achieve reparation. Students will feel capable and will no longer need to attack the teacher by projecting their fear of inadequacy. What the teacher can offer then will be experienced with gratitude and not with envy that stifles education.

As teachers, we must learn to understand and use projective identification, even when it comes in the form of an attack, because of what it communicates to us. Projections tend to exist in subsymbolic forms of communication such as body language or tone of voice, which can make them difficult to consciously process. But we can pick up on them by being receptive to the way they make us feel and reflecting on, rather than ignoring, them. When students project into teachers, teachers will experience a form of countertransference. Robert Waska defines Kleinian countertransference in a clinical setting as "the analyst's total reaction to the patient," which includes "all intrapsychic responses to the patient's projection of internal objects through the dynamic of PI [projective identification]" (160). We can use our countertransferences that take place in the classroom to better understand the needs and anxieties of students. We should not allow ourselves to be negatively affected by projective identifications from our students, even when they come in the form of attacks, and we certainly should not respond back with attacks—active or passive. Rather, we should take students' projections as forms of communication where students tell us that the class is either too stressful or too boring for optimal learning to take place.

Daniel Goleman discusses an optimal level of stress that is most conducive to education. If students have too much stress, their anxiety will inhibit their brain's cognitive and creative ability. Likewise, students with too little stress will become bored and apathetic (270–272). Our task as teachers, which Goleman describes as an "emotional task," is to achieve and maintain this optimal level of stress in the classroom (274). We can use projective identification to know when students are becoming too bored or too anxious in a classroom because they will make us feel bored or anxious. Students will often project their lack of interest into teachers who will then begin to lose interest themselves. Or, students may project their frustrations into teachers who will then become frustrated with students. The key is not to act out on our countertransferences through attacks, reprojections, or apathy, but to receive projections, and adjust our teaching accordingly—not because the students are controlling us but because we are understanding and empathizing with them. This may mean pushing a class that is bored, or making them more active participants in the material through different class activities. Or, it may mean easing off a bit or providing more support to a class that is experiencing overwhelming frustrations.

I would also like to stress here the importance of teachers within an institution meeting regularly to discuss their teaching experiences with each other. This kind of support group is common during many of our first teaching experiences as graduate students, but tends to disappear later when we become full-time faculty members. The insights of our colleagues can prove extremely helpful because the projections we receive and our reactions to them tend to occur on an unconscious level. Talking about our current teaching experiences with other teachers and getting their feedback can help us to realize more clearly what is occurring in our classes and how we feel about it.

We may ask here exactly what kind of object the teacher should be in a classroom to achieve an optimal level of stress and to encourage students to function in the depressive position. The teacher should not, for one, take on the role of the superego in either its idealized or its harsh, overly critical form. An ideal object makes students who need to take responsibility for their own education and development too dependent on the teacher. They will not be sufficiently engaged in material even though the class may appear to be running smoothly. A harsh superego is destructive to students' egos. It will overwhelm them with anxiety and a sense of inadequacy, and will only evoke envy and hostility toward the teacher. Students must be challenged, but must be able to cope with these challenges if growth and learning are to occur. We want our students to have strong identities so that they are able to tolerate the frustration involved in the educational process. At the same time, we do not want these strong identities to become overly rigid because education and development require a degree of openness. As teachers, we must take on a similar role. We must remain strong enough in our identities to tolerate the frustrations that students will project into us, but open enough to adjust to students' needs when necessary.

A major part of attaining strong but fluid identities as teachers involves gaining deeper self-awareness by constantly analyzing our teaching methods and constantly interrogating our motives. This is an area where regularly meeting with our colleagues to discuss teaching can be extremely beneficial, but it also requires looking inward. If we, as teachers, achieve an understanding of our own identities—our own needs, desires, fantasies, etcetera—we can avoid teaching practices designed to support our narcissism and enact those that are most useful or helpful to our students. Of course, we must maintain some self-interest in order to function as teachers, but our gratification comes when we see the resultant development in our students. When we become better able to respond to student needs, we develop a gratifying identity for ourselves as teachers, one of helping others to achieve. Mark Bracher explains, "The fullest enactment of our (teachers') identities occurs to the extent that we enable our students to develop their identities in ways that enable their greatest possible personal fulfillment, which is itself found...in prosocial activities that benefit others" (*Radical* 77). A teacher's identity can be both strong and flexible if we maintain it as an identity bound in our students and our field. We may change our teaching style and methods, but must remain committed to what we teach, and, above all, the people we teach. Bracher writes, "Truly ethical teaching is teaching that helps our students learn, grow, and develop their identity to its optimal extent" (156). Teachers with rigid egos will not be able to support student identities because they are too concerned with protecting their own identities. However, teachers who lack confidence and commitment, who have weak identities as teachers, will prove too vulnerable to the attacks and manipulations that frustrated or anxious students will project into them.

Student frustration is inevitable and necessary in any class that provides students with anything of educational value. Deborah Britzman writes, "Education is often the stage for painful fights, ... for the urgency of wanting to learn and the defense of needing to already know" (*Novel* 148). Not knowing can be difficult for the ego. It gives rise to anxiety based on the fear of inadequacy and envy toward the one who, one imagines, does know—the teacher. Because attacks and manipulations through projective identification are inevitable in the classroom, the teacher—like the mother with her infant or the analyst with the analysand—must be capable of surviving them. We must experience and survive the frustrations of our students and use these frustrations to support our students' development. As poetry therapist Deborah Eve Grayson writes, "[S]ome of our most memorable learning occurs because we successfully weathered the storm of fear or anger in order to reach the shore of safety, security, and knowledge" (83). Our ability to weather the storm will directly influence our students' ability to do so.

As teachers, we must become useable objects to students. We do this by showing that we can survive their omnipotent projections, through which they imagine they can control us, with our identities intact and without retaliating or moralizing. D. W. Winnicott discusses the difference between relating to an object and the more mature ability to "use" an object. He writes, "In object-relating the subject allows certain alterations in the self to take place...Projection mechanisms and identifications have been operating, and the subject is found in the object" (88). To make use of an object like a teacher, for example, the student must be able to place the teacher "outside of the area of subjective phenomena" (87). "Relating," Winnicott clarifies, "can be described in terms of the individual subject...usage cannot be described except in terms of acceptance of the object's independent existence" (88). The useful object is not a creation of the subject, not a result of the subject's projections, but is experienced as an independent object. Between relating and use "is the subject's placing of the object outside the area of the subject's omnipotent control; that is, the subject's perception of the object as an external phenomenon, not as a projective entity, in fact recognition of it as an entity in its own right" (89). When teachers show they can experience students' projections and keep their identities as teachers intact without counterattacking by either becoming aggressive toward students or apathetic toward teaching, they show they are not simply objects to be related to or controlled through projective mechanisms, but that they are separate objects, beyond students' omnipotent control, who have something of value to offer. Winnicott explains that the object must be destroyed in a sense, destroyed as an internal object, but must survive unchanged as an external object (90–91). Teachers show survival, or "object permanence," by patiently coming to understand what students' projections are communicating, not by acting out on them or allowing them to fundamentally alter the teacher (91–93). The teacher who survives shows students that they are not the objects of students' fantasy projections, and, instead come to be understood by students as separate, whole objects that they can use and learn from. To be of use to students requires us as teachers to maintain confidence in ourselves and in the abilities of our students—to believe in the educational process and to empathize.

Britzman points out that object permanence also applies to students (*Novel* 119–121). They must be able to survive our attempts to make them develop and learn with their egos intact. As teachers, we must not only educate but also help students survive their education. Eric Brenman writes of this phenomenon in terms of the psychoanalytic encounter, "[T]he pursuit of truth goes hand in glove with the ego strength to bear it. This strength is derived from supporting relationships" (3). Surviving students' projections with our identities as teachers intact, while remaining open to what these projections communicate to us, will help students survive our demands and remain open to what we can offer them. In this way, the educational process becomes one of mutual support and development between teachers and students.

One model that will help us to consider the way we can experience students' projective identifications and use them to offer support is Wilfred Bion's concept of a container. Teachers may act as containers through empathy, just as we encourage empathy in our students. The mother/infant relationship provides the prototype of the container/contained relationship. This primal object relationship enables the subject to tolerate and regulate affects. When an infant experiences intense emotions, the attuned parent reflects the experience back and then stabilizes it, soothing the child. This enables the child's capacity for diverse and intense emotional experience. Ruth Riesenberg-Malcolm defines the theory of containment

> as the capacity of one individual (or object) to receive in himself projections from another individual, which he then can sense and use as communications (from him), transform them, and finally give them back (or convey back) to the subject in a modified form. Eventually, this can enable the person (an infant at first) to sense and tolerate his own feelings and develop a capacity to think. (166)

Projected experiences, she continues, "go into the mother who modifies them through an emotional function that transforms the baby's raw sensations into something that—if all goes well—the baby takes back into herself and becomes the basis for the baby's awareness of her feelings and, eventually, thoughts" (168). In the prototypical relationship, the mother acts as the container for the contained projective identifications of the infant.

As teachers, we must allow for some frustration in our students, but must strive to keep it at an optimal level. When students do experience frustration and project it into us, we must be able to contain it and help students to cope with it. We can help students to cope by empowering and instilling confidence in them by both downplaying our authority and by listening attentively to their thoughts, ideas, and feelings about texts. Jeffrey Berman writes, "Empowering teachers are compassionate and attentive, and though their educational philosophy and pedagogical styles may vary, they affirm their students' curiosity for knowledge and self-worth" (89). Students will eventually learn to cope with the frustrations of the classroom on their own and delay evacuating their anxiety through projection. Bion writes, "The choice that matters to the psychoanalyst is one that lies between *procedures designed to evade frustration and those designed to modify it. That is the critical decision*" (29). In order to avoid immediate evacuation, the frustrating experience must be tolerated. Projected frustrations are contained and then returned by the attuned teacher so as to become more tolerable, so that students will not need to evacuate them in the future. Teachers can contain students' frustrations and respond to them in a number of ways that may include simply offering words of encouragement such as, "I know this is a tough assignment, but it's nothing you can't handle." Or we may have to respond to frustrations by making ourselves available outside of the classroom where we can offer more direct support, or by taking a different approach to material inside the classroom. The important aspect of the container, as it relates to teaching, is to remain patient and try to understand what students' projections communicate to us—to use them to empathize better with students.

To be a whole, useful object, the teacher must put the needs of students first, but this is not the same as putting their demands first. What students may demand is a lack of anxiety, which is not conducive to learning and development. We should not try to protect our students from stress, but should keep it contained, in part, through empathy and understanding. Goleman explains that "whenever teachers create an empathetic and responsive environment, students not only improve in their grades and test scores—they become eager learners" (284). The good teacher, like a good boss in the workplace, must provide students a "secure base" (277).

The term "secure base" comes from John Bowlby and attachment theory. Bowlby writes that the central feature of parenting is

> [t]he provision by both parents of a secure base from which a child or an adolescent can make sorties into the outside world and to which he can return knowing for sure that he will be welcomed when he gets there, nourished physically and emotionally, comforted if distressed, reassured if frightened. In essence this role is one of being available, ready to respond when called upon to encourage and perhaps assist, but to intervene actively only when clearly necessary. (11)

Jeremy Holmes lists several types of caregiver responses associated with secure attachment: "[R]esponsiveness, sensitivity, consistency, reliability, attunement, the capacity to absorb protest and 'mild-mindedness,' the ability to see the distressed child as an autonomous and sentient being with feelings and projects of his or her own" (9). We can compare this to Goleman's list of the characteristics of a good boss: great listener, encourager, communicator, courageous, sense of humor, empathetic, decisive, takes responsibility, humble, shares authority (277), and his list of the characteristics of a good teacher: responsive to needs, lets student guide interactions, pleasant and upbeat, warm and caring, clear but flexible classroom manager (283). Not surprisingly, Hynes and Hynes-Berry list similar characteristics as essential for the bibliotherapist: "A bibliotherapist should demonstrate the necessary therapeutic attitudes of empathy, respect, and genuineness. These attitudes grow out of the personal characteristics of maturity, integrity, adaptability, and responsibility" (118). By taking on these characteristics, we provide a secure base to our students so that they are encouraged to become independent thinkers and creators. We strive to contain their frustrations, provide support, make them active and responsible participants in their education, and encourage individual development.

Rejection, Placation, and Manipulation

What we seek in the classroom is for our students to learn in a way that encourages them to grow and develop. In a poetry classroom, we want students to attain a deeper understanding of the effects of poetry and its relevance for the reader so that it can lead to increased awareness of both self and other. Our pursuit of this goal can be aided by the clinical writings of the Kleinian theorist Betty Joseph, which deal with the issue of patients attaining the kind of understanding that leads to psychic change. Much of Joseph's clinical work may be applied to the classroom setting. Michael Feldman and Elizabeth Bott Spillius describe one of the major themes in

Joseph's work as an "avoidance of what one might call 'knowledge about' in favor of 'experience in'" (3). We want to enable students to experience a poem by having them invest in it emotionally and imaginatively; we do not simply want them to acquire empty knowledge of a subject that will get them through an exam. Students will not always prove receptive to this deeper understanding, and the awareness and development that it brings. Students bring with them to our classes an entire history of relating to poetry and education in a certain way, and participating in English classes that have taken a very different approach. We may refer to this renewing and reparative approach to teaching as what Britzman, using Freud's term, calls "after-education": a psychoanalytic education that seeks to move beyond the authority, indoctrination, inhibition, and anxiety involved in traditional education (*After-Education* 4–5). While some students will find this approach to poetry new and exciting, others will avoid any real understanding or insight that it might offer them. Joseph, in her essay "The Patient who is Difficult to Reach," discusses three ways in which patients avoid gaining real understanding, each of which applies to students and their use of projective identification in the classroom. I use the terms "rejection" and "placation" for the first two and use Joseph's term "manipulation" for the last.

Rejection represents the total breakdown of education that occurs when students completely discard a teacher, text, or subject. This can occur in a passive form where students simply refuse to read, work, or engage in the class, or in a more active form where students openly attack a teacher's methods or capabilities, or the authors or texts chosen for the class. Attacks that come with rejection may involve open defiance, or may come in more subtle forms such as a roll of the eyes or a private conversation held between students during a lecture. Rejection tends to be contagious and difficult to recover from once it occurs with a large number of students, so it is important to notice students' negative projections early and to deal with them effectively.

Some students will reject understanding, or the text, class, or teacher, due to envy of the good that these things possess, or because of immature paranoid/schizoid defenses. Students will use projective identification in its negative role to split and expel their frustration, self-doubt, social fear, fear of dependence (envy), or even genuine lack of interest into the teacher. Teachers receiving these projections may in turn tend to feel frustrated with students, begin to doubt their teaching abilities or the value of the subject, fear reprimands from students that may disrupt class or lead to negative end-of-semester reviews, begin to feel envy toward students for their power, or begin to lose interest in the class or subject. Teachers who are easily frustrated or, like many inexperienced teachers, prone to self-doubt are especially vulnerable to the destructive capabilities of these negative projections.

As teachers, we must use these projections for what they communicate to us, rather than retaliating against them. When students expel unwanted elements into us, they are also communicating their educational or sometimes emotional needs. When students begin rejecting a class, its teacher, or its material, they communicate their anxiety or boredom to the teacher. It is essential that a teacher survive, contain, and use students' negative projections to better respond to their needs and create an optimal stress level for education to take place. Surviving students' projections means not crumbling under self-doubt when things begin going badly in the classroom. Instead of showing self-doubt or doubting oneself into incapacity, teachers must show students that they are strong, permanent objects. A strong object, however, is not a stubborn one. Teachers must be prepared to interpret students' projective identifications and adjust to their needs. Teachers must stay committed to the students and the class, but not to their ineffective teaching methods.

It is also extremely important that teachers contain students' frustration and not respond by acting out their own. Nothing will perpetuate or broaden rejection like a counterattack. Frustration in the classroom is inevitable, but we must not act out on the frustration that students project into us. We must understand that students may envy our authority, but it will do little good to point out this envy or insist on our authority. We cannot force gratitude. It is much more productive to relinquish some authority by doing class activities that make students active participants and that put learning into their hands.

Rejection stems mainly from students' inability to tolerate frustration in one form or another. Poetry can be frustrating in its inexact, playful, at times even evasive, use of language. The teacher must act as a container for the students by not only allowing for some frustration but also setting up a nurturing environment where it is tolerable. Joseph stresses the gaining of understanding as well as "tolerating not understanding" as major goals (139). If we deemphasize meaning, the typical focus of studying poetry in an English course, in favor of experiencing, then poetry becomes less of a source of frustration. Students can then focus on learning how poetry functions and on involving themselves in the experience of poetic language without becoming frustrated when they cannot reduce a poem, a line, or an image to an equivalent meaning in conventional language.

Rejection is probably the easiest to recognize of the strategies students enact to avoid the frustrating process of learning. Other methods are less overt and easier to ignore because often there is no obvious problem in the classroom. Placation is perhaps the easiest for the teacher to fall prey to.

When students placate the teacher, they simply go along with whatever ideas the teacher presents in order to pass a test, write a paper, or, generally, to get a good grade, without really considering the information presented and its applications or relevance. With placation, students fear the anxiety that learning presents to their egos, and teachers are vulnerable when they fear this student anxiety as well. Bracher explains that

> [o]ften... the main impediment to education is not the opposition but rather the collusion between the two sets of identity needs, resulting in teachers and students engaging in activities that both parties find supportive of their identities but that do not contribute significantly to realizing the aims of education: learning and identity development. (*Radical* 79)

In the case of placation, students and teachers have the same goal. However, it is not to create an optimal educational environment, but simply to create a low-stress one. Placation often gives the appearance of active learning, but it represents the extreme in passivity. Students seem engaged when they appear to agree with and support the teacher's opinions and interpretations of texts, and when they are able to repeat these opinions and interpretations on tests and in class discussions. But it becomes an instance where no real learning, understanding, or insight occurs in students.

Placation puts the teacher in the role of the ideal object or the one who knows, but it is really an empty idealization because, though the teacher appears to have knowledge, it is empty knowledge that does not challenge students and does not lead them to attain real understanding of material or to see how the material is relevant to them. Placation typically arises as a defense against the anxiety and frustration that come with learning. When students placate, they are communicating their own self-doubt, social fear (the fear of looking bad or stupid to others), and envy or fear of dependence (since attaining only empty, unneeded knowledge would not make them feel dependent on the teacher). In this case, they are expelling through projective identification the split-off part of themselves that could engage in the material and could achieve meaningful understanding, but is afraid of the frustrating process of learning, into the teacher who already knows the material and can simply pass on information. Potentially anxious students then become bored students. They see the class material as irrelevant to them and placate the teacher who presents the material as irrelevant. The teacher whose goals are simply for students to answer objective questions and attain empty knowledge of materials will work very well with students who are bored, but who still want good grades. The students continue to desire a lack of conflict or stress in the classroom and are happy if their teacher provides it.

Placation is an easy trap for teachers to fall into, since its major characteristic involves a lack of conflict. Typically, we think of conflict as a negative in the classroom, and certainly a lack of conflict makes our jobs easier. But a complete lack of conflict in the classroom may also be an indication that students are not experiencing the texts in the ways we want them to, and are not using the texts to explore and challenge themselves. Teachers who are afraid of conflict themselves or who have fragile egos are especially vulnerable to placation because, just as it involves no real challenge to the identity of students, it involves no challenge to the identity of the teacher. There may be a degree of laziness or even narcissism in the teacher who allows placation, but essentially the teacher experiences the same fear of frustration and anxiety that students do. Projective identifications between students and teachers who fear the frustration and anxiety that go with teaching and learning will continue to reinforce placation and inhibit education.

Teachers must remember never to become too pleased with themselves or complacent with their teaching. Only teachers who constantly analyze themselves and the dynamics taking place in their classes will recognize when placation is taking the place of real education. Not only must we constantly question ourselves as teachers, but we must constantly question our students and make them responsible for their own education. The easiest way to avoid having students placate you as a teacher is to avoid telling them exactly what they should get out of a text. We must relinquish our total authority over the texts we teach and refuse to play the role of the ideal object or the one who knows. When students offer interpretations or responses to texts, we should always recognize and encourage them, but also keep them open to alternatives so that a particular student's response does not become the ultimate authority for the class either. We want to look at texts for their possibilities, both for possible linguistic meanings and possible reader responses, rather than their objective, closed meanings. At the same time, however, it remains important to establish clear goals and guidelines for the approach the class will take with poetic texts. We should make it clear to students that approaching texts is about exploring ambiguities and potential interpretations rather than establishing one master interpretation, and we should create a classroom space where students can express reactions to texts beyond linguistic meanings simply by encouraging and validating such responses.

When we do recognize that placation is taking place in the classroom, it is important not to change from the teacher who fears conflict to the teacher who attacks students for not engaging or for being brain-dead. These kinds of direct attacks on students who placate will only increase their anxiety and resistance to learning. We should, instead, engage students in activities that require them to actively assess the materials themselves, rather than passively take in our thoughts or opinions. This could include focused writing activities or small-group discussions with specific goals. We should make students do much of the work themselves when looking at a text. Our role should be to give them the tools to do this and to moderate open discussions. We should encourage open exploration of all of the things (images, affects, and thoughts) that a poem might give rise to, and even allow for other types of discussions on broader issues that a text might bring about. This approach may cause some frustration initially, because many students desire an idealized object to expel their conflicts into without having to attain meaningful knowledge, but most students will come to accept and even appreciate it when they discover the rewards.

Manipulation is similar to placation but tends to play more on a teacher's narcissism or image of a teacher's role as master than on fear of conflict. Manipulation often takes place with teachers whose intentions are to relinquish authority, but whose students are not comfortable with them in that role. With placation, students who desire a lack of conflict fit well with teachers who desire a lack of conflict, and together they create a classroom with a lack of conflict and, with it, a lack of learning. With manipulation, students force reluctantly authoritative teachers into the role of authority by stroking their egos, playing on an ideal image they may have of the role of the engaged teacher, or by making the classroom uncomfortable by regressing to something resembling rejection when teachers refuse the role of authority. When teachers take an approach that downplays their authority over texts, students who find this frustrating will try to manipulate them into giving interpretations and acting as the authority. Where placating makes things easier on the teacher and the students, manipulation makes things easier on the students. Teachers may easily fall back into this authoritative role themselves because, after all, they do, in most cases, have more knowledge about the text and the subject than the students do. Such a response also gives the teacher a sense of mastery, and with it a sense of respect or even awe from students.

But the teacher must, at times, refuse this role because it encourages passivity. Students' motivation for manipulation is essentially the same as that for placation—fear of frustration in learning—and involves a similar splitting off. Joseph explains that some of her patients are beyond understanding "because the part that could aim at understanding and making progress is split off and projected into the analyst" (146)—or teacher in our case. In other words, students split off the part of themselves that should take this role of interpreter or explorer of a text and project it into the teacher. The teacher experiences a kind of countertransference brought about by an outward demand from students, which may involve them asking the teacher a lot of questions that they should be trying to answer for themselves, or more passive demands, which often involve uncomfortable silences in the classroom when students refuse to engage, not because they are rejecting the material, but because they doubt they have anything of value to offer. Students may play on a teacher's narcissism by making comments that clearly posit the teacher as the authority over the material. Students will sometimes try to split the teacher off as ideal good object who masters the bad object of the frustrating text they are reading. But again, this makes the teacher into a false ideal who contains only empty knowledge, rather than a teacher who allows for necessary frustration and only contains it when it threatens to become overwhelming to education.

These countertransferences we feel as teachers, however, can make us desperate to take the role of the one who understands the text. Joseph writes, "It is more comfortable to believe that one understands 'material'" rather than play the role of one who does not (158), but we must play this role at times. Part of an approach to poetry that will bring about a deeper understanding of texts and their relevance requires us as teachers to put our understanding aside so that students can experience texts for themselves. We must refuse to answer questions at times, or, at times, we must turn students' questions back onto them. This may cause frustration, but through our encouragement and support, we can contain it. We must at times actively downplay our role as master of texts, because even if we feel we know a text well, we should recognize that it contains possibilities we have not considered. We must also learn to tolerate and survive long silences in the classroom rather than giving in to them because we feel uncomfortable. Silence that will lead to real engagement later is more valuable than filling silence with empty knowledge.

CHAPTER FOUR
THE POEM AS (SELF-, TRANSFORMATIONAL, TRANSITIONAL, AND REPARATIVE) OBJECT

Poetry, in its exploration of various, often intense, affective states, allows one to experience and explore the inner self in a safe environment. Poetry therapist Hirsch Silverman writes that "inhibited and negative emotions can be opened up through poetry therapy and the valuable energy within us used to create *interrelationships*. Experiencing psychotherapy through poetry as an unlocking of psychic energy makes one open to more intense physical, emotional and spiritual experiences than before" (22). Tolerance of anxiety becomes crucial for opening the self to the experiences that poetry offers. But poetry is useful to students because a poem maintains its otherness as an external, permanent object. Students will project their experiences and emotions into poems, but poems will reflect these projections back in a modified form where students are able to process and interpret them. Poetry's ability to return these projections in aesthetic form makes it an invaluable tool for raising awareness. Students can receive the parts of self that they have split off and become more integrated people.

Kleinian theorists provide an analytical model that helps us to understand the dynamics of reading poetry in terms of the projections and introjections of readers. This analytic model, applied to the reader/text relationship, involves readers reflecting on feelings, associations, and fantasies evoked by poems. Through this approach, students may have an experience with a poem that is analogous to psychoanalytic transference and countertransference. A poem in the role of analyst may act as a container for the reader through a process akin to transference where readers can emotionally invest themselves in, or project their internal objects into, a poem in such a way that encourages deeper awareness while offering recognition and support. In a phenomenon similar to countertransference, readers in the role of analyst receive projections from poems when the poet brings them into the experience that the poem is trying to express. Through receiving these projections, readers develop greater empathy with the writer or speaker of the poem—and thus with others in general. This relationship with poems functioning as objects offers one a rewarding experience in the external, object world. Such rewards in the realm of language and social relationships encourage further linguistic and social development. This development leads to a better balance between the need for object relations and personal independence. The reader's relationship to the poem serves the therapeutic purposes of increasing self-awareness and providing renewal, and guiding one toward reparation of self and improved relations with objects in the external world.

In this sense, the poem functions like Bion's container in a far more effective way than the teacher can. By allowing a poem to act as a container, we can avoid much of the anxiety involved in self-exploration. A more in-depth understanding of how a container works will help us to better understand how a poem may function as a transference object for the reader. As the prototypical container, the mother must take in the infant's unsymbolized, frustrating emotional experiences—what Bion refers to as beta-elements—passed into her through projection. The mother then interprets these elements, transforms them into a more elaborated, symbolized form (a form such as what dreams might be made of)—what Bion refers to as alpha-elements—where the potential for attaining consciousness arises. Beta-elements refer to obscure but strong emotions that infants cannot tolerate and therefore immediately evacuate and project into the mother. As Bion writes, "[B]eta-elements are suitable for evacuation only—perhaps through the agency of projective identification" (13). When beta-elements predominate, one experiences "an incapacity for symbolization and abstraction" (Grinberg 50). There comes no potential for understanding or awareness with beta-elements; they must be transformed into alpha-elements. Bion explains that "alpha-elements comprise visual images, auditory patterns, olfactory patterns, and are suitable for dreams, contact-barrier, [and] memory" (26). Alpha-elements do not equal consciousness, but produce a "contact-barrier" between consciousness and unconsciousness that creates the potential for realistic conscious awareness. Poetry also takes these raw, unsymbolized elements of self and puts them into a form where they may be interpreted, integrated, and understood. With the mother's help, infants will eventually develop their own alpha-functions. Likewise, through reading poetry and exploring the self through poetry, students can develop their own creativity and their own symbolizing functions.

In the mother, the projected bad object of the infant's internal world gets "modified in such a way that the object that is re-introduced has become tolerable to the infant's psyche" (Bion 90). Bion refers to the mother's capacity to act as a container—"to be open to the baby's projected need" (Grinberg 56)—as "reverie." "Reverie," Bion writes, "is a factor of the mother's alpha-function" (36). "By receiving the projections of beta-elements, and working them by her own alpha-function," Riesenberg-Malcolm explains, "the mother/analyst is 'a container' for these projections, which then can be called 'the contained'" (171). The capacity of the mother, or the analyst in therapy, to act as a container enables one to make use of emotional experience rather than simply evacuate it. Tolerance of emotion is necessary for the conversion of beta- into alpha-elements that create the potential for consciousness, thinking, knowledge, and symbol formation.[1] Real knowledge, or knowing, for Bion "is the activity through which the subject becomes aware of the emotional experience and can abstract from it a formulation which adequately represents this experience" (Grinberg 102).[2] Attaining knowledge is often a frustrating process to the adult as well as the infant. An inability to tolerate frustration disables one's ability to attain real knowledge of both self and other. Acting as a container, a poem can reflect the reader's emotional state back in a form that offers distance and greater tolerance, and thus enables the reader to gain awareness of and make use of emotions for positive personal development.

In the transference that takes place between reader and text, readers' projections are as complex as experience itself. Klein and her followers take a broader view of transference than Freud. Klein views the transference relationship as dynamic like all object relations. To Klein, transference involves not just previous relationships but all of the fantasies, emotions, defenses, love and hate, etcetera, that go with them. Klein writes, "[I]n unraveling the details of the transference it is essential to think in terms of *total situations* transferred from the past into the present, as well as of emotions, defenses and object relations" (*Selected* 209). Beyond referring only to direct references to the analyst, Klein's "conception of transference as rooted in the earliest stages of development and in deep layers of the unconscious is much wider and entails a technique by which from the whole material presented the *unconscious elements* of the transference are deduced" (209). One's earliest object relations provide a foundation for everything that comes out in relationships and transference, and, to Klein, "object relations are at the *centre* of emotional life" (206). As Betty Joseph explains, Klein shows "that what is being transferred is not primarily the external object of the child's past, but the internal objects" (156). As a transference object, a poem reflects "total situations" that we may relate to and, sometimes, find comfort in. As a container, it reflects our projected feelings back to us, offering awareness, tolerance, and recognition of emotion. Poetry puts emotions into symbolic forms (alpha-elements) of metaphor and linguistic image and gives them back to the reader so that they may become conscious, modifiable, and useful.

As an object of transference, the poem becomes what Heinz Kohut refers to as a selfobject, that is, an object that we experience as part of ourselves. In childhood, one's parents provide the first selfobjects who fulfill the child's early needs and create a foundation of self-esteem, vitality, and creativity for the child. We internalize our selfobject functions, and they serve to stabilize the self throughout our adult lives. However, Kohut often finds this selfobject function lacking in his adult patients. A cure is effected in his self-psychology model via the analyst serving the patient as a selfobject whose function is gradually internalized. Poems can serve in a similar capacity, as what Kohut calls "cultural selfobjects" (*How* 220). Kohut describes three kinds of selfobject transferences, each of which are relevant to how readers experience poetry: mirror transference, idealizing transference, and twinship or alter-ego transference (192–193). In the mirror transference, the selfobject reflects back our sense of grandeur by offering conformation and approval to the self. Poems can serve in this capacity when they improve a reader's self-esteem by offering recognition, particularly of an ambitious or grandiose self. Idealizing transference occurs with poetry when we find ourselves in awe of a poet's intellectual and creative power. Those of us who profess to love poetry or literature are familiar with this experience. Here, we "experience [a] merger with greatness, strength, and calm" (194). This does not imply losing the self to the other of the poem, but internalizing the power found in a creative work. When we internalize the creative power of an other, our own creativity is stimulated. Lastly, the twinship transference gives us "confirmation of the feeling that one is a human being among other human beings" (200). This occurs when poems offer us recognition of our emotions and thoughts and show us that we share in a common humanity. One may argue that by fulfilling these primary needs in the selfobject transference, the analyst or poem essentially treats adults like children. But what Kohut finds with his patients is that by serving as a gratifying selfobject, he allows them to recover the sense of self-regard, vitality, and creative energy from childhood. Reality will gradually temper these in a healthy way, but a lack of a gratifying internalized selfobject leads to despair.

Like the analyst, a poem helps us translate our inner world back to ourselves, ideally in such a way that offers deeper awareness. Reading an author's poetic expression of familiar emotions that one experiences as shameful or illegitimate offers a sense of normalcy. Poetry, because of its regressive, primal nature, is specifically adept at helping people to cope with negative emotions such as anxiety or depression, which find their roots in infantile frustration and object loss from birth, weaning, and an increased sense of reality. Pain is ubiquitous, since we all sense a primal loss of our experienced omnipotence in the womb and of the nurturing maternal object that we must renounce. Akhtar defines "mental pain as a sharp, throbbing, somewhat unknowable feeling of despair, longing and psychic helplessness" (231). Since most humans repress this primary loss, we often experience the mental anguish that arises from it as objectless and without a definable cause. James Hamilton points out, in his response to Akhtar, that the difficulty in defining such pain may be because it finds its roots in pre-symbolic loss (1221). Akhtar, and other therapists who use poetry, see the value in finding language and images described in poetry to capture the inner turmoil of the reader. Akhtar describes using Tennyson's elegy "Break, break, break" with a patient having difficulty dealing with the death of a loved one. The patient found that the poem "provided a psychic space for necessary mourning...In giving voice to [the patient's] hitherto mute agony and in witnessing her pain, the poem functioned as good mother and a good analyst!" (237). Poems can function this way for students in the classroom as well, if we create a space for them to do so.

As objects, poems renew us when we project ourselves into them and receive these projections back in a form that we can interpret and integrate into ourselves. A poem can act as what Christopher Bollas calls a "transformational object"—an object that enables the subject to alter and renew itself (*Shadow* 115). Bollas writes, "Persons rich in self experiencing, who take pleasure in the dialectics of the human paradox, seek objects with evocative integrity that challenge and stretch the self" (*Being* 31). As we seek these objects out in poetry or in the object world in general, we open ourselves up to new experiences and renew ourselves through object relations. Again, the primary relationship with the mother provides the prototype. We first experience the maternal object that integrates our experience as relational, rather than as a completely separate object. We experience poems the same way. The search for such a transformational object, Bollas tells us, continues into adult life. "The memory of this early object relation," he writes, "manifests itself in the person's search for an object...that promises to transform the self" (*Shadow* 14). Poems can function as these objects, as they integrate our experiences in specific ways that bring about a new self. This occurs through a process of projective identification where we subjectify our object world—putting personal meaning into objects to find ourselves reflected back in sometimes surprising ways. Bollas writes, "This type of projective identification is ultimately self enhancing, transforming material things into psychic objects, and thus furnishing an unconscious matrix for dreams, fantasies, and deeper reflective knowings" (*Being* 23). Bollas refers to this process where objects give rise to greater creativity and awareness as "lifting." He writes, "Some objects...release us into intense inner experiencings which somehow emphasize us. I think of this as a form of *lifting*, as encounters with objects lift us into some utterance of self available for deep knowing" (*Being* 29). Poems can lift us in this way, enhancing our inner experience and making us more attuned to ourselves and our relationship with the external world.

Poems connect us with the external world and others by evoking and developing empathy. Kohut defines empathy, which he calls "vicarious introspection," as "the capacity to think and feel oneself into the inner life of another person" (*How* 82). To J. Brooks Bouson, "empathy is central to the reading experience" (26). Bouson stresses that in Kohut's model of empathy, it is both a cognitive and an emotional phenomenon—it is both "subjective and objective" (28). Bouson explains, "[T]he model of reading as an empathic event recognizes that the critic/reader, in the acts of reading and interpreting, is simultaneously cast in the roles of reader/analysand and critic/analyst" (27). Empathy is both an intellectual activity and natural human response. We cannot help but empathize when we read, so reading can help us develop our empathetic capacity. Teachers can also assign classroom exercises designed to specifically focus on the empathetic aspect of reading, like having students write from the perspective of a character, for example.

Developing empathetic capacities in individuals is of great social value. Kohut recognizes the crucial role of empathy not only for analysis, but also for the survival of the world in general. "The expansion of the self, its increasing capacity to embrace a greater number and a greater variety of others through a consciously renewed and cultivated deepened empathy may be [a way of psychological survival in our world]." Kohut explains that as infants the empathy of our parents protects us from the external world.

> [I]t is human empathy, as we mirror and confirm the other and as the other confirms and mirrors us, that buttresses an enclave of human meaning—of hate, love, triumph, and defeat—within a universe of senseless spaces and crazily racing stars...it is with our last glance that we can retain, in the reflected melancholy of our parting, a sense of continuing life, of the survival of essential human sameness, and thus protection against the fallacy of pairing finiteness and death with meaninglessness and despair. ("Future" 682)

In Kohut's view, human beings are inherent empathizers, but a lack of empathy and a propensity for aggression often comes to dominate our adult lives. He writes, "I believe that man's destructiveness as a psychological phenomenon is secondary; that it arises originally as the result of the failure of the selfobject environment to meet the child's need for optimal...empathic response" (*Restoration* 116). Our empathy begins with the reciprocal primary relationship to the mother and is, ideally, sustained as an introjected object. People will not automatically hold aggressive attitudes, their natural state is empathy as long as their empathic function is stabilized by the parent. When this empathic function fails, it must be rebuilt both by the reparation of a good object and by recognition of the need for object relations. Poems acting as objects can serve in the restoration of empathy and of self.

A poem can help us connect with the external world and reject narcissism, where the world is only considered in terms of the self, by acting as what Winnicott calls a "transitional object." A transitional object, prototypically, refers to the first object belonging to a child (a blanket or a toy perhaps) that the child forms a strong bond with. This object serves the child, on one level, as "a symbol of the union of the baby and the mother" (96)—the primary bond—though it is clearly not the actual mother; it belongs to the child as well as to the external world. We could not describe such an object as primary because the relationship the child has with it moves away from the mother and the narcissistic view of self where there is no differentiation, but, at the same time, the relationship with the inanimate object does not constitute a real secondary object relation. "The transitional object," Winnicott explains, "is *not an internal object* (which is a mental concept)—it is not a possession. Yet it is not (for the infant) an external object either" (9). Thus, Winnicott describes the object as transitional, providing a space—what he calls a "potential space"—existing between self and other, between dependence and separation, that moves one gradually toward reality and meaningful relationships with real external objects.

We can see children at play making use of objects that are under their control, reflecting their inner fantasies, but that also clearly have external existence. Winnicott writes, "The transitional object is never under magical control like the internal object, nor is it outside control as the real mother is" (10). Play occurs in this transitional boundary between fantasy and reality. Thus, like Freud, Winnicott sees the child's imagination as the root of artistic creativity and enjoyment in adults. Winnicott locates art, or cultural experience, "in the *potential space* between the individual and the environment" (100). As Peter Rudnytsky explains, "Art provides a lifelong refuge to which we can turn as we negotiate our precarious oscillations between illusion and reality" (xiii). Art and other transitional phenomenon (play, religion) may function in this capacity because they are accepted forms of illusion. Winnicott explains that "the task of reality-acceptance is never completed, that no human being is free from the strain of relating inner and outer reality, and that relief from this strain is provided by an intermediate area of experience which is not challenged" (13). We can think of poems as offering a potential space for the reader, which could aid in the transition into greater and more realistic awareness of self and objects needed to attain real reparative object relations. In order to separate from the primary object and to form symbols, Winnicott explains, the child must have a strong foundation in the primary relationship. The attuned or "good-enough" mother must give the child a sense of love, continuity, and object permanence. This foundation gives the child the ability to make the transition into the external world. Poems may also offer a sense of love through recognition, continuity through the creation of form, and permanence as they survive as objects or even celebrate survival as a theme. As objects, poems can lead one in the transition toward a renewed and repaired self by giving both support and deeper awareness of objects. This renewed and repaired self will have a strong sense of reality and a capacity for object love.

In the classroom, the poem provides a "third object" that allows for a transition into remunerative object relations. Virginia Goldner writes, "Poetic action is a densely layered one- and two-person process that achieves its psychological effects by potentiating the mental space that is *thirdness*" (110). Goldner describes thirdness as "that quality of mental space that allows us to connect to another's mind and negotiate meaning" (115). This space between self and other creates a genuine sense of human empathy, and poetry opens up this space. Goldner explains that reading a poem creates a third that is not the poet or the reader but rather a kind of meeting place where the relationship exists between the two (115). The words we read belong to another whom we relate to, yet at the same time they become our own. Poems may act as supportive objects through their regressive qualities that return us to the loving mother, the good object or the container, of infancy. Goldner refers to this aspect of poetic thirdness as the "transcendental third": "the music of universal laws and meaning." She writes, "A poem's rhymes and meter, the elemental pleasure of sounds making music, must call up the infant's coos and babbles, the mother's harmonic responsiveness" (110). Poems not only evoke our earliest experiences and communications, transcending norms of experiencing and communicating, but also, like the good mother, reflect our experience back to us in aesthetic form that we can make use of.

Of course, any effort to strictly categorize the experience of poetry in terms of what we project into poems and what poems project into us will not prove altogether successful. Transference and countertransference, renewal and reparation, and increased self-awareness and increased empathy are all constantly occurring at the same time and building upon each other because of the profound effect objects have on our subjectivity and because when we learn about our objects, we are also learning about ourselves. Bollas writes, "Each entry into an experience of an object is rather like being born again, as subjectivity is newly informed by the encounter, its history altered by a radically effective present that will change its structure" (*Being* 59). Poems as objects can transform us in a number of positive ways that affect our image of self and our relations to others. As loving objects, they offer support and recognition by reflecting or containing our intense experiences. They also project into us, giving us new experiences and deeper empathy with the experiences of others.

Klein, Art, and Reparation

Melanie Klein introduces the concept of reparation in her 1929 essay "Infantile Anxiety Situations Reflected in a Work of Art and in the Creative Impulse," where she considers two instances of reparation in works of art: one in a fictional character and one in a creative artist. Klein begins with a consideration of the libretto of Ravel's opera *The Magic Word* based on a story by Colette. The opera begins with a small boy expressing aggressive feelings toward his mother. He refuses to do homework and desires to "eat up all the cake in the world" (showing his excessive oral greed for the nourishing maternal body) and "to put mama in the corner" (showing his desire to control the mother). The child's mother then appears as an excessively large figure and tells the child that he may only have a meager dinner of dry bread and unsweetened tea, thus frustrating his oral desires (*Selected* 85). This throws the boy into a rage in which he begins to destroy all of the objects in his room, representing to Klein an attack on the maternal body. Soon, however, the objects retaliate against him and mount their own attacks. Here, we see the fear of retaliation realized. The child takes refuge in a nearby park where the animals turn threatening and violent. When a small squirrel is injured in the violence, however, the boy picks it up and begins to tend to its wounds. As he does this, he says the word "mama," thus symbolically repairing the primary object relationship through an act of compassion. In doing this, Klein says, "[h]e is restored to the human world of helping, 'being good'" (86). The child has conquered his own threatening aggressive impulses by reestablishing his capacity for love. Klein writes, "[W]hen the boy feels pity for the wounded squirrel and comes to its aid, the hostile world changes into a friendly one. The child has learnt to love and believes in love" (89). This restores the primary relationship with the mother, and as Kristeva points out in her reading of Klein's essay, provides a necessary separation from the primary object as love is displaced into the external world. "It is through this process [of reparation]," Kristeva writes, "that [the child] finally becomes capable of autonomy and culture" (*Colette* 130). Here, Klein shows us the act of reparation performed within a work of art. Though Klein does not make the argument at this point, we begin to see here how a literary work might provide a model of reparation for the reader by representing the reparative process—making one aware of dangerous aggressive instincts and showing how they may be overcome through a cultural, symbolic achievement.

In the second part of the essay, Klein considers the role of reparation in the artist's creative process. She discusses an article written by Karin Michaelis on the real-life story of an artist named Ruth Kjär entitled "The Empty Space." Klein describes Kjär as "beautiful, rich and independent," though "subject at times to fits of deep depression." She had no "pronounced creative talent," but possessed "remarkable artistic feeling," which she put into collecting art and decorating her house (*Selected* 90). When a favorite painting of hers is removed, the empty space on the wall comes to symbolize the deep depressive state that she falls into. One day, she decides to take up painting and fill the space on the wall herself. Through this act, she realizes her artistic talent, and this gives her the ability to restore herself and overcome her depression. Later on, she paints two pictures, which Klein points to as particularly reflecting the process of reparation of the primary, maternal object. In the first painting, Kjär portrays a sickly looking older woman. According to Klein, this reflects her natural aggressive tendencies toward the maternal object. The second painting, however, is a portrait of the artist's mother standing up tall and strong. Through this painting, the artist has repaired the previously attacked mother by creating an image of her as a resilient, loving object. Klein comments, "It is obvious that the desire to make reparation, to make good the injury psychologically done to the mother and also to restore herself was at the bottom of the compelling urge to paint these portraits of her relatives" (93). Klein comments here on the creator rather than the appreciator of the work, but we may infer that a renewed image of the loving object in a work of art could have a similar reparative capacity for the viewer or reader as it does for the artist.

In this early essay, as Sandra Gosso points out, Klein views reparation as essentially a reaction formation against aggression toward the mother (4). When Klein introduces her central concept of the depressive position in her 1935 essay "A Contribution to the Psychogenesis of Manic-Depressive States," reparation takes on a much more important role. Here, the maintenance of the depressive position against paranoid/schizoid and manic defenses becomes key to the mental health of the subject. According to Klein, the reparation and restoration of the maternal loved object "are determining factors for all sublimations and the whole of ego development" (*Selected* 124). The road to mental health involves creating and sustaining positive and realistic relations with one's objects. Klein writes, "Along with the increase in love for one's good and real objects goes a greater trust in one's capacity to love and a lessening of the paranoid anxiety of the bad objects—changes which lead to a decrease of sadism and again to better ways of mastering aggression and working it off" (144). Along with mastering the aggression associated with the previous paranoid/schizoid position, the subject must also manage the depressive position itself to avoid overwhelming guilt that would lead to severe depression. Reparation, now, becomes the process through which the subject both maintains and manages the depressive position.

In 1937's "Love, Guilt, and Reparation," Klein explores the various modes through which one may achieve reparation. Here, she specifically considers the importance of balancing negative emotions and impulses with the reparative capacity of love. She writes, "This making reparation is, in my view, a fundamental element in love and in all human relationships" ("Love" 68). Object relations, as they move away from the original maternal object, dilute the intensity of the primary relationship with all of its aggressive and anxious elements. For these secondary relationships to exist, a good loving object must be maintained internally through the process of reparation. This loving object provides one a sense of security and a sense that one is loveable, allowing for the comfortable entrance into the social world where other object relations become possible. This capacity for love and the sense of being lovable proves essential for the preservation of life itself, just as the original love of the mother proved essential for survival during infancy. The dominance of love over the self-destructive elements of hatred involves a feeling of guilt associated with destructive instincts that leads one to constantly repair one's loving objects through acts of creativity. As one makes reparation, empathy, "a most important element in human relationships" becomes possible, and with it arises a sense of responsibility for one's objects (66). Only the self capable of love and reparation may engage in positive relationships with others and maintain a healthy interest in the external world.

To Klein, reparation and aggression interact in an ongoing cycle where both positive and negative instincts self-perpetuate. "The struggle between love and hate," Klein writes, "is active all through life" ("Love" 63). Impulses of love and aggression develop in connection with each other and engage in a constant struggle that threatens one's relationships and one's self. Feelings of hatred become linked from early experience with the fear of annihilation. Feelings of guilt give rise to the fear of losing love—of abandonment. The security one experiences with a strong, loving object allows one to accept gratification from relationships—and this, in turn, increases one's capacity to experience gratification in general. These feelings of gratitude and security, according to Klein, "are apt to increase [one's] creative powers...and to influence [one's] capacity for work and for other activities" as well (73). But if one feels incapable of love and reparation, one will never master the life-threatening destructive impulses.

Real relationships in the object world offer mutual happiness, shared with the other. They bring about reparation while also increasing confidence in one's reparative capacities. The feeling of gratitude and security achieved in a loving relationship—with parents, sexual partners, or friends—increases one's essential creative capacity and diminishes inhibiting aggressive instincts. The initial move into the world of object love, away from primary narcissism, is toward the father and then toward others who help the subject to repair the damaged primary relationship to the mother. Fears of annihilation in the primary relationship lead to a debilitating sense of dependence on the mother and a greedy desire to possess the maternal body for one's own gratification. Overwhelming feelings of guilt over the maternal relationship may prove equally debilitating as they can lead one to employ manic defenses where love is rejected altogether. Though one must ultimately move away from the maternal relationship into the world of object love, the good, loving mother of early infancy provides an important foundation for love, which gives one the experiences of pleasure and security and enables one to adapt to frustrations. The child must detach from this foundational relationship for fear of overdependence, but it remains the paradigm for all relationships throughout life. "These conflicting feelings [of the need for love and the need for separation]," Klein explains, "together with the emotional and intellectual growth of the child which enable him to find other objects of interest and pleasure, result in the capacity to transfer love, replacing the first loved person by other people and things" ("Love" 91). Love, to Klein, is a displacement of the relationship with the primary good object onto people, things, and interests in the social world. As one displaces this primary love onto objects, the emotional intensity of the primary relationship, with its destructive and threatening elements, decreases. As attachments are lessened, one experiences a conflict with the still-strong desire to maintain love. However, Klein explains, the decrease of guilt and fear that comes with separation from the mother actually increases one's capacity for reparation and one's ability to avoid negative or unrealistic defense mechanisms. Klein writes of the subject, "[B]ecause his feelings towards these new people are less intense, his drive to make reparation, which may be hampered if the feelings of guilt are over-strong, can now come more fully into play" (93). This increased capacity for reparation allows object relations to flourish so as to continue increasing a sense of love and goodness in the self.

Klein offers some insights into the reparative value of literary works for the reader. She first considers characters from fictional works in their capacity to become displaced loving objects. Heroes, or characters who represent ideals to the reader, can offer the same sense of security and trust that real objects can. Klein describes them as "people towards whom is turned the love and admiration without which all things would take on the gloom of hate and lovelessness" ("Love" 97). As readers react to these characters emotionally, favorable feelings are evoked along with images of strength associated with the good object. Like the primary good mother, the ideal character represents the pure and unspoiled loving object, preserved in word and image. The fictional hero stands in as an image of the loving parent "preserved in the unconscious mind as the most precious possession, for it guards its possessor against the pain of utter desolation" (98). The opposite can also occur, in terms of villains and characters who arouse negative emotional reactions, but these characters also have value for reparation. Klein writes, "It is safer to hate these people who are either unreal or further removed, than to hate those nearer to one—safer for them and for oneself" (97). Imaginary figures offer a safe distance for the subject to experience feelings of both love and hatred. This experience allows one to examine characteristics and emotional states so that, ideally, love and loving objects will emerge as favorable to hatred and bad objects.

Klein also discusses the literary text itself as a loving object offering recognition, support, and encouragement. Feelings of desire, curiosity, and love emerge in reading. These emotions encourage exploration, which Klein relates to the child's early interest in the maternal body. "The desire to re-discover the mother of the early days," Klein explains, "is also of greatest importance in creative art and the way people enjoy and appreciate it" ("Love" 105). The pleasure found in reading brings about positive feelings in the reader that give rise to a sense of security and joy in the external world. Klein considers reparation in terms of the reader by looking at John Keats's poem "On First Looking into Chapman's Homer." In the poem, Klein explains, "Keats is speaking from the point of view of one who enjoys a work of art" (106). Keats the reader experiences the poetic work—Chapman's translation of Homer—as a good object as he becomes a kind of explorer of the self and the outside world through it. From the poem's support and stimulation, Keats the reader grows elated with positive feelings toward the outside world that will lead to further explorations and their promise of reward. The reader as explorer also becomes an explorer of the internal world. As inhibitions break down, one becomes better able to gain awareness of objects and of reality in the external world, as well as of the self.

The reader experiences both the anxiety and the desire to repair that motivate the creation of a work of poetry. Reading poetry can counteract fears of annihilation and abandonment and help one to maintain the depressive position. Reparation found through poetry offers feelings of love and stimulation of creativity. Constructive means of coping with negative emotions lead to positive object relations, as well as a positive relationship with the self. Object reparation, Klein points out, is also self reparation, since our relationships with others are always linked to our internal experience. Klein explains, "[A]ll that we have received from the external world and all that we have felt in our inner world...makes part of our selves and goes to build up our personalities" ("Love" 111). We experience the hatred within ourselves with revulsion, but we also project our love onto the external world. If we have good, loving internal images, we experience the world as more loving. But our own hatred creates the experience of a more hateful world. Klein writes,

> These phantasy-relationships, based on real experiences and memories, form part of our continuous, active life of feeling and of imagination, and contribute to our happiness and mental strength. If, however, the parent-figures, which are maintained in our feelings and in our unconscious minds, are predominantly harsh, then we cannot be at peace with ourselves. (114)

The images we have of the external world, based on our images of and feelings toward our primary objects, directly affect our political attitudes and largely determine whether we react to social problems with distain or indifference, or if we choose to engage ourselves in seeking solutions. But art can repair these images. New objects of pleasure, including creative works, link us to the original maternal object of pleasure—the good breast. Feelings of guilt and fear give rise to a willingness to accept substitutes for the original object. This necessary detachment from the mother allows for an enlarging range of interest in the world. In reparative acts, we recreate and rediscover endlessly, in other people and interests, our capacity to love. "A good relation to ourselves," Klein says, "is a condition for love, tolerance and wisdom towards others" (119). Reparation allows us to forgive our parents for infantile frustrations that lead to feelings of hate. It allows us to find peace with ourselves and gain the ability to love others.

In her later writings, Klein makes an important contribution to her theoretical framework with her concept of envy, which carries implications for the theory of reparation and creativity. By "envy" Klein refers to a desire to destroy any good objects based on the power that these objects are perceived as holding over one.[3] Envy disables one's capacity to feel gratitude toward a good object and, thus, disables one's capacity for positive object relations or other positive experiences in the external world. The first object of envy is, of course, the mother's breast that contains the milk that the infant needs. Klein sees the enjoyment of the gratifying breast in infancy as the key to future object relations. She writes, "[T]he breast in its good aspect is the prototype of maternal goodness, inexhaustible patience and generosity, as well as of creativeness" (*Envy* 180)—but envy of the breast makes enjoyment impossible, disabling the capacity growth, creativity, and love. It stands as the enemy of reparation. Klein writes, "Envy of creativeness is a fundamental element in the disturbance of the creative process" (202). The envious subject cannot create and cannot reap the benefits of reading or appreciating the creative work of others.

Another important aspect of Klein's later writing on creativity comes with her greater consideration of the role of the paranoid/schizoid position in the creative process. This step broadens and clarifies her earlier theories of reparation and art. Clearly, all creative works cannot, strictly speaking, reflect reparation or arise from a desire to make loving reparation. Not every work of art creates a more realistic or positive image of the other, or brings out the more positive elements of the self. Many creative works, such as many modern horror films, enact sadomasochistic fantasies with few if any redemptive human qualities. Other works, such as some forms of propaganda, encourage hatred and aggression, or servitude and simplistic thinking. In a short and seldom-cited essay published in 1942, Klein offers some explanation for this phenomenon. She explains that the depressive position and its reparative drive create an ethical system where "good" is reparative to the primary loved object and "evil" is destructive to it. However, she warns, this ethical system "is capable of manifold variations and distortions, and even complete reversal." Using Nazi Germany as an example, she refers to the Nazi attitude as a distortion or reversal. She explains, "Here the aggressor and aggression have become loved and admired objects, and the attacked objects have turned into evil and must therefore be exterminated" (*Envy* 322). We see here how the reparative function may be corrupted. A work of art that is also a work of pro-Nazi propaganda still restores a loved object and attempts to suppress anything that would destroy that loved object, but here the loved object itself is corrupt. Such corruption of the loved object, Klein argues, comes from an overwhelming, unmanaged fear of the other. We must differentiate then between positive, normal, healthy forms of reparation and negative, distorted forms in the same way we differentiate between positive and negative defense mechanisms. The corrupt form of reparation functions through paranoia, not within the depressive position. True reparation, in its positive form, remains consistent with and aware of reality, and does not convert hatred into the object of love.

This brings up the important point, however, that works of art and creativity do not necessarily arise from or reflect the depressive position alone—though this position remains important for achieving the separation needed for social interaction and symbol formation. Toward the end of her career, Klein moves away from a strict definition of art as reparation. In her reading of *The Oresteia*, Klein explains the dramatic trilogy symbolically as what we might call a Kleinian allegory. Her central argument is that Orestes is saved in the end because he operates in the depressive position; he feels guilt, symbolized by the Furies, for his murderous deeds and wants to make reparation. Agamemnon and Clytemnestra, in contrast, feel no remorse for the murders they commit. They operate in the paranoid/schizoid position and are punished accordingly by the gods, or fate, that represent the punishing superego. While this reading still ultimately stresses the importance of reparation and the depressive position, Klein puts more emphasis on the artist's reflection of the complexity and fluctuations of the inner world through symbolism. "The creative artist," she writes, "makes full use of symbols; and the more they serve to express the conflicts between love and hate, between destructiveness and reparation, between life and death instincts, the more they approach universal form." The artist's use of symbols finds its roots in infancy where the capacity for symbol formation first emerged. Klein explains that infantile emotions and fantasies attach to objects "real and phantasied—which become symbols and provide an outlet for the infant's emotions... The child puts his love and hate, his conflicts, his satisfactions and his longing into the creation of these symbols, internal and external, which become part of his world" (299). Here, Klein clarifies her views on art. Gosso explains, "What is worth underlining is the necessary integration of *Ps* [paranoid/schizoid position] and *D* [depressive position] in the creative process." In other words, art often reflects the fluctuations between the two positions. Gosso explains, "[T]o insist on reparation, and therefore on harmony, does not allow for the fact that the artistic process, as also the creative process, is born from the chaos of primary impulses and affects" (7).

This development in Klein's work represents more of a clarification than a revision of her theory of art and reparation. We can see evidence of this view from her earliest essay on reparation where the child from the opera goes through paranoid/schizoid processes before making reparation, and where the artist paints the sickly old woman as a paranoid/schizoid attack on the mother as bad object before restoring her as good object in a later painting. We must recall that the Kleinian subject is one in constant fluctuation between the two positions. The fact that we are able to function in the depressive position does not mean that paranoid/schizoid mechanisms disappear. Art reflects this fluctuation, which makes it valuable for raising awareness and for self-assessment. In another later essay, Klein writes, "Though the rejected aspects of the self and of internalized objects contribute to instability, they are also at the source of inspiration in artistic productions and in various intellectual activities" (*Envy* 245). Here, Klein makes it clear that all art does not simply reflect or perform reparation, but rather, offers a reflection of the inner self with all of its conflicts. It is this element of art, however, that enables it to raise awareness and offer recognition, which makes it a useful tool in attaining the depressive position and achieving reparation.

Social Reparation

Reparation is a social as well as a symbolic act. Of course, language itself is social; we use it not only to think, but to communicate and interact with others as well. Language proves key to establishing our object relations, including those of love. Kristeva, following Klein, places love firmly in the symbolic, seeing it as a speech act. "Love is something spoken," she says, "and it is only that" (*Tales* 277). In the analytic situation, this comes into play through positive transference. "I speak in favor of imagination as antidote for the crisis," Kristeva writes, calling imagination "a discourse of transference—of love." Freud turned love into a cure, she tells us, "not to allow one to grasp a truth, but to provoke a rebirth" (381). Language and love move us away from the narcissistic structures of infancy where we cannot reflect on the world in relation to anything outside of ourselves, and offers us the capacity for understanding and empathizing with others. As we enter the social world, we separate from our primary objects and learn to take responsibility for ourselves. But to function at our full potential in the object world, we must also recognize our dependence on others, and with it our social responsibility toward others. We cannot simply ignore social problems and isolate ourselves; we must recognize that social problems affect everyone in a socially interconnected world.

Those who, even in adulthood, continue to function primarily in the infantile state of the paranoid/schizoid position, will be debilitated with fears of annihilation—whether literal annihilation or the loss of an identity structure. They will experience the world as threatening and will constantly seek out enemies—immigrants, homosexuals, various racial groups, etcetera—to project their internalized fear and hatred onto. They will also tend to split the world into oversimplified categories of good and bad. Their enemies will be purely bad objects and their heroes become pure good objects. Complex thinking about issues and understanding of other points of view become impossibilities. Poetic language can help to move one into the depressive position by creating empathetic others as speakers and characters, and challenging black-and-white thinking through its complex use of language, approach to themes, and examination of emotions and thought processes.

In the depressive position, our view of objects, or people, becomes more realistic. We no longer separate the world into good and bad, or heroes and enemies. The depressive position, however, brings its own anxieties. Our fear of annihilation becomes quelled when we lose our paranoid fear of our perceived bad objects, but we also feel guilt because of our aggressive tendencies toward objects who we now realize are not altogether bad, but whole and complex. Our primary anxiety now is not over annihilation but the fear of abandonment. We fear that our objects will abandon us, that we are essentially unworthy of love, because of our negative impulses. Part of our anxiety in the depressive position also stems from the loss of the pure good object, which, though unrealistic, offers a great deal of comfort. We must keep in mind that the Kleinian subject is a fluid one. Even the best of us will sometimes regress into paranoid/schizoid thinking as a defense against the anxiety of the depressive position. A black-and-white world of hated/ing and loved/ing objects is simple and easier to deal with. In part, reparation refers to the maintenance of the depressive position in the face of paranoid/schizoid regression. When poetry offers complexity in the face of simplistic thinking, or empathetic others in the face of hatred, it assists in this maintenance.

The negative aspects of the depressive position can, themselves, also create major obstacles to prosocial attitudes and activities. Even if the defensive regression to the paranoid/schizoid position is avoided, the realistic assessment of the world with its lack of pure good and its recognition of destructive impulses can sometimes lead to severe depression where silence, apathy, hopelessness, and inactivity prevent prosocial activity. Kristeva relates depression specifically with a loss of self in the symbolic as it compels one "to silence, to renunciation" (*Black Sun* 3)—the opposite of poetic expression. But the realistic assessment of the depressive position remains essential. Subjects who are more realistic about themselves will be more able to cope with hateful emotions and invasive paranoid/schizoid thoughts, and the depressive guilt that comes with them. Those who assess the world more realistically while maintaining their own psychic equilibrium will be capable of taking effective actions for social change. Poetry can help raise this realistic awareness through its examination of human nature and external reality, and the recognition poetry offers can give one a sense of normalcy. Self-aware subjects who function primarily in the depressive position will be able to recognize and accept the mental fluctuations and regressions their mind takes without being overwhelmed with guilt and stifled in the external world through silence and renunciation.

Reparation can only take place within the depressive position. It is not simply the maintenance of this position, but also a healthy way of coping with the position itself. The subject may be personally and socially stifled within the paranoid/schizoid or the depressive position if reparation is not made. In the traditional Oedipus complex, we must move away from our narcissistic mental structures, separate from the primary attachment to the mother, and enter the social world. This entrance into the social world is key to Klein as well as Freud and Lacan, but in Klein, the motivation for entering the social world, which is also the world of language, is not fear of imagined or symbolic castration via the father, but the promise of rewarding interaction in the social world with the ultimate reward being love. Kristeva picks up on Klein's view with her concept of the "imaginary father" who provides us with a positive image of the social, symbolic world that we must move into. In response to the depressive loss of the pure good object of the maternal realm, the entrance into the paternal symbolic "allows me to block up that emptiness, to calm it and turn it into a producer of signs, representations, and meanings" (*Tales* 42). Kristeva reminds us that love and reparation occur in the symbolic—the realm of language and, of course, the realm of poetry and creativity. Reparation is a creative way of coping with the external world. It takes action, but, just like the maintenance of the depressive position, it is not absolute but ongoing. The social implications of reparation are enormous. Reparation involves hope in the face of apathy, a voice raising itself out of oppression and silence, and creative action that helps one personally and can lead one to helping others.

We perform reparation through symbolic acts that offer awareness, support, and ultimately self-control in relation to our objects. This capacity to maintain a loving image of our objects proves crucial for the attainment of mental health and a rewarding relationship with the world. The act of reading and experiencing poetry offers awareness of complex emotional states, while also putting emotions at a manageable distance. Poetry provides us with recognition of familiar emotions—evoking a sense of calm and arousing pleasure. Poems themselves can take on the role of loving objects, stimulating our interest and providing us with loving support. The mental and emotional stimulation we gain from poetry can lead us to our own creative capacity where we may recreate and constantly renew ourselves by performing reparation. A consideration of poetry for its reparative capacity gives us a unique appreciation of the genre, which also has practical value for teachers of literature who seek to stimulate prosocial development in their students, or for therapists who use poetry in their practice.

Chapter Five
A Poetry Therapy Model for the Classroom

The goal of the classroom model that follows is to make the study of poetry more valuable for both students and society by maximizing its developmental potential. This model is designed to increase empathy, validate emotional experience, increase self-awareness, and develop and encourage creative capacities—essentially, to bring about renewal and reparation in response to a poetic text. The field of poetry therapy provides us with some useful guidance as to how we might achieve these classroom goals. Nicholas Mazza and Arleen Hynes and Mary Hynes-Berry illustrate models for poetry therapy that are useful for considering how to structure a class around a therapeutic approach to poetry. Many aspects of these two models went into the creation of the classroom model outlined below. What follows is meant to be a flexible model that others may adapt, alter, and borrow from to fit the needs of their classes.

In this therapeutic approach to poetry, teachers must always proceed with some level of caution. Mazza warns of several issues that occur in poetry therapy that can lead to negative outcomes (27). One potential problem with poetry, and other works of art, is that a poem may be used as an intellectualization of a real personal issue, especially when a reader simply applies an emotionally detached analysis to it. This intellectualization can prevent students from attaining deeper emotional awareness or it can prevent them from experiencing recognition of their emotions through a text. Teachers can try to engage students in poetry in more emotional and imaginative ways in order to make poetry more vital and less purely intellectual. In fact, a therapeutic approach to poetry is far less guilty of intellectualization than traditional classroom approaches that do not take emotional experience into consideration.

We must also be careful not to put our agenda as teachers above students' needs. We cannot force students to experience personal revelations or to appreciate us for offering them the opportunity for such experiences.

Our role in this approach is to provide students with opportunity, guidance, and support. The major concern with a therapeutic approach to poetry, which is an ethical concern in the classroom, is of evoking feelings in students that they cannot cope with. Of course, traditional pedagogies can also evoke such feelings, especially when dealing with emotionally intense texts, without offering students a productive way to cope with them. We must always be careful, however, to let students progress at their own pace. Teachers cannot analyze students in the way that therapists do; it is unpractical in a classroom setting as well as unethical. What we are offering students is an opportunity to learn more about themselves and their relationships. The degree to which they do this must be left largely up to them. In my experience, however, students are nearly always enthusiastic about this approach to poetry, and its benefits frequently evoke a response of gratitude.

Another potential concern with this approach is that it neglects teaching students about other important elements of literature by focusing solely on therapeutic benefits. However, this approach does allow a space to discuss the typical concerns of a literature class and does not preclude traditional outcome goals. Students may learn about and experience therapeutic benefits of poetry while also learning about prosody, genres, and literary movements, as well as, political, cultural, and historical contexts. In fact, the kinds of individual, emotional responses that this approach focuses on are often tied to formal elements and cultural contexts. A deeper understanding of the form and context of a poem can enrich the emotional experience of it. And, likewise, an appreciation of a poem's therapeutic benefits can lead a reader to a greater appreciation of its form and the context in which it was produced. A therapeutic approach and a more traditional approach to poetry are not mutually exclusive. While some teachers may embrace literature's therapeutic elements as the primary focus of a course, these elements can also add to a course and to students' understanding of poetry in a supplemental role.

Mazza's brief poetry therapy model uses poetry to provide ego support, help one to improve one's relationships, and help one to deal with specific problems (26).[1] Mazza begins his four-phase model with the "supportive phase" where he introduces poems that offer support and instill hope, without yet delving into personal issues that arise in deep self-exploration.[2] Once support is established, Mazza moves to the "apperceptive phase," which involves the "development of insight regarding specific problems" (29). Mazza's third phase is the "action phase." Here, his clients are encouraged to take action and become the agents of their own change. This may involve keeping a personal journal or choosing to adopt a poem or song as one's own.[3] Mazza's final phase is the "integrative phase" where clients consolidate what they have gained in therapy while making goals for the future. Mazza also deals with separation issues during this phase by introducing songs or poems about saying good-bye and accepting independence.

Hynes and Hynes-Berry's four-step bibliotherapeutic process follows a different format, but is compatible with Mazza's work. Hynes and Hynes-Berry's first step is "recognition" where clients locate something in a text that engages them personally: "[S]omething that piques interest, opens up the imagination, stops wandering thoughts, or in some way, arrests attention" (44–45). Recognition is primarily an emotional response that may remain vague at this stage. In step two, "examination," "we must move beyond the flash of recognition to examine the concept or feeling for ourselves" (49). Here, clients take the initial intense response to a literary work and ask themselves questions in order to uncover the psychological sources of their response. They now begin to increase self-awareness through a text. The next step is "juxtaposition," where clients come to a more complex understanding of themselves by comparing and contrasting "two impressions of an object or experience" (50). Here, clients come to understand ambivalences, while also looking at alternatives through their impressions of a text. Hynes and Hynes-Berry end with "application to self." In this final step, clients evaluate their experience in the previous steps to gain deeper self-awareness and to integrate this awareness by applying it to their lives. This may involve creating new goals or committing to new kinds of behavior.

An indebtedness to both Mazza's and Hynes and Hynes-Berry's models is evident in the classroom model outlined below. It begins with a phase that seeks to establish poetry as a supportive object for the reader and also as an object that evokes empathy. In this "supportive/empathic" phase, students objectively consider how poems can offer emotional support, and students develop their own empathetic capacities by imaginatively relating to and adapting the voices of others. This phase is followed by a "response/examination" phase, which parallels Mazza's apperceptive phase and essentially combines Hynes and Hynes-Berry's first two steps, recognition and examination. Perhaps these should remain separate stages, but they overlap so often in classroom practice that it is difficult to separate them completely. Here, students use poetry to become more self-aware by responding subjectively to poems and by examining their subjective responses. The third phase is the "action/application" phase, which is a merging of Mazza's final two phases of action and integration and Hynes and Hynes-Berry's final step of self-application. Following Mazza's model, students choose the text that they want to more closely examine their relationship with. This phase relies on two other therapeutic models to achieve its goals: Alvin Mahrer's experiential therapy and Richard Kopp's metaphor therapy. These models work extremely well for integrating one's personal experiences of a text, raising one's awareness, and getting one to apply therapeutic gains to one's life. The final phase is a "creative" phase where students apply their deeply explored experience with a text by creating their own work of art in response to their chosen poem.[4]

Supportive/Empathic Phase

Following Mazza's approach, students begin with a supportive phase, which, in this model, includes a particular stress on empathy. They start by reading poems that offer recognition to affective states—poems that offer a realistic recognition of human suffering as well as those that offer hope in the face of suffering. We begin with a primarily objective approach to poetry and its therapeutic value early in the semester, where students are able to emotionally connect with poems without having to explore or reveal their personal thoughts, feelings, fantasies, or associations in detail. Students will begin to find recognition in poems and develop what Mazza calls "empathic understanding" (28–29) by focusing on the others they find in poetry. They will begin to see themselves and others, and themselves through others, in a safe environment, which will get them more comfortable with thinking of poetry in this way. Here, poetry is established as a potentially supportive object for the reader, and defense mechanisms that might lead students to resist achieving deeper self-awareness are relaxed.

Many of the approaches typically taken in literature classes are of value to a therapeutic approach to poetry at this stage, though teachers can do more to build on the rewards that literature offers. The conventional practice of identifying and discussing themes or predominant moods of poems, for example, is useful because it allows students to objectively consider elements of human nature that are being treated by a poem. One of the first steps in increasing students' awareness of themselves and their relationships is to identify psychological phenomena or truths revealed in poems, which students can later consider in more personal ways. Most literature teachers already engage students in issues of poetry's thematic elements. In a literary theory class, teachers may even use poems to exemplify or clarify psychological or social concepts of various schools of theory. These common approaches get students thinking in different ways and considering their worlds and their selves more perceptively and comprehensively.

We can take this objective approach to poetry a bit further in order to get students thinking more adequately about emotional and psychological issues by encouraging them to think about poetry in terms of its potential therapeutic value. Mazza suggests a number of useful questions that apply specifically to the therapeutic value of poems in his "poetry therapy training exercises for practitioners" (149). First, students consider what type of person might find a particular poem helpful. Some poems may speak more specifically to, or may have more relevance for, a certain gender, ethnicity, or age group. Students can also consider if there are particular issues or problems that a specific poem could help someone address. For example, poems can often help one cope with depression or anxiety by increasing awareness or offering recognition to emotions that are experienced as shameful. Students can determine if a poem might offer hope to readers that would enable coping. They can also ask if a poem could have harmful effects on a certain reader's identity. Some poems express despair but offer little hope to a suffering reader. Some offer false hope that a reader may reject. Others may express racist or misogynistic views that will offend and alienate certain readers. Thinking about poems in these ways increases empathy in students by helping them to imagine how others might read from their unique points of view.

Once students have begun thinking about poetry in this way, there are a number of creative response activities that can engage their imaginations, while helping them to develop empathy. Imagination proves essential for empathy as it takes imagination to put oneself in the position of the other. Rich Furman uses poetry therapy methods with his students in social work and other helping professions, seeing empathy as a "prerequisite for social justice" (104). Furman begins by having students remember a time in their lives when they "felt deeply accepted and understood by someone" (105). In a poetry class, students might write about a time they experienced a work of literature or another art form that made them feel understood or accepted. This "remembering empathy" exercise works well for establishing poetry or art as a supportive object. When students feel empathized with, they are more likely to empathize themselves.

Other exercises can specifically help students to develop empathy for others. Furman does a letter-writing assignment where his students write empathetic letters to clients they are having a difficult time with. Poetry students can write empathetic and supportive letters to speakers or characters from poems. While this exercise can encourage empathy, some students may offer judgments or chastisement. We can try to avoid negative letters, and encourage more empathy, by having students write to the speaker or character as if they were a good friend or a close family member. This is clearly a challenge, but it forces students to empathize with someone who they do not necessarily easily understand. I have used Coleridge's "Pains of Sleep" and several of Charlotte Smith's elegiac sonnets in this exercise. Students are often able to relate to the speakers' suffering, and even when they cannot, they are usually able to offer genuine words of support. Of course, each individual student will relate to certain poems more easily and will have a more difficult time relating to others. Doing this exercise with a variety of poems encourages students to respond with empathy even when it is more difficult for them to relate to a speaker or character. In their therapeutic practice, Phyllis Klein and Perie Longo encourage these kinds of "poetic conversations" where readers respond to poems, because it deepens "the possibility for empathy and sympathetic identification" (123).

After responding to others from poems, students can then write from, or take on, the perspective of an other from a poem. One writing exercise that works well is to have students write their own poems or narratives in the voice of either a speaker of or a character in a poem. This exercise often involves filling in gaps in a text. This is essentially what Tennyson does in his Mariana poems or what Browning does in "Caliban upon Setebos," where the poets write from the perspectives of Shakespearian characters, and we could certainly list other literary examples.

Another empathy exercise that builds upon this one involves having one student play the role of a speaker or character from, or an author of, a poem and having another student interview them. If a student were playing an author, for example, another student could ask them what was happening in their lives when they wrote the poem, how they felt when writing the poem, how they felt after the poem was written, where they came up with a certain image or metaphor, or what they meant by a certain ambiguous phrase. For a narrative poem, the interviewer may question a character as to why certain actions were taken, or they may ask how the character felt during a certain scene. Whatever the scenario, the student being interviewed must try to answer the questions by empathizing with an other through imagination. Students can transcribe and even perform these interviews for their classmates in order to share a broad array of responses.

The last part of this phase applies what we have done previously to relationships where many issues of human nature and empathy come into play. Poems are frequently addressed to someone specifically, so we can use poems that reflect various types of relationships to get students to not only consider the inner self expressed in the poem, but the relational self as well. Not only do our inner experiences arise during reading when we identify with a poetic voice, but all of our relationships and memories associated with these experiences come out. Again, during this phase, students do not consciously explore these things in terms of their own experiences, but they lay the groundwork. Poems about relationships can get students to think objectively about the nature of relationships, and to imaginatively empathize with someone as they exist within a relationship. I have used a variety of poems reflecting different types of relationships during this phase: Hemans's "The Dreaming Child," expressing parental love, Shelley's somewhat narcissistic love poem "To Harriet," and Caroline Norton's treatment of dying love, "Be Frank with Me." One poem that students tend to respond very strongly to is Norton's "Recollections." Addressed to her brothers, this poem deals with issues of death and survival within a family. With these poems, students write from the perspectives of the implied audience in response to the speaker of the poem. Here, students must again empathetically put themselves in the perspective of an other, while also gaining insights into the dynamics of relationships, which they may later apply to their own relationships.

Response/Examination Phase

In the response/examination phase, students move from objective considerations of poetry in terms of therapeutic value and generalized human nature, to subjective responses that focus on the self, with the goal of increasing self-awareness. This phase begins by introducing students to the concept of reading through the three registers of experience—affective, imagistic, and linguistic. When readers experience language, it gives rise to thoughts that are also in the form of language; this is the typical focus of a literature classroom. However, readers also form mental images when they read, particularly when reading vivid descriptions or metaphors. And, of course, readers respond to texts at a visceral, emotional level. This approach to poetry encourages students to realize and examine not only their cognitive, but also their imagistic and affective responses to poems.

It often proves productive to have students focus on a specific word, line, or image in a poem that has special significance to them (Mazza 19). Students are encouraged to locate and share parts of poems that they respond to intensely, either emotionally or imaginatively. This provides an opening for students to focus on and clarify their responses to texts. Students can then describe their emotional responses aloud or in writing, and describe or even draw on paper the mental images that poems evoke.[5] Bringing affects and images into consciousness and into language begins to get students engaged in responding creatively to texts while also getting them to begin looking inward to gain self-awareness.

Students share their affective and imagistic responses either in small groups or as a whole class. Holland and Schwartz describe how when we, as a class, all share our unique ways of reading and experiencing texts, we create a potential space between self and other where we come to see texts through the eyes of others and have our own experiences of texts shaped by them (12–13). Students come to recognize their unique responses, but as we share, everyone's responses will become altered somewhat and enriched by the responses of others. In this case, reading becomes a collective experience where we open texts up to multiple possibilities, and empathize with multiple ways of reading and experiencing.

As students gain increased awareness of their affective and imagistic responses to poems, they are also encouraged to explore personal associations through poetry. Students move beyond simply recognizing their affects and images to considering the personal experiences and memories associated with them. Here, students begin to get into even more personal explorations and self-analysis that will help raise their self-awareness. Words, images, and emotions are linked to events, people, places, and objects. Making these links between poems and the self can be quite a leap for many students. One way to start out slowly and get students to use association without necessarily getting too personal is to use intertextual associations instead of personal ones. We can ask students if the poem reminds them of a song, a movie, another literary work, or another piece of art. This offers students some distance as they begin to follow their associations. Instead of linking directly to personal experience, which might make them uncomfortable at first, they link the poem to a third object that is linked to the self as a work of art that has meaning to them, but that clearly has its own separate existence. Following these types of associations can provide a foundation from which students can later learn to relate poems specifically to past memories or to their current life situations.

Since allowing for personal meaning is so important in these exercises and in this approach to poetry in general, teachers should consider using poems that are more open ended. Students should be able to examine a multitude of responses to a text without settling in on or being pushed toward one specific master reading. Some poems are more prescriptive or, as Umberto Eco puts it, "closed" (4–5) than others, and students are more likely to be put off by these poems. But when we introduce open-ended poems, students are able to project their own personal meaning into them. These kinds of poems lend themselves to the kinds of creative exercises that are included in this phase. Imagistic experience, the experience of mental images in the mind, provides a foundation for creativity. Getting students in touch with this kind of experience can raise self-awareness particularly in terms of allowing them to realize their creative potentials. Students create their own narratives when they fill in gaps and ambiguities in texts with their imaginations. Later they can analyze their creative readings to come to a better understanding of their fantasies, desires, and emotions. Creative reading allows students to take action, and this is empowering in a way that can carry over into other aspects of their lives. Exercises that encourage creative responses from students foster the emergence of a self who is open to creative possibilities that may be used to alter the self or the external world in positive ways. Students will hopefully take these newly discovered elements of self with them beyond their formal literary studies.

As students begin using poetry for self-exploration in order to gain deeper awareness, the poems themselves will often validate student responses, but our role as teachers is mainly to not invalidate them. We should encourage personal judgments based on taste, values, or relevance to self, because these judgments can be used to teach students about themselves. It is essential, however, to always go beyond simply having students react to texts. We always want them to analyze their reactions based on their experiences or personality traits, to consider what their reactions are in all three registers of experience, but also to examine the roots of their reactions. Students may simply respond and share responses at first, but later they should follow up their responses and creative readings with self-analysis. Since many students are less comfortable sharing personal revelations with classmates, this is usually done in writing—either freewritings in class or journal responses at home. Here, students are asked to consider, based on their understanding of themselves and their experiences, why they react in certain ways to texts or why certain texts give rise to certain fantasies. Again, we must be careful never to push students to reveal anything that makes them uncomfortable in their self-analysis. This approach simply offers them the opportunity to explore themselves through poetry. What they do with this opportunity is largely up to them.

In this phase, along with selecting more open works, teachers should select poems that are either emotionally intense, reflect a variety of emotional states, use a lot of imagistic description and figurative language, or all of the above. Keats's and Shelley's odes work well for the purposes of this phase, but students also tend to be strongly affected by Romantic nature poetry. They respond very positively to excerpts from Smith's "Beachy Head" and a number of Wordsworth's nature poems including "Tintern Abbey," "Daffodils," and excerpts from *The Prelude*. These poems elicit profound, self-reflective responses in students, and tend to bring up concrete associations. Typically, students will recall specific moments and places where they had experiences with nature similar to those described by Smith and Wordsworth. Darline Hunter and Shannon Sanderson, in their blending of poetry and nature in therapy, recognize the psychic healing demonstrated by the "expression of connection, insight, awe, mindfulness, and gratitude" in the face of nature (216). In the classroom, the poem can allow students to explore their relationship to nature, and nature becomes an object that allows them to more deeply experience the poem on a personal level. Such explorations often lead students to consider the environment and the social issues surrounding it as well. Hunter and Sanderson write that "there is no more serious business than remembering, acknowledging, and protecting the awareness that there is an inherent sacred bond and responsibility between human beings and nature" (215). Those interested in the intersection of literary studies and ecopedagogy may find many of the exercises in this model useful for their classroom goals.

Action/Application Phase

Mazza sees value in having clients choose their own poem for further exploration, and this can work for students as well. The act of choosing is a form of expression that is open even to students who are not artistically inclined. Once students have become comfortable with responding to poems on a personal level and examining their responses, they can select their own poem that carries meaning for them. This process of selection is something nearly everyone can relate to since nearly everyone has had some kind of profound experience with a poem or work of art at some point in their lives. Typically, one would limit students to poems covered during the course, so it is important to provide a large and varied set of options. By choosing their own texts, and then writing about their unique experiences of them, students enact a kind of creative agency that moves them closer to becoming creators themselves, which is what they ultimately become in the final, creative phase of this model.

This action/application phase employs exercises based on Alvin Mahrer's experiential therapy and Richard Kopp's metaphor therapy. Both of these exercises are designed to achieve change in the individual. Through these exercises, students locate an intense personal response to their chosen poem. They respond through the three registers of experience, explore personal associations, and engage creatively with their chosen text. They move on to analyze these affective, imagistic, and creative responses. Here, they gain personal insights and deeper self-awareness on an individual and relational level. Finally, students complete each of the exercises by applying their newly gained insights to their lives.

Experiential Therapy Exercise

Alvin Mahrer's experiential therapy provides a model through which we may use poetry as a vehicle to explore personal affective experience in the context of a poetry class. This model, however, goes beyond affect to include memory and associations, as well as creative expression, serving the goal of bringing about personal renewal or a new sense of self. Mahrer's sessions have several attributes that make them applicable to the classroom and ideal for our goals in the teaching of poetry. Mahrer believes in the personal construction of the external world—that the way we, as humans, experience the world largely depends on our imagination or our fantasies. Experiential sessions involve creative activity so that a new self emerges with a more positive and profound image of self and of external reality. Mahrer's sessions are not grounded in any particular theoretical framework, though they are consistent with the goals of poetry therapy. These sessions are each independent and, ideally, each lead to a gained sense of renewal. This makes them useful in achieving therapeutic benefits with students during the relatively short time span of a semester. These sessions can be done in any setting or context. Mahrer even suggests that they may be done independently without the therapist (or teacher), which is helpful because teachers rarely have the capacity to give students the kind of in-depth personal attention that most forms of therapy require. The following exercise is heavily based on Mahrer's four-step experiential model.[6] In this classroom model that follows, the order of Mahrer's steps is altered. The classroom model is also expanded to six steps and transformed into a writing exercise. This exercise tends to work best as a homework assignment, though the instructor may want to give some guidance beforehand. Doing it during class time can help make it more structured, but most students find it more comfortable to do it outside of the classroom setting. The teacher may want to go through and explain each step before assigning it. However, sometimes less explanation, though it may frustrate some students, leads to surprising, positive results.

Mahrer's premise is that people generally function in their lives with operating potentials for experiencing but rarely discover their "deeper possibilities or potentialities for experiencing" (8). Experiential therapy seeks to discover one's deeper potential for emotional experience in particular, but also encourages one to locate creative potentials. In Mahrer's first step, the subject should locate a scene of intense emotion. Mahrer makes this scene the focus of the session rather than the therapist or client. Mahrer suggests using either a scene from real life or an intense dream, but because the session can start from or jump off from any scene of intense emotion, a poem that one experiences intensely can serve in this capacity.

To begin, each student chooses a poem that serves as the focal point throughout the entire exercise. Once the poem has been chosen, students try to isolate the exact moment of intense emotion—the exact stanza, couplet, or line within the poem where they experience the most intense feelings. Students, as they focus in, should try to get outside of themselves in order to discover something deeper, beyond their operating potentials for experiencing. They should imagine themselves within the scene of the poem as if they were the central character in the poem or an actor in a performance of it. As they continue to penetrate the exact moment of peak feeling in the poem, they should narrow the moment down even further to a specific word or phrase where the visceral experience of the poem grows most intense. It does not matter at this point what the quality of the feeling is, only where the reader quantitatively feels most intensely. Students will write their selected word or phrase at the top of their paper.

As students continue on to step two, it is important to remain with the experience uninterrupted. Students should continue to penetrate and intensify the deeper experience of the poem. In their minds, they should begin to fill in details associated with the experience like mental images and memories. Students should keep in mind that this is meant to be an enjoyable exercise. Locating this deep, rarely sought-after potential for experiencing should be both positive and exhilarating even if the focal experience is painful or negative.

Step two of Mahrer's process involves welcoming and accepting the deeper potential for experience located, but not defined, in step one. In Mahrer's sessions, participants act out and talk through the activities in this and the following two steps, but, for the purposes of the classroom, it is done as a writing exercise. Students begin by naming and describing in writing the deeper experience located in step one—whatever they feel, think, envision, or experience through the most intense moment of the poem. The goal is to integrate the experience by bringing it into language. As they write, students should admit both their positive and their negative reactions to the experience, so that they may come to recognize their complexity. Often, for example, a strong sense of fear and panic linked with a negative experience can also give rise to a feeling of courage or inner strength—a deeper potential—that comes from facing the experience unflinchingly. Here, students begin to explore personal memories and relationships associated with their intense experience of the poem that can bring up potentially painful feelings. Students continue by describing or discussing people they know who might exemplify, or whom they associate with, this experience. They recall times in their lives when they felt this experience or something close. Finally, they consider this as a deeper, new potential in themselves by asking how this quality of experience is not them or does not match how they see themselves or how others see them.

The final four steps deal in imagination and fantasy, but remain deeply rooted in personal experience. The prompts in these steps are similar to those in creative writing exercises. Students learn through these prompts to locate and be their creative, renewed selves open to broader possibilities and deeper potentials that they can realistically apply to their lives. This model rearranges and expands on Mahrer's model in order to better fit the purposes of the classroom.

In the third step, students are asked to inhabit the poem. They write a scene where they are the speaker of or a character in the poem experiencing the scene of the poem as the speaker does, but also as themselves. Again, it may be useful for students to think of themselves as actors trying to take on another character by relying on their own experiences. This is similar to the empathy exercises from the supportive/empathic phase of the larger classroom model where students must write from the perspective of an other. Here, students will strengthen their connection to the object within the poem—speaker, poet, or character—that gave rise to the intense experience. Again, the perspective they write from is both them and not them. Whether students write themselves as the speaker of the poem or a character in the poem, their focus should remain on their deep experience as they recreate the scene of the poem through this new perspective. They are the character experiencing the intense emotion, but within the context laid out in the poem. This and the fantasy scenes that follow may be done from any grammatical person (first, second, or third) or in any format (prose fiction, dramatic scene, or expressive poem). Again, we should remind students that this should be a fun-and-free exercise.

In step four, students will now apply the deeper potential for experiencing to a past scene. Students should find a specific real-life scene from their past where they either came close to this experience evoked by the poem, or where this experience was strikingly absent—appropriate or even preferable, but not present. This step sometimes evokes painful memories and may not be appropriate for all classroom settings. However, even though these past scenes sometimes prove painful, students are given the opportunity to act in them playfully in such a way that aims to repair negative feelings. Students will be in their past scene, again, as if replaced by a character or actor who exemplifies the deeper potential for experiencing discovered through the poem—a character both me and not me. Students should write, creating their own fantasy where they play out this real-life past scene with the me/not me character in their place. Students may try to make this a corrective fantasy or just an absurd and funny one that greatly exaggerates the deeper potential experienced in the past scene—or whatever; it is up to them.

Step five asks the student to apply their gains and practice being the qualitatively new person. Staying in the me/not me character, students create another fantasy scene where they play this character in a likely future scene—something that they anticipate taking place in their real life. This might be something they are looking forward to or something they are anxious about. Though this scene is realistic and likely to occur in some form in the future, this exercise is a complete fantasy; anything can happen. Ideally, the discovery of a deeper potential will allow one in the future scene to face down fears or repair an important relationship, or it may simply provide a more intense experience of the scene, broadening and deepening the potential for experience. At the end of the exercise, now that students have enacted this new potential in fantasy, they will hopefully consider how they might carry, use, or be this new person of deeper potential for experience in real life.

Once again engaging their imagination and their connection to this deeper experience, students follow up with a sixth step where they create a character sketch of their me/not me fantasy character from the first five steps of the exercise. They describe, in writing, how their character walks or talks, what they look like, how they carry themselves, how they interact with others, their general attitude or demeanor, what quirks they might have, where and in what situations they feel most comfortable, where and how they are most likely to excel. This follow-up helps to give students a clearer image of their new potential and what they can achieve with it. It also continues to strengthen their connection with their deeper potential. As they accomplish these things, they will likely gain a clearer picture of how to apply this deeper potential within them to their lives in a positive and constructive way.

After having completed this exercise, the vast majority of students acknowledge it as a positive experience. Through engagement in a poetic text, this exercise leads many to gain awareness on various levels. Some students discover, through poetry, newfound inner strength or a new level of self-confidence that they can apply to relationships and other interactions in the social world. Some discover a deeper sense of compassion or empathy. From these newfound discoveries of their emotions or desires, some students realize new goals for themselves or envision previously unimagined potential futures. This exercise allows some to reevaluate where they are in their lives in comparison to where they want to be. For some, this exercise provides a helpful means through which to cope with negative experiences, especially death and other personal losses. It allows students to reevaluate relationships. It allows for a cathartic release of negative emotions or stress-inducing concerns. It also allows students to have fun and live out whatever wild fantasies they can come up with, while giving them insights into their own imaginations.

Metaphor Therapy Exercise

Another useful exercise derives from Richard Kopp's metaphor therapy. Kopp's therapeutic model focuses mainly on personal images, but involves the integration of all three registers of experience. The basic premise of metaphor therapy is that human beings structure their reality metaphorically. Kopp writes, "Metaphors are mirrors reflecting our inner images of self, life, and others" (xiii). These metaphors are key to achieving awareness and change. In order to achieve renewal of self, Kopp explains, one must restructure one's mental imagery—one's metaphors. Metaphor therapy seeks to bring about change by raising awareness of both internal and external reality, and by integrating the registers of experience through metaphoric language and imagery.

Metaphor therapy, like a number of other therapeutic approaches, stresses individual creativity. Kopp sees metaphor as "the root of creativity and openness of language" (93). Metaphors, as the primary vehicle of poetic language, bridge the gap between visual imagination and verbal expression. They help individuals express things beyond normal language through the creation of verbal images. Kopp explains that "the metaphor-maker [or, we might say, the poet] draws out of his or her creative imagination an image that resembles a pattern of meaning present in a specific situation to which the metaphoric image refers" (96). Through exploring metaphor in poetry, not only do readers gain deeper awareness, but they can achieve a sense of openness by escaping the normal confines of traditional linguistic expression. Kopp writes, "Imaginal cognition is essential to the creation of new ways of looking at things" (96). When bringing the image into the verbal, people can express something new and liberating through metaphor.

Kopp divides the process of metaphor therapy into seven steps that should be followed loosely. Again, the exercise below transforms a therapeutic approach that engages in poetic language into a writing exercise appropriate for the literature classroom. One major difference between this classroom approach and Kopp's approach as a therapist is that while he stresses using client-generated metaphors as a focus, this approach asks students to locate a metaphor in a poem that they relate to in terms of their view of, or relation to, self, life, or other. While this may not serve quite the same therapeutic purpose, using a poet's metaphor as opposed to deriving a personal one offers a degree of separation that may be more appropriate or comfortable in an academic setting.

The first step simply involves the location of the metaphor. Students choose a metaphor from their chosen poem to explore more deeply. The poetic metaphor may be a few words or an extended conceit that lasts the length of a poem; either could potentially work, though a smaller focus may be preferable since students will expand the metaphor themselves during the exercise. It may also be more useful, though not necessarily, for students to choose a metaphor that they relate to negatively, or that they associate with negative emotions, as they will be transforming or reimagining it.

Once the metaphor is located and copied down on paper, students will describe in writing their mental image of the metaphor. During this second step, they transform the poet's verbal metaphor into their own unique and personal mental image. Then they describe their mental image of the metaphor, the picture it brings up in their minds, in their own words. At this stage, students should just focus on describing the image itself without making a relation to their lives or any real situations. It helps to have students do these first two steps independently with various poems several times in classes leading up to the metaphor therapy exercise in order to get them familiar with how linguistic metaphors bring up images in the mind. Such practice also gets them accustomed to noticing and working with metaphors before going through all seven steps of the exercise.

In step three, students will creatively expand on the mental image described in step two. Kopp suggests a number of ways that one may do this. One can expand on the scenery and the action of the image by describing what else is happening in the mental scene. One can bring in other imaginary-sense impressions beyond the visual—hearing, smell, touch, and taste. Lastly, one can expand on the time frame of the image by exploring what happened before and what happens after the mental scene (7–8). This step engages the imagination more deeply while also giving students good practice in descriptive writing.

In the next step, students shift from the imaginative to the emotional register by describing "feelings and experiences associated with the metaphoric image" (Kopp 8). By the end of this step, students have engaged all three registers—language, image, and affect—around a specific poetic metaphor.

Step five is key in terms of transforming the image in order to ultimately achieve a sense of personal renewal. Now, students go beyond simply recording their images and emotions to taking control of them. Working with the expanded image of the metaphor created in step three, students consider how they would alter this image or narrative to make it more favorable to them. For example, if their mental image was of someone drowning, they might alter the image to that of someone being rescued or swimming to safety. Students are encouraged to produce a corrective fantasy, taking potentially negative images and putting them in an idealized form, or making positive images even more positive. This step allows students to create something new and better out of their images, and gets them to break away from their set ways of imagining.

In the final two steps, students come "out of the domain of metaphoric imagination, back across the 'metaphoric bridge,' returning to the domain of logical discourse and the external world of everyday life and literal meanings" (Kopp 11). These two steps get more specifically personal by asking students to examine what their chosen metaphor represents to them in their lives, and how they might apply their alteration/idealization of the metaphor to their lives. In step six, students make explicit this connection between the metaphor they explored in steps one through four and their real life. Here, they write about why they relate to their chosen metaphor and what the metaphor represents to them in terms of their self, life, or relationships. In the seventh and final step of the exercise, students relate the changed image or narrative they reimagined in step five to the real-life situation described in step six. They apply their altered image to how they might alter something in their lives.

This exercise encourages students to personally relate to poetic metaphors. This exercise can also help in raising awareness on various levels (to self, to other, and to reality, in general), particularly in terms of examining one's personal mental images. Lastly, this exercise encourages openness and change through the alteration or expansion of mental images. Kopp explains, "Instead of being imprisoned in the current metaphoric reality reflected in a particular metaphor or early memory metaphor, the client is freed by changing the metaphor, which can result in a change in the client's perception of reality" (107). Like the experiential exercise, students generally find this to be a positive experience. By engaging the poetic imagination, students create a more ideal image of self, life, or other and then relate it to their own lives.

At the conclusion of this action/application phase, students write a personal essay where they discuss and examine their relationship to the chosen poetic text. They are welcome to draw from the experiential and metaphor exercises or any other class activities. In the essay, they should have some kind of central focus, similar to a thesis. They might make their focus about how the poem helped them cope with something, how it helped them gain awareness, how it guided them toward new goals, or how it inspired them in some way. They will discuss their reactions to the poems in the three registers, discuss personal associations and memories that the poem brought up, and analyze themselves through their experience of the poem. The personal essay allows students to take their gains from this poetry therapy model and put them into a structured linguistic format.

Creative Phase

In the final phase, the creative agency established during the earlier phases is pushed further when students respond to their chosen poems with their own creativity. For their final project, students take their chosen poem that they have a strong response to, whether it is an emotional, associative, inspirational, or vividly imaginative response, and they create something artistic that expresses their response. Students can write a poem of their own, or the possibilities for the creative project can include any artistic medium (though collecting and returning larger projects can become a task). In the semesters that I have opened up the possibilities for the response, students have responded by taking an astonishing variety of approaches. Projects have included photo collages done on computers or with scissors and glue, paintings and watercolors, pencil and charcoal sketches, clay sculptures, bead sculptures, foam sculptures, computer slide shows, films of various sorts including animation, comic strips, pamphlets, letters to poets, and many excellent poems. At the end of the creative project, students again engage in self-reflection. They are required to include a brief written explanation of the project that talks about why they chose the poem, what their project means to them, and how it engages with the poem.

Mazza's brief poetry therapy, Hynes and Hynes-Berry's bibliotherapeutic process, Mahrer's experiential therapy, and Kopp's metaphor therapy all promote greater self-awareness while allowing for and encouraging the imagination of a new self. The classroom model presented above offers these therapeutic benefits to students of poetry. Poetry provides a vehicle through which students can delve into personal experiences in order to enrich their lives. Of course, it is difficult for teachers to judge when and to what degree an encounter with poetry gives rise to a genuinely intense experience and when that experience leads to personal change. It certainly does not happen with every reader and every poem. We can see this change, however, when students write about their encounter with a poem and discuss how change occurred in them, or when their poem leads them to create something thoughtful and imaginative in response. A therapeutic approach to poetry in the classroom allows students to deeply experience and to examine the profound effects that poetic texts can have on them. I have witnessed the success of this approach in the many students who have expressed gratitude for the opportunity to explore their identities through poetry in this way. My students will frequently say that they had never connected with a poem before doing these exercises.

Chapter Six
Cultivating Empathy:
Wordsworth's *Lyrical Ballads*

In his book *The Political Brain*, neurologist Drew Westen describes a series of experiments he and his colleagues performed supporting the hypothesis that emotion trumps reason in people's political views (x–xv). He goes on to describe how, in recent years, conservatives have been much more effective at appealing to voters on an emotional level particularly by creating narratives that appeal to moral values rather than making arguments based on facts or policy. Thus, Westen stresses the importance of creating emotionally compelling narratives for progressive political values. More recently, cognitive linguist George Lakoff has also stressed the need for progressives to do what conservatives have done so effectively in recent years, create and repeat narratives that activate positive emotions toward their worldview and negative emotions toward the worldview of their opposition. At stake, he argues, is nothing less than our democracy (1).

Lakoff defines the progressive worldview as one centered on empathy. This empathetic "mode of thought" that progressives use leads to a sense of social responsibility and ultimately to positive, prosocial action. Lakoff sees this mode of thought as fundamentally different from both a neoliberal mode of thought that may have good intentions, but ultimately centers on an old view of reason and self-interest, and a conservative mode of thought, which centers on obedience to unquestioned authority and discipline to maintain this obedience.[1] Lakoff explains the differences between progressive and conservative thought through the conceptual metaphor of the nation as a family.[2] In this metaphoric structure, the ideal conservative family/nation is one with a strict father who always knows best. The ideal progressive family consists of nurturing parents who must earn the respect and trust of their children by protecting and empowering them. To Lakoff, the ideal government provides such protection and empowerment to its citizens.[3]

Both Westen and Lakoff see a need to abandon the old Enlightenment view of reason that has continued to influence our understanding of political reality.[4] This view separates reason from emotion and assumes that people will act politically in their best interests when presented with facts and logic. Ignoring the central role of emotion in people's political and moral reasoning has been disastrous for the progressive movement in recent years. Progressives need to do more than appeal to citizens in terms of policies and their effects; progressives need to get people emotionally engaged in moral issues in ways that they can understand, identify with, and empathize with. Westen and Lakoff propose how we can use our contemporary understanding of the emotionally motivated brain, through neuroscience and cognitive science, to influence people toward more progressive political views and actions.

The prevalence of the eighteenth-century, reason-based view of the mind also helps us to understand the frequent ineffectiveness of social justice pedagogy in English classrooms. Bracher describes the typical approach of those in literary studies who seek to contribute to social justice as, "[E]xposing as false and harmful certain dominant cultural representations of various Others."[5] He continues, "To date, however, there has been little evidence that this pedagogy accomplishes its aims." Citing findings of social psychology and cognitive science, Bracher suggests that these traditional approaches to teaching for social justice are, in fact, likely ineffective ("How to Teach" 363).[6] The reason for their ineffectiveness is that they seek to appeal to students' reason more so than to their emotions. Bracher writes, "[A] fundamental reason that current practices of literary study are ineffective in reducing injustice is because the persistence of injustice is not due ultimately to lack of knowledge, lack of analytical skill, or even lack of the right principles or values; it is due to lack of emotional change" ("Teaching" 469). Teachers try to change students' views on a strictly cognitive level, without getting them emotionally and empathetically engaged with texts. Literature can serve as a powerful ally for cultivating prosocial attitudes because it provides emotionally compelling narratives that humanize issues. Our new understanding of the brain's role in political thinking could have great significance for literary studies and social justice pedagogy especially if we can maximize the emotional impact of texts on individual students and get them to examine their experiences with texts.

In recent years, social psychologists have taken a great interest in empathy as a motivation for prosocial attitudes and actions. C. Daniel Batson and his colleagues have led the way in providing empirical evidence for many of the complex dynamics surrounding human empathy. They have gathered support for Batson's "empathy-altruism hypothesis" showing that empathy evokes an altruistic, rather than self-interested, motivation to improve the welfare of victims ("Empathic Joy"). They have shown that empathy for a member of a stigmatized group can lead to more positive attitudes toward the group as a whole ("Empathy and Attitudes"). And, they have shown that these improved attitudes do often lead to prosocial behavior toward a stigmatized group ("Empathy, Attitudes, and Action"). Like Bracher, Batson attests to the ineffectiveness of revising stereotypes simply by providing information. Instead, Batson's experiments show that engaging emotional empathy is far more effective for changing attitudes toward stigmatized groups ("Empathy and Attitudes"). In one experiment of particular significance for literary studies, Batson examines whether empathy has the same effect if it is shown toward an individual that the participants of the experiment know to be fictional. While his results "do not warrant a firm conclusion," they suggest that emotional empathy is a more significant factor than whether or not the individual presented was real or fictional ("Empathy, Attitudes, and Action" 1665–1666). This supports the case for the positive social effects of literature, as well as the need to focus more on empathy in our approach to teaching it.

Empathizing with fictional characters does, of course, come with some potential ethical issues (most significantly, that it can offer escapism from real issues) and practical limitations (for one, that you cannot relieve the suffering of a fictional character) that we must acknowledge. Suzanne Keen offers a somewhat cynical scrutiny of "the literary version of the empathy-altruism hypothesis" (224). However, Mary-Catherine Harrison writes, "It is essential that we examine the potential failures of narrative empathy, but also that we give an equally rigorous account of its potential successes" (258). Harrison is particularly concerned with ethics of narrative versus interpersonal empathy—that is empathy for fictional characters versus empathy for real, suffering individuals. The ethical dilemma that narrative empathy brings about is whether feeling empathy for a fictional character leads to empathy with actual people and whether that empathy translates to action. Drawing from the research of Batson in particular, Harrison proposes a synechdocal model for understanding the effects of narrative empathy. She writes, "Research on discourse processing suggests that readers engage in a metaphorical, or what we might call synechdocal interpretation of character: taking the part (individual) to refer [to] the whole (group). In this way, readers' emotional responses to fictional individuals can be parlayed into an emotional, *and* ethical, response towards groups of people whom they represent" (258). By empathizing with fictional individuals, we generalize and empathize with the oppressed or stigmatized groups that they represent.

Cultivating emotional empathy should be a valued classroom goal for any social justice pedagogy. While not everyone agrees on an exact meaning of empathy,[7] Elaine Hatfield et al. provide a useful definition for the term that we can aspire to promote in our teaching. They write, "[T]rue empathy requires three distinct skills: the ability to share the other person's feelings, the cognitive ability to intuit what another person is feeling, and a 'socially beneficial' intention to respond compassionately to that person's distress" (19).[8] One of my classroom goals is to develop emotional empathy in my students while also making them more aware of their emotional responses and how they may be manipulated (including by me or by the texts I value). While I do not push any agenda in my classroom beyond this, both of these goals for the literary classroom are consistent with Westen's and Lakoff's strategies for a more socially progressive society. I want to make students more aware of the effect of language on their neural networks, particularly those emotional ones that influence their political views, because such awareness makes them less susceptible to manipulations. And, I want to encourage and foster empathy in my students. The focus on empathy will activate progressive frames in students that neurologically strengthen their prosocial values.[9]

I do not consider activating empathy in this way manipulative or unethical because, for one, it is essential for a more just society, and because the human brain already contains a natural capacity for empathy. Lakoff writes that many people are biconceptual, that is, they use different modes of thought for different issues. Even self-identified conservatives will at times, often unconsciously, use empathetic modes of thought in many areas (70). What I want to do, to use J. D. Trout's terminology, is bridge empathy gaps. Trout describes several common failures of human empathy. For example, we tend to empathize more with those who are similar to us or in our in-group, and withhold empathy from cultural, racial, or other types of outsiders (22–23). We also tend to empathize more with those who are geographically closer to us and withhold it from those who are far away, even when their level of suffering makes them more deserving (24–25). Because empathy is tied so closely to altruism, Trout argues that society must enact policies that take these empathy gaps into account. Bridging empathy gaps first requires a conscious effort to recognize when and where these gaps are occurring. One of the things I try to get my students to do is to become aware of their empathy gaps, and then practice bridging them through imagination.

The primacy of human empathy has been established by various fields. Kohut has made a case for the primary function of empathy from a psychoanalytic perspective where the infant's survival is dependent on the reciprocal primary relationship with the parent (*Search* 682; *Restoration* 116).[10] Evolutionary psychologists Elliott Sober and David Sloan Wilson link altruism or unselfish behavior that can arise from empathy to greater species survival.[11] In recent years, the field of social neuroscience has used the discovery of mirror neurons in the brain to argue that human beings have a natural, primary, biological capacity for empathy. Marco Iacoboni writes that mirror neurons "are the foundation of empathy and possibly of morality, a morality that is deeply rooted in our biology" (5). Essentially, I try to bring out the best of what is already inside my students by developing their empathetic capacities so that they will, hopefully, be more broadly applied.

Westen and Lakoff propose several ways that progressive politicians and social activists can be more effective, many of which are relevant to the literature classroom. As human beings, we have systems in our brains that activate pleasure and anxiety, and these systems become neurologically bound to certain words and ideas. The Right has understood and used this neural binding to frame issues in ways that encourage a conservative worldview, enabling them to push a radically conservative agenda. The framing of our continued presence in Iraq during the second Bush administration is a great example: do we "cut and run" (which evokes cowardliness, weakness, and anxiety) or "stay the course" (which evokes strength, determination, and positive emotions). The Right creates and repeats such frames, narratives, and metaphors so that they become physically ingrained in our neural networks and affect our political opinions based on the emotional responses they evoke. Discussing the logic of our positions on issues or appealing to the interest of those who might benefit from progressive policies simply does not work. We must, instead, create and repeat emotionally compelling narratives and metaphors for a progressive moral worldview. This means evoking empathy for victims of social injustice. It also involves examining causality within a narrative structure in order to challenge harmful stereotypes. We must create positive associations with a democratic, empathetic, socially responsible, and nurturing worldview, while creating negative associations with an antidemocratic, self-centered, strict authoritarian worldview. We must repeat these narratives and metaphors so that they become neurologically bound in the brains of those we are trying to reach. We should also raise awareness in our students of how the brain works by examining the effects language has on us in terms of our neural networks.[12] Such knowledge is critical for avoiding destructive types of manipulation that lead to injustice and suffering.

There are a number of strategies we might draw from to learn how to effectively use literature for the purpose of increasing emotional empathy. To achieve my classroom goals, I begin by selecting emotionally compelling, prosocial narratives to teach. Literature is already a powerful tool in encouraging empathy and social responsibility, and what you teach is often as important as how you teach it. Batson, when creating a "high-empathy" group for his psychological experiments, simply instructs certain subjects to read, or view as the case may be, with empathy. This may appear overly simplistic, but it has proven effective within his research. Beginning by valuing empathy and encouraging empathetic reading in the classroom provides a solid foundation for later, more specific assignments.

Beyond choosing texts that lend themselves to empathy and encouraging empathetic reading in our students, we can use several exercises that engage empathy by engaging students' imaginations. Here I am reminded of Shelley's quote from "The Defense of Poetry": "A man, to be greatly good, must imagine intensely and comprehensively; he must put himself in the place of another and of many others; the pains and pleasures of his species must become his own. The great instrument of moral good is the imagination; and poetry administers to the effect by acting upon the cause" (106). As I discuss in chapter five, poetry therapists often do exercises with poems that are designed to develop empathy through imagination.[13] I find many of Wordsworth's poems from the original 1798 version of *Lyrical Ballads* particularly useful for my pedagogical approach because they offer emotionally compelling narratives—focused on people, not policy—that are consistent with progressive values of social justice: empathy, responsibility, and interconnectedness.[14] Wordsworth's poems seek to activate empathy for victims of social injustice. They challenge stereotypes about the underprivileged that remain prevalent today. They bind positive emotional associations with socially responsible actions, and negative ones with greed and self-interest. They link Wordsworth's love of nature to love of humanity in general. And, finally, they reject an enlightenment view of mind that is based primarily on human reason in order to create an emotionally expressive and evocative poetry.

The term "empathy" was coined in the twentieth century, but Wordsworth did write about "sympathy," a similar phenomenon and one that was central to his poetry.[15] In part one of his "Essay upon Epitaphs," Wordsworth defines "general sympathy" as the "common or universal feeling of humanity" (*Wordsworth's* 129). Contrasted with individual particulars, this universal feeling binds us together as human beings. As a poet, Wordsworth seeks to capture human emotions and to evoke our sympathy by sympathizing himself. In the 1802 preface to *Lyrical Ballads*, Wordsworth writes, "[I]t is the wish of the Poet to bring his feelings near to those of the persons whose feelings he describes, nay for short spaces of time perhaps, to let himself slip into an entire delusion, and even confound and identify his own feelings with theirs" (*Wordsworth's* 78). While empathizing is clearly a goal of Wordsworth's, we may certainly question whether he always genuinely achieves it. John Keats's criticism of Wordsworth's egotism is well known, and there is potentially some conflict between empathy and the Romantic elevation of the individual that we see throughout Wordsworth's poetry.[16] Wordsworth does come off as self-righteous in his treatment of social issues at times, and one sometimes gets the sense that the poor exist to Wordsworth primarily so that he can write his poetry. However, I have seen no evidence in any of my students' responses to Wordsworth that suggests that they were put off by him on the grounds of his egotism, whereas, I have seen much to support the emotional and empathetic impact of his poetry.

In the classroom, I transparently frame discussions of Wordsworth's poems in terms of awareness, empathy, and social justice as valued goals. Students consider the emotional effects (positive and negative) of characters and speakers, and their narratives, along with the social value of these narratives. While doing this, they also consider counternarratives that these narratives challenge, such as stereotypes or socially harmful worldviews. I also have students complete a poetry project that seeks to engage them personally, empathetically, and creatively in Wordsworth's poetry. For the project, students choose one Wordsworth poem to focus on. They are instructed to empathize with their text, and told that the purpose of the assignment is to get them emotionally and imaginatively engaged in a poem. The project involves two parts. For the first part, students create a written response to express their experience of or reaction to the poem. I give students two options for this part: for option one, students may write a poem in response to the Wordsworth poem. This could be a reworking of the poem that offers some new perspective, or a poem expressing their personal reaction to the original poem. Their poem may be addressed to Wordsworth, one of his characters, or a general audience. It could also be written from the perspective of a character. For option two, they can write a letter to Wordsworth or to one of the characters from one of the poems. For part two of the project, students write a brief reflection on their creative responses. Here, they can talk about why they chose their poem, how their project engages the poem, or what their project means to them.

The poem "Lines Left upon a Seat in a Yew-Tree" provides a good starting point for the course section as it is about a personal failure of one with prosocial ideals to effectively act socially in the world. The poem begins with a speaker describing a man to a passing traveler. This man was "no common soul" (13). In his youth, he went forth into the world "pure in his heart" (15) with "lofty views" (14). This young man is prepared to meet any opposition, but he is not prepared for the neglect that he encounters. His spirit is dampened and his pride is hurt, so he withdraws from the world of humankind to live a secluded life in the wilderness around the yew-tree seat. The natural setting that he retires to is one that "shall lull thy mind / By one soft impulse saved from vacancy" (6–7). As we often see in

Wordsworth, the natural setting makes the young man feel connected to humanity in general. This loving feeling toward humanity makes him feel a "mournful joy" (39), a feeling of regret because he has severed his connection with mankind. In the final verse, the speaker turns to the young traveler warning him not to be a victim of pride, and to remain empathetic and engaged with humankind. "True knowledge," he advises, "leads to love" (56). The poem activates positive neural networks associated with nature and with humanity, but it also activates negative neural networks associated with self-centered pride and a lack of social responsibility. We fault the main character for his flaws, but we also empathize with his feelings of regret. The poem creates a powerful metaphor—the yew-tree seat—for the negative aspects of isolation (in nature). This metaphor is particularly effective as a space of enclosure implying concepts of isolation as burial and death. This narrative of regret brings about sadness, yet also empathy for one who fails to act on his convictions. Students are typically able to empathize with the character's regret and frequently express a wish to avoid such regrets in their own lives. His failures bring about negative emotions in readers associated with isolation and a failure to act socially. Thus, social action is encouraged as a way of avoiding the same kind of regret that the protagonist must live with.

"The Female Vagrant" activates empathy for a lower-class victim while challenging conservative frames about issues like homelessness, crime, and war. The eventual female vagrant of the title is the speaker of nearly the whole poem, though there is a brief frame at the beginning and at the end. She begins by telling of the rural life she once lived with her fisherman father. Her father is "a good and pious man" (10) who works hard. The speaker, her father, and her eventual husband are all described as hard workers. My students always admire this trait, and it keeps them from blaming the victim later on when the family falls into misfortune. Trout discusses this common bias where the poor are blamed for their situation. This bias, of course, becomes an obstacle to prosocial action (40–41).[17] Wordsworth is careful throughout the poem to show the causality of the suffering that the vagrant and her family go through by showing them to be hardworking and moral individuals who simply fall on extreme hard fortune. Wordsworth activates negative neural networks associated with greed and selfishness early on in the poem as the heroine and her family are driven from their land by a ruthless landowner in the interest of commercial progress.

The poem also challenges common pro-war frames. The female speaker has some reprieve when she marries and she and her father move in with her weaver husband. They have three children, but soon her father dies and her husband can no longer find enough work. Desperate for their hungry children, the vagrant's husband joins in the war against America—an antirevolutionary war that Wordsworth saw as unjust.[18] Before shipping off to America, the family spends months in an impoverished, overcrowded seaside town. When they come to America in the midst of war, she recalls their previous poverty as preferable. Wordsworth offers many brutal descriptions of the inhumanity of war. This narrative undercuts the frame of war as heroic and glorious, and of soldiers as heroes who fight honorably for a cause they believe in. Her husband only joins the war effort out of financial desperation, and the American soldiers are portrayed murdering and raping their British adversaries. In one year, we learn, the speaker loses her husband and all three of her children. She is forced to return home to Britain where, having nothing and no one, she will ultimately become a vagrant.

Upon returning to her homeland, the speaker turns first to crime as a means of survival. Again, Wordsworth challenges conservative frames of criminals that simply see them as bad human beings. The descriptions that Wordsworth gives of the vagrant's physical experiences of hunger, in particular, make readers empathetic to her situation. When she joins a band of thieves, most readers cannot fault her. Students will often say or write things like "I would have done the same thing in her position." The thieves are also the only people who show her kindness when even her husband's family shuts her out. The speaker, however, cannot continue a criminal lifestyle for long. Her morals prevent her, since she was "brought up in nothing ill" (242). In the end, she is left alone and, however uncomfortable she is about it, must beg for a living. She writes, "Forgone the home delight of constant truth, / And clear and open soul, so prized in fearless youth" (260–261). Even though she is a victim of circumstances, she remains regretful about the decisions she's made. Because Wordsworth establishes the moral character of the vagrant and shows the uncontrollable circumstances that lead to her vagrancy, readers must alter any frames they might have about homelessness that blame its victims as deserving of their plight. They typically respond with empathy for the female vagrant and anger at the social injustice of which she is a victim.

"Simon Lee" provides a heroic narrative for a small act of social responsibility. The poem achieves its emotional effect by using what Lakoff describes as a rescue narrative (33–37). This is a commonly used narrative structure designed to achieve a powerful emotional response. The rescue narrative includes several prototypical roles: a victim who needs to be rescued, a hero who does the rescuing, and a villain from whom the victim needs to be rescued. This structure is compelling to human beings, since we all fear victimization, in whatever form. Sometimes our life or well-being is threatened, other times, our identity or pride is threatened. Politicians use this type of narrative frequently to evoke fear in voters who are potential victims of, for example, terrorism or economic inequality. Politicians then position themselves as the heroes who will rescue the public from such threats. Commercials also use these narratives to manipulate consumers. The product is set up as the hero who will rescue consumers from hunger, dandruff, static cling, or whatever ails them. Rescue narratives begin by enacting negative fear, but then offer relief from fear that creates positive associations with the hero. Giving students an understanding of how these narratives are designed to manipulate them, empowers them to transcend such emotional manipulations.

However, as we see in the case of "Simon Lee," these types of narratives can also enact positive emotions for prosocial ends. In "Simon Lee," we come to sympathize with Lee who is a victim of old age and unfortunate circumstances. The poem activates empathy networks for poor and elderly people by describing Lee's physical decrepitude. It challenges common negative frames of the poor (they are lazy and deserve it) by showing what a determined huntsman Lee was as a young man. This contrast makes his current state all the more sympathetic. Students respect his work ethic as a youth and also tend to admire his continuing perseverance as an old man. The conversational tone of the poem also creates a sense of kinship with readers that further encourages an empathetic reading. Michael O'Neill writes that the poem depends "on a reader's readiness to 'kindly take it,' to respond, that is, in a spirit of human kinship" (36). He describes poems like "Simon Lee" as having a "suggestion of mutuality" (37), where the reader is invited to reflect on the situation. Once Lee is established as a sympathetic figure, the poem ends by activating positive neural networks associated with social responsibility when the speaker helps Lee with what for the speaker was a fairly simple task, digging up a root. As readers, we tend to identify with the speaker of the poem who, in this case, plays the role of hero within the rescue narrative structure. By positioning his speaker as the hero, Wordsworth shows that a small act of kindness toward another human being is heroic and can make a difference.[19] Students will often use this poem to reflect on the importance of helping the elderly and the responsibility that younger generations have for their elders.

"The Convict" challenges conservative frames of crime, criminals, and ways of dealing with them by evoking empathy for one confined in inhumane conditions. The poem begins by activating positive neural networks associated with nature, before contrasting the beauty of nature with the conditions the convict lives in. The poem's speaker is a visitor to the jail. His descriptions of the horrid jail, a "comfortless vault of disease," (32) and the convict's declining physical state, "That body dismissed from his care," (18) are designed to activate empathy networks for a confined criminal. Wordsworth challenges conservative frames of criminals (they are just bad people), by showing the convict's sincere remorse. In a powerful rhetorical analogy, Wordsworth activates negative neural networks associated with state-sanctioned violence, like war, which causes much more destruction than any common criminal could create. The poem ends with the speaker expressing the wish to "plant thee [the convict] where yet thou might'st blossom again" (52). This metaphor frames criminals as people who might, with the proper care, be rehabilitated rather than simply confined as punishment for their supposed natural lack of morals.

"The Convict" is, however, a complicated poem in terms of evoking empathy. My students are often very concerned with the actual nature of the convict's crime, and the ambiguity of the poem on this issue frustrates them. Sometimes students will withhold empathy because they do not know what the convict's crime was. Others will express an initial empathetic response with the convict, only to question it later. Batson shows in one of his experiments that the sense that one is responsible for one's suffering is a major factor in whether others will empathize with them ("Empathy and Attitudes" 107), so this selective empathy is not surprising. Students' inability to tolerate the poem's ambiguity leads many of them to fill in the gap in the text during their writing projects. Some will portray his crimes as severe and then argue that he deserves his punishment. Others will want to think better of the convict and will show his crimes as minor or his conviction as a result of a misunderstanding. Some students, however, will empathize with him regardless of his crime simply because of a natural response to human suffering.

"Tintern Abbey" creates positive links with the natural environment and links these to positive feelings toward humankind in general. We see an ecological consciousness at work in the poem where nature is valued, not as a resource, but as something that restores the soul. Ecocritic Jonathan Bate explains that in the poem Wordsworth does not approach nature with the purpose of mastery, but one of submission to an "inner vision" (146). This poem is probably the most famous of Wordsworth's *Lyrical Ballads* and is always a popular choice among my students for their projects. Many are predisposed to the poem because they too are "worshipper[s] of nature" (153). College-aged students also tend to identify with "Tintern Abbey" as a coming-of-age narrative where Wordsworth reflects nostalgically on his transition from childhood to adulthood. He reflects that he is "changed, no doubt, from what I was when first / I came among these hills" (67–68). He reflects on the more wild and pure relationship he had with nature in his youth when nature to him was "all in all" (76). Students will also at times express remorse for inevitably growing up and losing the joyful experiences of youth. In this sense, they experience a general empathy for the human condition. The poem also has relational value. Students will often write about the desire to share nature with others as Wordsworth does with his sister, Dorothy, near the poem's conclusion. He sees that in Dorothy, "Nature never did betray / The heart that loved her" (123–124). In her youth, she is still able to experience a pure form of joy in the natural setting.[20] Some students will even write about sharing nature with a younger sibling or relative and seeing them see nature the same way Wordsworth sees Dorothy experiencing it—which is also the way they saw it themselves when they were younger. Sharing nature with others and, in particular, with someone younger has further ecological implications as it points to the need to preserve nature for future generations to enjoy.

"Goody Blake and Harry Gill" was based on a supposedly true story, and it is easy to see why this story resonated with Wordsworth.[21] The poem tells of an old woman named Goody Blake who lives alone and is struggling to keep warm during the winter. To keep her fire going, she takes some wood from a hedge that is on the land of a young farmer named Harry Gill. When Gill catches her taking his wood he grabs her "fiercely by the arm" (91), and she is forced to let her bundle fall. Blake responds by looking to the heavens and praying, "'God! Who art never out of hearing,' / 'Oh may he never more be warm!'" (99–100). As a result, Gill becomes constantly cold for the rest of his life, stuck in bed under a pile of blankets with teeth clattering and no relief.

The poem activates empathy networks for the poor and elderly by describing the suffering of Goody Blake. It challenges framing of the poor as lazy and the old as useless by showing that Blake continues to work hard in her old age. The poem also challenges stereotypes about crime, however petty Blake's crime is, by showing causality. With its violent description of the strong and stout Harry Gill's accosting of Blake, it activates negative neural networks associated with greed and selfishness. It creates a powerful metaphor for a lack of social responsibility—the curse of relentless coldness that befalls Gill. Many will see this as poetic justice, along with the fact that Gill, through his curse, is essentially being forced to empathize with Blake who stole wood for a fire because she was cold. "Goody Blake and Harry Gill" is, however, problematic in terms of its treatment of social justice because it is not only a narrative about upper-class greed and the suffering of the lower classes, but it is also a narrative of revenge where the revenge is rather severe. This poem is a popular choice of my students for their projects. I get a variety of responses that illustrate the complexity of empathy.

Some students will be vehemently anti–Harry Gill. Often they respond with self-righteousness or anger toward him, chastising him for his lack of empathy and social responsibility. More radical responses will even challenge concepts of class and private property. Essentially, these students feel that Gill gets what he deserves. Yet, their lack of empathy for Gill for his suffering is similar in some ways to Gill's lack of empathy for Blake. Some students will write from Gill's perspective in order to show a transformation in him where he regrets what he's done and changes his unempathetic mode of thought. This approach may be idealistic, but it does involve a level of empathizing with Gill. Some students are clearly against Gill's selfish actions, but also sympathize with the severity of his punishment. Then there are students who respond to the poem with more conservative, less empathetic modes of thought. These students value personal discipline and obedience to authority or law above or equal to empathy and social responsibility. They will see Blake's act as a result of her lack of discipline rather than understanding it as a desperate act for survival. Stealing is simply wrong, and Gill is a hardworking, successful landowner who is victimized both by Gill's theft and her curse. Still, even most of these students show a capability for biconceptual thinking and at least show some empathy for Blake.

What becomes strikingly evident in students' responses to "Goody Blake and Harry Gill" is that you can get students to use empathy, but you cannot control exactly where their empathy is placed. Certainly a teacher does not want to force students to respond to texts with political views and modes of thought that they find more favorable. This would cause many students to reject a teacher or text altogether and would cause many others to simply go along with the teacher's point of view for the sake of a grade. Either way, no real change would have occurred in students. This does not mean that we should simply act as values clarifier where one morality is as good as another. By encouraging empathy in general, we are encouraging a prosocial value that will encourage everyone to use biconceptualism. This can potentially bridge an empathy gap between progressive and conservative modes of thought. We can use the different points of view that students bring to the classroom to discuss how different people think in different ways, and we can use student responses to discuss the texts in terms of the different modes of thought that students bring to them. This raises self-awareness as well as awareness of others. We could also consider the social value of these modes of thought as a class, but must be careful not to make any students feel like they are being attacked. When handled gracefully, this approach provides a classroom opportunity to explore empathy gaps and different modes of thought, while also cultivating empathy.

Chapter Seven
A Reparative Text: Tennyson's *In Memoriam*

In his 1802 preface to *Lyrical Ballads*, William Wordsworth famously describes good poetry as "the overflow of powerful feelings," which "takes its origin from emotion recollected in tranquility" (85). Arthur Hallam, in his 1831 review of his friend Alfred Tennyson's first volume of poetry, *Poems, Chiefly Lyrical*, maintains this valuing of emotion, but sees the reflective aspects of Wordsworth's poetry as overly intellectual. Hallam puts forth, through Tennyson, the concept of a poetry of sensation—as opposed to one of reflection. He admires Wordsworth for "awakening the minds of men, and giving a fresh impulse to art," but argues that "it is not true...that the highest species of poetry is the reflective" (184). Hallam values the more primary aspects of poetry, sound and image in particular, as they evoke sensations in the reader. He makes the weighty claim for great poets: "[T]hey speak to the hearts of all, and by the magnetic force of their conceptions, elevate inferior intellects into a higher and purer atmosphere" (189). Great poets like Tennyson give us greater awareness of ourselves because they take such detailed notice of human experience, and they are able to express what they notice. William Johnson Fox wrote of Tennyson's *Poems, Chiefly Lyrical*, "Mr. Tennyson...seems to obtain entrance into a mind as he would make his way into a landscape" (76). Tennyson does this by noticing the totality of human experience—sensory as well as intellectual.

It was Hallam's death at the age of 22 that lead Tennyson to create his poetic masterpiece, *In Memoriam*. A long elegiac poem made up of 133 shorter lyrics written over a 17-year span, *In Memoriam* offers a detailed account of one man's experience of mourning his lost friend that many readers from Queen Victoria onward have related to and found comfort in.[1] Tennyson's insights into the mourning process, his accuracy and honesty in portraying both his thoughts and the depth of his feelings across all three registers of experience, make the poem a reparative text. Perhaps

Hallam, writing of poetry's reparative power, puts it best: "[T]he strong musical delight prevails over every painful feeling and mingles them all in its deep swell until they attain a composure of exalted sorrow, a mood in which the latest repose of agitation becomes visible, and the influence of beauty spreads like light over the surface of the mind" (195).[2]

The deep internal realism that we find in Tennyson's elegy, with its aim of capturing the truth of affective experience in humans, corresponds directly with the goals of achieving renewal and reparation through poetry. His realism makes us more aware of our own affects and those of others. It also gives recognition to affective states that we may feel uncomfortable with or repress, so that we see the commonality of them. We empathize with an other, the poet or speaker of the poem, while also seeing ourselves in them. Our view of the world and people becomes more realistic and potentially more hopeful as we gain understanding. Finally, we see how affect may be expressed through image and language, so that we may then attempt our own poetic expressions. Poetry therapists Sherry Reiter and Lila Lizabeth Weisberger explain that "[r]eading or hearing the words of others may touch our pain and inspire us to write and communicate our grief in words" (110). This kind of self-expression allows one to contain the sometimes overwhelming experience of grief that may be inhibiting them from reaching their potential. Also, as students begin to express themselves through poetry, they often come to see new possibilities for themselves and the world. This may include adopting social views that are more humane and account for the desires, emotions, viewpoints, and experiences of others, or creating goals that involve helping others. Dealing with and understanding the pain of mourning and loss in oneself often leads to compassion for others and a desire to help.

One may think of reparation as a form of mourning—mourning the loss of the original good object of infantile fantasy. Klein makes this connection in her 1940 essay "Mourning and its Relation to Manic-Depressive States," and Hanna Segal has focused on this aspect of reparation in her work on creativity and art. To Klein, normal mourning due to a real loss repeats the process of the early loss of the good object or good breast when one enters the depressive position. Klein writes, "[I]n mourning the subject goes through a modified and transitory manic-depressive state and overcomes it, thus repeating, though in different circumstances and with different manifestations, the processes which the child normally goes through in his early development" (*Selected* 157). In mourning, we repair the loss of the real external good object by reinstating it as a good inner object. To Klein, as with Freud and other theorists on mourning, this involves testing of outer reality. A loss can shatter one's inner world. Feelings of love and goodness must then be reestablished by new positive experiences in the external world. The "pining" for the loss of a real object brings about a depressive state parallel to the original depressive position that one must manage through reparation, but that often gives rise to manic defenses until one develops the capacity for reparation. "The fluctuations between the depressive and manic position are an essential part of normal development," Klein writes (151). Likewise, Klein sees the process of mourning as manic-depressive in that the mourner fluctuates between manic fantasies of omnipotent control and feelings of triumph over the lost object, which then give way to feelings of guilt, sorrow, and depression. Manic fantasies that deny feelings of guilt and sorrow, as well as overwhelming feelings of hatred and triumph over the lost object, can severely impede mourning. Klein sees them as forms of denial in that the subject must "deny his impulse to make extensive and detailed reparation because he has to deny the cause for the reparation"—painful feelings of guilt and sorrow (155). However, these are also normal parts of the mourning process just as they are normal parts of infantile development. One must learn to master these more primal and negative impulses in order to make loving reparation.

Klein also observes a manic elation in mourning due to idealization of the lost loved object. She writes, "The passing states of elation which occur between sorrow and distress in normal mourning are manic in character and are due to the feeling of possessing the perfect loved object (idealized) inside" (158). Though this idealization must be relinquished, it provides a foundation for reinstating good inner objects later on just as a positive image of a good mother in the paranoid/schizoid position provides a foundation for later positive object relations in the real world. Klein explains, "Only gradually, by regaining trust in external objects and values of various kinds, is the normal mourner able once more to strengthen his confidence in the lost loved persons" (158). Through this process, one can realize that the mourned object is not perfect without losing a sense of love for the object. Reparation takes place in normal mourning within the depressive position where one must reinstate the inner good, loved object and rebuild a harmonious inner world. This involves a realistic acceptance of loss and the sorrow that comes with it, just as one must accept the loss of a pure good object in infancy.

Toward the end of her essay on mourning, Klein begins to relate mourning to the creative and artistic aspects of reparation. She writes,

> [W]hile grief is experienced to the full and despair is at its height, the love for the object wells up and the mourner feels more strongly that life inside and outside will go on after all, and that the lost loved object can be preserved within. At this stage in mourning, suffering can become productive. We know that painful experiences of all kinds sometimes stimulate sublimations, or even bring out quite new gifts in some people, who may take to painting, writing or other productive activities under the stress of frustrations and hardships. (163)

Segal has taken this aspect of Kleinian reparation to create her own aesthetic theory of art. She explains Klein's premise, "The memory of the good situation, where the infant's ego contained the whole loved object and the realization that it has been lost through his own attacks, give rise to an intense feeling of loss and guilt, and to the wish to restore and re-create the lost object outside and within the ego." According to Segal, "This wish to restore and re-create is the basis of later sublimation and creativity" (187). Creative activity for Segal comes from mourning and reinstating the primary good object. She writes, "[A]ll creation is really a re-creation of a once loved and once whole, but now lost and ruined object, a ruined internal world and self" (190). Like Klein, Segal sees that "symbol formation is rooted in the depressive position" (196). A mature assessment of the realistic loss of the good object proves essential for creative reparation. "It is only when the loss has been acknowledged and the mourning experienced," she explains, "that re-creation can take place" (190). Reparation involves reacting against negative instincts that prove harmful to self and other. This renunciation of aggression is part of Freud's reality principle, which, as Segal explains, proves key to artistic sublimations. "One of Freud's greatest contributions to psychology," she writes, "was the discovery that sublimation is the outcome of a successful renunciation of an instinctual aim; I would like to suggest here that such a successful renunciation can happen only through a process of mourning" (196). The subject renounces not only the enactment of destructive behavior, but also the unrealistic relationship with the pure, idealized, good object. This renunciation must occur if one is to function in the social or symbolic world where real relationships form, and where art is created. "Every aspect of the object," Segal writes, "every situation that has to be given up in the process of growing, gives rise to symbol formation." She relates this renunciation to mourning, "In this view, symbol formation is the outcome of a loss; it is a creative act involving the pain and the whole work of mourning" (196). Art, to Segal, reflects and arises from the need to mourn the original loss of a pure good object. Reparation then refers to the symbolic restoration of this object that takes place through art. As readers, we often find ourselves brought back to this primary good object and the original loss of it—particularly with elegies or other texts dealing with death. This gives us some insights into the profound emotional effects that such works of art can have on us.

I describe Klein's model of mourning here because I find it useful in explaining the power of Tennyson's *In Memoriam*, which lies in the accuracy of its portrayal of the mourning process. It is surprising that critics of the poem who have dealt specifically with its mourning have typically approached the poem through a Freudian view of mourning based on his essay "Mourning and Melancholia."[3] In "Mourning and Melancholia,"

Freud argues that successful mourning comes to a decisive end when the subject gives up the libidinal attachment to the lost object and reinvests in a new object. The problem with Freud's economic view of mourning is that it implies that the people we love are replaceable, and that our attachments are narcissistic and transient rather than empathetic and enduring.[4] My students, on the other hand, tend to be more familiar with the "5 stages of grief" model made popular by Elizabeth Kübler-Ross.[5] Reiter and Weisberger explain, however, that while this model has value in identifying some common elements of grieving, it also implies that there is a correct way to grieve. Furthermore, the model becomes problematic because it is so commonly misunderstood in the popular imagination as a sequential process when it was not intended to be viewed as such (111–112).

The Kleinian model of mourning accounts for several closely related elements of Tennyson's *In Memoriam* that the limitations of the Freudian model and the Kübler-Ross model call attention to. First, Kleinian theorists recognize the primacy of the mourning process, which Tennyson expresses at various times in his elegy. Furthermore, Kleinians recognize mourning as fragmented where the subject fluctuates frequently between various states. Like *In Memoriam*, the mourning process is made up of many moments and does not follow a neat narrative arch where one moves progressively from one phase or stage to another. George Bell focuses on this aspect of capturing moments in his approach to poetry therapy. Bell writes, "Because poets focus on moments, they have had, and perhaps always will have, unique access to reality in human experience" (178).[6]

Klein's model also accounts for the endlessness of the mourning process, or the impossibility of completely abandoning the object. The mourned object is not replaced, as in Freud's model, but its internalized existence is repaired by the mourner so that it may continue to represent a whole, loving object that the mourner can continue to love and to make use of.

The loss of Hallam represents to Tennyson not only the literal loss of a beloved friend, but also a repetition of the loss of the internalized pure good object that provides a foundation essential for achieving positive loving relationships. Aidan Day and James Hood have both recognized the primal loss that Hallam's death represents to Tennyson. Day refers to the "mythologisation of Hallam" (121), where Hallam takes on archetypal status for the poet. Hallam, first, represents an archetype of love for Tennyson. The loss of Hallam then becomes the loss of love itself. Day explains, "Hallam's death succeeds a prior loss...Grief over that death caused the already existing heart sickness to crystallize in—among other things, perhaps—the writing of *In Memoriam*" (126–127). Hood describes Day's Tennyson as questing for preconscious infantile wholeness (5), while concurring that Hallam serves as "an archetypal symbol of all loss, all grief, all human yearning" (118). In Kleinian terms, this primal loss is the loss of the good object, essential for relationships and action in the external world. This is the lost object that Tennyson must repair.

When we look at the various lyrics in the poem as individual moments that lead to a greater capacity for reparation, we can come to a clearer understanding of *In Memoriam* as representative of a mourning process. Throughout the poem, we see moments of manic reparation and resistance to it, paranoid/schizoid anxiety, depressive guilt, and, especially in the later lyrics, real reparation where Tennyson is able to reaffirm Hallam as a loving object and take a more loving view of the world, of life, and of others. In Tennyson's mourning process, Hallam is an object of love, reminiscent of the primary good object. But because he is a lost object, one that has abandoned Tennyson, he is also the object of Tennyson's grief and brings about overwhelming depression. Tennyson remains concerned throughout the poem with abandoning his grief by also abandoning his love for Hallam; such a manic denial of love would ease his grief. But Tennyson is generally conscious of his need to maintain Hallam as an object of love while coping with the feelings of grief that his loss brings about. He is careful throughout most of the poem not to split Hallam as grief-object/love-object, or to abandon the object altogether, but tries to maintain him internally as whole—as lost, as the cause of pain, but still as loving and as loved. In his reparative moments, he experiences a connection with Hallam as loving, and this leads him to action and participation in the social, external world.

In Memoriam is not only a very deliberate and self-conscious poem, but one portraying a very deliberate and self-conscious mourning process. Because he remains conscious of using manic or regressive defenses, Tennyson is generally successful throughout the poem at maintaining an image of Hallam as whole and loving—though he is often overwhelmed within the depressive position for his loss. Where Tennyson does make paranoid/schizoid splits is in his view of the external world, nature, and in its personified creator, God. In his moments of deepest despair, Tennyson associates God/nature/world with death, chaos, destruction, and cruelty. Tennyson reacts to this bad object with anger and hopelessness. This image of God/nature/world as bad object is split off from the loving, creating image of God/nature/world as good object. This bad object threatens Tennyson with a paranoid/schizoid fear of annihilation; the same force that took Hallam will someday take Tennyson. But the good object associated with life, order, meaning, and love, the object that gave the gift of Hallam, is the same as the bad object. Tennyson makes this split by associating God with love, and splitting God from nature that, in his most desperate moments, becomes a destructive, threatening bad object famously described in Lyric LVI as "red in tooth and claw" (15). Both Sacks (199) and Isobel Armstrong (263) have pointed out the Oedipal nature of this split—moving from maternal nature to paternal God. But Tennyson must eventually go beyond this Oedipal resolution to maintain God and nature as a whole, good object. He comes to repair this split when he accepts that God and nature are essentially the same, or part of the same force. He repairs this split mainly by imagining that the cycles of life and nature are part of a greater plan of a loving God, and that man is ultimately progressing toward some greater goal. In his reparative moments, Hallam also merges with this greater force in Tennyson's imagination.

When Tennyson functions within the depressive position, he experiences both the depressive anxiety based on his loss and depressive guilt for his attacks on the object God/nature/world. We see this in his pleas for forgiveness in the poem's prologue: "Forgive these wild and wandering cries" (41). The loss of Hallam leads to the fear of abandonment by the love object that is the major fear of the depressive position. Suddenly Tennyson's image of a good object has lost its permanence. His reaction to the depressive position at times involves manic defenses, and at other times a regression to paranoid/schizoid splitting of the object. The image of God/nature/world represents Tennyson's view of life that must remain ultimately positive for psychic, and perhaps literal, survival. The death of Hallam, however, has shattered his psychic foundation—his image of a good, loving object. When he can come to the realistic acceptance of this loss and accept that life will bring both grief and love, then he can experience moments of real, positive, loving reparation. This reparation involves the maintenance of Hallam as a loved and a loving object that the poet can keep with him internally, and who can serve as a support and a model for seeking loving relationships in the external world. Similarly, Tennyson also repairs the image of God/nature/world that he comes to see as both whole and loving. Tennyson must restore the good object in a realistic way, not by maintaining a paranoid/schizoid position where God and nature are split, or where Hallam is the good object and the remainder of the external world is persecuting. The poet is driven, for his very psychic survival, to creatively find a way to cope with this threat to his own identity. He writes in Lyric XXI, "I do but sing because I must" (23). The journey of *In Memoriam*, a poem made up of individual lyrics, sometimes connected but mostly representing individual moments of intense emotion, is one of a poet struggling to achieve reparation and balance through the act of writing—through symbolization.

There is no absolute closure to the processes of reparation or mourning, and *In Memoriam* by its very scope, resists such closure. The motivation behind the poem is not to escape grief, but to confront it and repair the loss of both object and self. Herbert Tucker explains, "[K]eeping the poem going provides a reliable means of maintaining contact with the experience of grief" (384). A. C. Bradley writes that the development in the poet over the three years during which the poem appears to be set gives "the impression of a very gradual and difficult advance" (23). As a long poem made of individual lyrics that each capture individual moments, the poem does not follow a smooth narrative progression, but shows the fluctuations in the author's moods and thoughts. Donald Hair describes it as expressing "its grief in fits and starts rather than in a continuous and fully worked out discourse or narration" (93). Helen Hayward also discusses how *In Memoriam* is structured to resist closure: "[I]n its movement, it at once repeatedly ends only repeatedly to begin again, and, with its circlings back on itself and self-revisions, seeks to eschew the conclusiveness and finality of endings" (3). The various fluctuating moments of the poem imply the endlessness of the mourning process and the temporary nature of reparation. Of course, the poem does end, and it ends with a moment of reparation, leaving both the writer and the reader at a positive place. The love object is not rejected or replaced, but internalized and repaired. But the poem's ending, while serving an aesthetic purpose, is only one in a series of moments. We remain aware that the process of mourning the lost object will never end completely.[7]

In Memoriam works well with the experiential and metaphor exercises described in chapter five. I will often have students choose a lyric from the poem as the focus of these exercises. The exercises allow students to explore their affective states, to evaluate their lives and their losses, to find comfort, and to better cope. When reading through my student's responses to the poem, I, like Tennyson, often feel both saddened and comforted by the universality of loss. These exercises enable students to explore various types of loss and mourning—including but not limited to death. Building on Klein's view of the primacy of mourning, Susan Kavaler-Adler uses the concept of "developmental mourning" to describe mourning as a fundamental, ubiquitous process in human development. Kavaler-Adler writes that "through the pain of regret based on disillusionment with oneself, and the pain of loss related to disillusionment with the other, we open the door to consciousness" (13). My students discover that mourning is unavoidable and that, while loss remains painful, they can use it for personal growth. Nearly everyone has dealt with death—a surprising number of my past students have lost friends (often to drunk driving). Others have lost parents, siblings, grandparents, or other family members. Some are able to express empathy for their friends who have experienced major losses (parents, siblings), or for their parents who have lost friends. Some will discuss the loss and mourning involved in ending a relationship with a boyfriend or a girlfriend. Some will write about the mourning involved in leaving their old high school friends and going off to college. Some write about personal failures in terms of mourning, such as having to give up on a dream or goal. Others will write about traumatic experiences that caused them to grow—injuries, illnesses, losses of innocence, or other changes. All of these cases involve a traumatic change that took place where one had to learn to tolerate the loss of something external, but also a loss within the self. Below I will discuss some selected lyrics that my students tend to have strong responses to.

Significantly, from *In Memoriam*'s opening lyric, we see Tennyson functioning in the depressive position—the position necessary for reparation to occur. This proves an important achievement early on within the poem's structure, since the achievement of the depressive position allows for and brings about the reparative drive that leads him to create the lyrics of *In Memoriam*. In Lyric I, we see his immediate concern with feelings of triumph over the dead, a manic aspect of mourning that Klein warns will inhibit reparation. Tennyson worries "that the victor Hours [of time and death] should scorn / The long result of love" (13–14). Tennyson appears to recognize these manic feelings of triumph, and experiences guilt because of them. He insists, however, "Let Love clasp Grief lest both be drown'd" (9), expressing a commitment to experience grief from the loss of the loved object, rather than to manically reject the need for the object altogether. This early awareness of manic processes allows the poet to continue to create elegiac poetry out of his reparative drive in order to recover the internalized image of the lost love object.

Students will sometimes respond to this lyric in general terms about dealing with life's difficulties or their fears of the future, which include dealing with personal failures as well as object loss. Students will seek clarity about the suddenness and absoluteness of death that often leads to existential questions of "why?" These, of course, are questions without answers. Students will reflect on ways of coping, which range from self-destructive methods like alcoholism to more positive personal commitments to hope and faith. What ultimately resonate with students are the lyric's commitment to experience and its examination of the relationship between grief and love—an issue that is central to the entire poem and central to individual development in general. Grief is a by-product of love. Love may come in the form of a personal goal that one is committed to, and that one may fail in, or, love may come in the form of a relationship that may end for any number of reasons, including, of course, death.

Students will use this poem to discuss the importance of accepting grief as a part of life. Often they will discuss loss in terms of what the lost other would want; they would want the survivors to live a positive life without regrets. This is an internalization of the lost, repaired good other. To make further reparation, one must learn to cope with grief in order to both enjoy life and to remain engaged in the world so that they may help others and accomplish positive things. Students see through the poem that a commitment to grief often accompanies a commitment to love, but this commitment is essential if one is to rise to "higher things" (4) in their own lives, as Tennyson wonders if the dead rise to higher things spiritually.

Tennyson also recognizes in these early verses the lack in the symbolic, or the limits of language and symbolism. He understands that words and symbols can prove useful to him in making reparation as he writes the poem, but he sees their inability throughout the poem for capturing the depth of his grief. He writes in Lyric V, "For words, like Nature, half reveal /And half conceal the Soul within" (1–4). But words, he recognizes with some reserve, are also essential in his process of coping with this loss.

> But, for the unquiet heart and brain,
>   A use in measured language lies;
>   The sad mechanic exercise,
> Like dull narcotics, numbing pain. (5–8)

Here he recognizes the comfort that words may offer him, while remaining painfully aware of their limits. Richard Turley writes that the lyric "describes the pull of two competing conceptions of language: one in which words seem to offer a dependable representation of experience; the other in which they are revealed as hollow and misleading" (171). While writing poetry allows Tennyson to begin to express his grief, he knows that, if we catch his double meaning, "measured language" ultimately "lies." He also feels guilt at this point over any comfort that symbolism might offer him, afraid of making manic reparation that would keep him from maintaining Hallam as a love object.

Again, students will use this poem to discuss various kinds of life struggles and losses including ending relationships and deaths of friends and family members. What they focus on in this poem, however, is this conflict of expression. Many will write about their difficulty or total inability to express their affective experience of grief. Part of this issue, as Tennyson understood, lies in the inability to know oneself. Students will often write about invasive thoughts and emotions they have about loss that they do not feel comfortable or at home with. This is a major strength of

Tennyson's poem. He offers words that one feels match experience even as he expresses the inability to do so in any perfect, completely accurate way. His insights into their limits teach us a great deal about language and self-knowledge, and about the difficulties we have with them in our own experience. However, Tennyson also recognizes the value of expression. Many of my students have experienced this as well. They will often write about how writing, in a journal perhaps, or another form of self-expression, has helped them to cope with losses and disappointments. Of course, this allowance for self-expression is a major strength of the experiential and metaphor classroom exercises. Many students will discuss the value of the assignment in these terms when they reflect on it. Again, students will use their self-expression to consider their reactions to loss and find strength in grief, and to use the mourning process to develop from a past self to a new improved self who is personally repaired and socially engaged.

Lyric XVI also deals with the difficulty of self-awareness and the internal conflicts that one recognizes in the self. In a moment of self-reflection, Tennyson recognizes his own internal contradictions. He asks,

> What words are these have fall'n from me?
>   Can calm despair and wild unrest
>   Be tenants of a single breast,
> Or sorrow such a changeling be? (1–4)

Of course, the answer to these questions is "yes," and by recognizing his internal contradictions and emotional fluctuations, Tennyson begins to gain deeper awareness of his self. Later in the same lyric, however, he shows how the recognition of the self as fragmented can bring about anxiety. He wonders if his sorrow genuinely changes, or

>   knows no more of transient form
> In her deep self, than some dead lake
>
> That holds the shadow of a lark
>   Hung in the shadow of a heaven? (7–10)

Students will often choose this complex, yet brilliant, metaphor to reflect on. On the surface, a lake changes when it reflects a bird flying over head, but this change only occurs on the surface. All of the lake that is below the surface, that is, nearly all of the lake, remains the same. Tennyson wonders here if the apparent change in sorrow that he sees in his poems is only superficial, like a reflection on the surface of a lake, without affecting the depth of the water. Is the same essential sorrow simply taking different external forms? As he begins to gain insights into his sorrow and its relation to his creative process, the conflict drives the poet deeper into despair. In another metaphor, he imagines himself as a sinking ship and has lost "my power to think / And all my knowledge of myself" (11–16). While Tennyson begins to gain awareness of his fragmented self here, he is unable yet to integrate his various intense experiences of emotional despair and creative inspiration. Here, as is often the case in moments of newly gained awareness, we see an anxious experience of a loss of self. He sees himself as a

> delirious man
>   Whose fancy fuses old and new,
>   And flashed into false and true,
> And mingles all without a plan. (17–20)

Of course, this description would prove accurate for most human subjects, but the poet here has difficulty coping with his self as a complex, fragmented object.

Mourning brings about complex shifts in emotion that prove confusing to the individual. Students will use this poem to discuss death and other traumatic changes that occur within their families (like illness or injury) and relationships. These kinds of changes lead to feelings of uncertainty. The self and the world we were familiar and comfortable with get turned upside down. Our once-strong identity is now one of uncertainty as we feel a mixture of emotions and thoughts that do not necessarily match the concept we have of ourselves. Students will use the lyric to discuss this confused feeling and to consider the detachment they feel between their emotions and their concept of themselves. As with the lake metaphor, they reflect one thing on the surface, or different things at different times, but, internally they are dealing with a constant pain that goes unseen. The natural imagery of the lyric will lead many students to discuss nature as a means of coping. Being in nature and witnessing the cycles and order of the natural world can provide a source of comfort. Students will also discuss the importance of friendship and love in the mourning process. Tennyson uses both the natural world and personal relationships as two major sources of coping and achieving reparation throughout *In Memoriam*. Students will also discuss how a change occurs in themselves as a result of the mourning process. This process forces them to mature and to reorganize their priorities in order to live a more positive and productive life.

Lyric L is perhaps the most moving and powerful lyric of *In Memoriam*.[8] It reflects a moment of deep despair while also expressing the human need for love. Many of the poem's metaphors show that the speaker's experience of life grows sluggish at times. "Blood creeps" (2) and his "wheels of Being slow" (4), implying a depressed state, void of stimulus. His "light is low" (1) in this state and his "heart is sick" (3). This figurative language describes one deep in despair through its use of metaphoric imagery. The poem gets at the intense pain of despair as the "nerves prick and tingle" (2–3). The experience of the external world becomes wholly negative; time is "a maniac" (7), life "a Fury" (8). Along with this despair, or perhaps as a result of it, comes the profound awareness of mortality. Men are simply "flies" (11) whose lives are "petty" (13). The speaker has given up hope and lost a sense of meaning; his "faith is dry" (9). Through it all, however, he repeats, "Be near me," acknowledging the need for the loving other, a good object, to make life bearable in these moments of despair, suffering, and, finally, death. As Timothy Peltason explains, "[T]he request for comfort and company is all that he can manage, all that keeps him from the complete despair of silence" (80). This lyric provides recognition and awareness by expressing the depth of the poet's negative emotion, but it also points the reader toward the love that is necessary for one to cope with and to recover from debilitating thoughts and feelings.

Many students will focus on the issue of time in this poem. Time continuously passes, beyond our control, and eventually robs us of everything. It is an issue that comes to the forefront in the mourning process. As time passes, we age and so do the people we love. Sometimes death comes suddenly or unexpectedly, and we feel that those lost have been robbed of time or that we have been robbed of time with them. Memory also frequently arises as a theme associated with time. We try to connect with those we have lost through memory, as Tennyson does, but memory too fades with time. These considerations of time can be bleak, but they also teach us to value time and cherish life. Students will often reflect on loss in terms of how they plan to live in the future. Again, the idea of what the lost other would want often emerges. But, mainly, loss simply puts life in perspective. Students are led to think about how they use time and what they want to accomplish in the world.

Students will also frequently use Lyric L to discuss the conflicting desires of dependence and independence. Lisa Friedlander describes how this is a central conflict that she finds in working with couples. "The central struggle of couples in therapy," she writes, "often has to do with finding room to be an individual in close proximity to the other" (228). We value our individuality and often take pride in our independence. This is a particularly significant issue for young college students who are living away from their families and the friends of their childhood for the first time. Many are anxious to develop their individuality and feel held back by the expectations of family and others. Love can also prove frightening, as discussed above, because with it comes the potential of grief. Love takes a degree of courage—a kind of courage that can have great prosocial consequences. While Tennyson's lyric often leads students to write about the value of independence, it also gets them to consider their need for others. The idea of loss, again, provides perspective on the value of loving relationships. More broadly, this idea of human dependence can lead one to consider the dependence that all human beings have on each other and the universality of our need for love.

After Tennyson reaches the height of his despair in the poem, the later lyrics become gradually and generally, though not absolutely, more reparative.[9] In Lyric XCVI, Tennyson reflects on how he has gone through "honest doubt" (11) and come "[t]o find a stronger faith his own" (17). Using Hallam, who went through his own crisis of faith, as a model, Tennyson comes to accept his internal fluctuations between "the darkness and the light" (19), but ultimately comes out on the side of faith but not dogma. Students respond to this poem with their own experiences with doubt and faith. Sometimes students will write about doubt in general as a negative, debilitating emotion that has a negative impact on their lives. These students will often express a commitment to be more positive and perseverant in their pursuits. More often, students will write specifically about religion. Sometimes they write about having an experience similar to Tennyson where they strayed from their faith, only to return to it. This lyric validates the experience of doubt to them, and they typically feel good about achieving redemption in their religion. Other students have, like Tennyson, found their own individual form of faith, outside of religion. Lyric XCVI also validates this and provides self-confidence. For these students, individualism and independence provide sources of pride.

Another lyric that resonates with college students in particular is Lyric C. This is the first of three poems that Tennyson included in *In Memoriam* about his family's move from Somersby to High Beech, Epping Forest, in October 1837 (Tennyson 261n). Most of the students in my classes have recently moved from home to attend college and have had to say good-bye to family and friends. While they will see their home and most of the people from there again, they will never again recover the life they had there. Moving, too, involves a process of mourning. Longo and Rolfs write, "[P]hysical relocations are so commonplace as to almost go unnoticed, yet they are often accompanied by innumerable small losses and a deep cumulative sorrow" (40). For Tennyson, moving from Somersby brings a renewed sense of loss for his friend as he recalls the memories they shared there. As he surveys the land he will soon leave, he finds "no place that does not breathe / Some gracious memory of my friend" (3–4). And as he leaves, he is struck by the feeling that "once more he seems to die" (20). Students respond to Lyric C by considering their relations to places, but these places contain many things that are also lost. Furthermore, moving often comes with other major life changes. Going to college and becoming an adult is one, but students will sometimes write about having to move because of a divorce or because of the loss of a parent. Students will often find comfort in memories and the internalization of others. They will also come to value the relationships with friends and family that they will continue to have, even though these relationships will necessarily change with new circumstances.

It is through continued relationships with the living that Tennyson finds many of his moments of reparation in *In Memoriam*. Students will respond to many of these more positive later lyrics to discuss their own methods of coping with inevitable loss. In Lyric CVIII, for example, Tennyson insists on relinquishing his isolation and vows, "I will not shut me from my kind" (1). For, he asks, "What profit lies in barren faith" (5). He accepts the reality that he cannot be with his friend, and sees the futility of pining for the lost object when he can maintain the internalized love object as a model for future object relations in the world. He will accept his loss as part of the whole experience of life, and, from this depressive position, he will continue to make reparation by using his creativity, experiencing life, and forming relationships with others. He explains, "I'll rather take what fruit may be / Of sorrow under human skies" (13–14). Students respond to this lyric by reflecting the value of others when coping with loss, and the value of internalizing the lost object through memories and actions. This lyric also brings up the theme of faith in many students who find the strength to cope through belief in a higher order.

Similar themes arise in student responses to some of the other later poems. In Lyric CXXII, Tennyson imagines his friend was with him as he began to achieve a greater capacity for reparation through writing and contemplating the self and the world. In this moment he comes to recover a sense of "placid awe" (5), as he begins to see the ultimate order of the universe that is all in "motion with one law" (8). In the following lyric, CXXIII, Tennyson reflects on all of the changes the earth has known, which were a source of despair earlier in the poem, and now finds comfort in them. Though change always occurs in the material world, he "cannot think the thing farewell" (12). The soul remains immortal. Students will often find comfort in these ideas and will discuss their own experiences where they were able to see a profound order in the natural world that provided them with the hope that they may someday reconnect with their lost loved ones in another realm. Like Tennyson, they commit to "dream a dream of good / And mingle all the world with thee [their lost loved ones]" (CXXIX 11–12). By expressing his sorrow honestly and acknowledging his creative empowerment, Tennyson becomes able to repair his image of a good object. For the reader, Tennyson offers a path to reparation and renewal via honest expression that leads to deeper self-awareness, and by offering supportive recognition of emotions. Tennyson also integrates intense emotions from loss into the imagistic and linguistic registers by finding metaphors. He eventually alters his negative images and ways of thinking, and finds new positive ones that allow him, and allow his readers, to repair the image of a good object and with it a good world.

CHAPTER EIGHT

INTEGRATING EXPERIENCE: MORRIS'S
*THE DEFENCE OF GUENEVERE AND
OTHER POEMS*

William Morris's *The Defence of Guenevere and Other Poems* is the least canonical of the four texts I treat here. Yet, it is generally considered a quintessential example of the Pre-Raphaelite aesthetic—an aesthetic that lends itself to a therapeutic approach to poetry. Pre-Raphaelite poetry may seem like an odd choice for an approach that is ultimately concerned with social transformation. The Pre-Raphaelites are rarely overtly political and often accused of being escapist.[1] I maintain, however, that personal change and development on an individual level must come before social change on a broader scale. Renewal and reparation are the prerequisites that predispose one to prosocial behavior, and I find the Pre-Raphaelites particularly useful for attaining these goals. The Pre-Raphaelites share Tennyson's attentiveness to the senses—with a particular focus on the visual. They create with an ambiguity of meaning that allows readers to actively participate in the reading process. Elizabeth Helsinger explains, "Pre-Raphaelite poetry represents but also in turn demands of its readers what might be called acts of aesthetic consciousness." It calls for our deep attention to the details of a poem but also to the details of our responses. "Such attention," Helsinger writes, "demands active imaginative participation" (3). Pre-Raphaelite poetry avoids the closing off of meaning and identity by keeping desire in play, engaging the reader creatively in the text. It also orders fragmented experience, integrating images and affects with words. And, it presents psychological processes realistically, offering recognition and the potential for greater self-awareness.

The Pre-Raphaelite movement has its foundations in the visual arts, so the integration of the visual into language that we frequently see in Pre-Raphaelite poetry remains consistent with many of the original aims of the movement. Armstrong describes the new principle of poetry put forth by the Pre-Raphaelites as being "to move away from expressive theory by attempting to extend a *visual* theory to language and poetry in general" (234). She continues, "The idea of representation through the visual and, by extension, the verbal sign, is the strength of Pre-Raphaelite thoughts" (235). The Pre-Raphaelite poets' extensive use of images and objects engages readers in their imaginative capacities by encouraging them to bring up mental images and experience these images both visually and emotionally on their own, not through the subjectivity of the poet. Carol Christ discusses the tendency in both Tennyson and the Pre-Raphaelites to attempt to show objects in themselves, or, "to anchor feeling in the qualities of objects rather than in the imagination of subjects" (*Victorian* 7). She writes of Dante Gabriel Rossetti, for example, "Rossetti is against interpretation of natural objects...He does not attempt to convert them into emblems of general truths. Rather, he tries to portray the sensuous immediacy of a particular moment of perception" (*Finer* 47), and this is equally true of Morris. Because Pre-Raphaelite poets do not interpret their objects, readers are left to do so, and, in doing so, will also come to explore their own relationships with images and objects.

The Pre-Raphaelite focus on image and affect leads to a poetry that contains a great deal of linguistic ambiguity. Pre-Raphaelite poetry remains ever aware of the limits of linguistic expression. It often draws attention to these limits, and in doing so enables readers to more easily read themselves into poems. With its focus on primary processes, Carole Silver has argued that Pre-Raphaelite poetry is essentially dream poetry. She defines literary Pre-Raphaelitism as "a movement to which dream is central, a movement which utilizes accounts of actual dream, dream language, dream symbol, and, most significantly, a movement with the characteristics of dream itself" ("Dreamers" 5). She discusses this poetry in terms of the Victorian philosophical, medical, religious, popular, and literary writing about dreams, which predate Freud, but include many of the same elements he would later discuss in *Interpretation of Dreams*. Dreams, in the mid-nineteenth century, were seen as containing truths about the inner self and as using associative logic ("Dreamers" 6–9). The Pre-Raphaelite use of dream distinguishes itself "by a special concern with accurate accounts of 'real' dream experiences and by increased emphasis on capturing dream logic and structure" (12). Their poetry contains associative logic, rapid shifts in scene and image, condensations, displacements of self, private symbols, lack of temporal and spatial consistency, gaps, and lack of cause and effect (23). Like dreams, they involve images and scenarios that evoke intense feelings without offering any obvious meaning. Essentially, the poetry allows readers to act as what Walter Pater calls the "aesthetic critic." What is important to the aesthetic critic is "the power of being deeply moved by the presence of beautiful objects" (72).

Along with linguistic ambiguity, Pre-Raphaelite poetry allows for moral ambiguity by resisting moral judgments that many readers find off-putting. It is not didactic and allows us instead to make our own explorations. Ambiguity is important for opening readers up to possibility and potential without imposing specific views or morals on them that they may not want. The capacity to tolerate ambiguity and ambivalence is also a frequently cited objective in poetry therapy. Perie Longo and Alma Maria Rolfs write that this capacity is "a mark of mental health" and a "hallmark of creativity" (41). We should remain cautious about offering poetry as a moral guideline to readers and students, but we can engage them in poetry in such a way that leads to deeper self-awareness, offers identity support, and encourages empathy and creativity—all essential to a capacity for social ethics.

In my therapeutic approach to poetry, I often use the dream or fantasy poems from *The Defence of Guenevere and Other Poems*. Like dreams, many of these poems lack clear or specific meaning, and thus they force readers to focus more on visual, imaginative, and sensual experiences. Constance Hassett explains, "*The Defence of Guenevere* works in a variety of ways to scrutinize, qualify, or prevent settled meanings" ("Style" 107). These poems are mysterious and atmospheric, and often unrealistic. They function through primary processes of image and tone. Their action often lacks clear causality, and they further confuse by using nonreferential pronouns. Some of the poems avoid clarity in key areas, while giving elaborate descriptions of minor details. They lack narrative concerns for logic and coherence and draw attention to the ambiguities of language and the pre-symbolic functions of poetry. Readers can use these poems to explore their own images, feelings, associations, and to create their own interpretations or responses. Poems like Morris's that confound linguistic meaning allow students a broader experience of poetic language.

Walter Pater refers to *The Defence* as "the first typical specimen of aesthetic poetry" (521). The term "aesthetic" tends to bring to mind Oscar Wilde's statement that "all art is quite useless" (48), but Morris's volume is useful for both encouraging individual development and the development of social ethics. J. M. S. Tompkins writes, "Morris is interested in the psychology of his subject, rather than the ethics" (61). Yet, while Morris's poems lack clear moral judgments, his explorations and evocations of human emotion increase our awareness of both self and other, which can lead to increased empathy and ethics. Later in his career, Morris became especially concerned with the class inequality he saw in industrialized Victorian England. In his 1894 lecture "How I Became a Socialist," Morris reflects, "[A]part from the desire to produce beautiful things, the leading passion of my life has been and is hatred of modern civilization" (*XXIII* 279). One can see the seeds of this rejection of the status quo even in Morris's early poetry, and this still resonates with many contemporary readers. In an age where we can very easily lose our identities to the mass media and to mass consumer culture, Morris's emotional and imaginative poetry takes us to something more real within us. Blue Calhoun writes of the poetry in *The Defence*, "Morris is interested in the individual struggle for self-definition within the larger social context that seems variously dull, uncomprehending, and destructive" (40). I seek to engage my students in Morris's poetry so as to allow them to feel intensely and to envision imaginatively. This intense engagement in poetry is very much in opposition to the kind of escapism that is often associated with aesthetic poetry.

Morris's poems put us directly into the experience of his subjects without making judgments, while also making us share their experience. Often, these experiences confound his characters and his readers alike. Inga Bryden writes, "[T]he poems typically combine the tactile, vivid imagery of a ballad, or dream, logic with psychological confusion and exploration of the boundaries (or lack of) between different states of being" (104). The strange fantasy or dream elements of the poems are often confusing, incoherent, or unrealistic, but the experiences of Morris's subjects and his readers are always very real. Frederick Kirchhoff writes of these poems, "[T]heir willingness to explore the raw output of the unconscious mind is simply another aspect of Morris's psychological realism" (51). Morris's realism might also be described as affective realism. Charlotte Oberg writes, Morris "emphasizes the immediate feelings of his speakers and makes us share their anxieties and frustrations as we try to fathom the meaning of their experiences" (135). Typical of Pre-Raphaelite poetry, Morris's early dream poems make us sense and feel intensely, and offer us a level of poetic experience that is beyond and more primal than what we would get from simply interpreting linguistic meaning. Margaret Lourie writes that if we can discover how Morris's dream poems "operate, we will perhaps have learned something essential about the Pre-Raphaelite contribution to English poetry" (195). This contribution, I believe, lies in the emotional, sensual, and imaginative elements of Pre-Raphaelite poetry that create a unique and multilayered experience for readers.

Ekphrastic Poems

One of my first goals is to encourage students to notice, explore, and describe the visual images that arise in their minds when reading poetic texts. Morris's ekphrastic poems "The Blue Closet" and "The Tune of Seven Towers" provide examples of poems derived from visual images, as they were both inspired by watercolors painted by Dante Gabriel Rossetti.

I use these two Morris poems along with their respective paintings in order to get students thinking about how the mind transforms images into language and language into images. Jerome McGann writes about this specifically in terms of Rossetti, "Rossetti shows every artist's understanding, that the only adequate interpretation of a work of art is a responsive work of art" (*Dante* 21). He explains, "In this kind of model, images call out to images and their dialogue is the action of an artistic process of thinking" (23). Helsinger describes one of the most influential strategies of Pre-Raphaelite poetry as what she calls "translation" (2).[2] This refers to translating texts into different languages, but also translating across different media as a way of creating a new art object out of the author's relationship to a work of art that is already in existence. I constantly encourage this kind of response in my students. I want them to use the imaginative works of others to engage their own imaginations, and to create new objects through creative translation.

Before having students read the poems, I devote one class period to the paintings. I begin with *The Blue Closet*, and have the students describe the contents of the image—translating the visual into language.[3] After this, I have students engage their imaginations more deeply by asking them to create a broader scene in their minds. They start with Rossetti's image and expand it spatially by considering what else might be happening in the scene. Many imagine that the women portrayed in the painting are giving a concert or are performing at a festival surrounded by people. Others see them alone singing praises to God in an old church. After expanding the image spatially in their minds, I ask students to expand the sensory experience from the visual to include other senses. Many will hear music. Some imagine either a musty or perfumed smell in the air. Next, I ask students to create a short narrative based on the scene they built from Rossetti's painting. This requires them to expand the image temporally by considering what might have come before and what might happen after the scene.

After finishing *The Blue Closet*, the class does the same activity with Rossetti's painting *The Tune of Seven Towers*. With this painting, students may imagine a dying queen, a princess meeting an undesirable suitor, or a lonely woman whose beautiful music captivates those around her. By the end of this activity, students have essentially created their own imaginative works in writing from the two paintings, which is exactly what Morris did in creating his poems. Among the many benefits of this exercise, students learn to relate to Morris's creative process before reading his works.

For the following class, I have students read the two poems. Beginning again with "The Blue Closet," I hand out a storyboard sheet with six frames on each side (the kind that filmmakers use) to each student and tell them to imagine that they had to film the poem in six scenes. They then draw, to the best of their ability, each of the scenes on the storyboards. Instead of transforming an image into language, they transform language into a series of images. This activity gets students thinking about the poem visually, and also forces them to come up with an imaginative interpretation of the poem. Because of the poem's ambiguity, students' visualizations of it differ greatly and offer a starting point for discussions about how we might possibly interpret it. The different interpretations that necessarily arise also help students toward a more relativist approach to poetic interpretation.

For "The Blue Closet," as for "The Tune of Seven Towers," a number of questions and ambiguities arise. In "The Blue Closet," the setting is not completely clear, and the action is only slightly less vague. The poem presents four women, two queens and two damozels, who are trapped in some mysterious setting where they are allowed out only once a year on Christmas Eve so that they may sing in the Blue Closet. One of the queens, Lady Louise, recalls her dead love Arthur who may have been murdered. In the end, Arthur returns from the dead and takes the women from their prison to the land of the dead with him.

The atmosphere or mood of the poem is perhaps more important to the poem's overall effect than the story. Throughout the poem, a bell tolls for the dead, only to fall silent near the end. The setting never becomes clear, but the women exist "between the wash of the tumbling seas" (2), and at one point water oozes up through the "tiles of the Closet Blue" (33). Perhaps they live in an underwater realm, or near water. The poem is full of strange and often vague images that allow the imagination to roam. In one of the more interesting images in the poem, Arthur says that he cannot weep for his love because his tears are "'hidden deep under the seas'; / 'In a gold and blue casket she keeps all my tears'" (44–45). In one of Louise's early memories of Arthur, he comes to her with snow in his hands and places it upon her head to melt. Then, one of the ladies questions whether Arthur was strangled with the scarf that she wore. In the scene leading up to Arthur's return, a lily rises up from the tiles of the Blue Closet. These strange details and images set a mood for the action, but explain very little. They invite the reader to interpret and imagine—filling in the elisions.

Lourie refers to the poem as "the quintessential example of Pre-Raphaelite dream-poetry" (202). Like a dream, not only are the contents of the poem somewhat vague, but the meaning of it is entirely confounding as well. The poem functions mainly through its eerie atmosphere and dark language in order to achieve its emotional and imagistic results in the mind of the reader. Lourie explains,

> [I]t is largely the refusal of this poem to mean anything or to lend itself to rational interpretation that provides its special power; for in "The Blue Closet" Morris transcends the normal processes of waking thought and cuts off the usual orientation of the mind toward the phenomenal world. As a result, he can journey down into the pre-logical and primary image-making reaches of the psyche. The many critics who accuse Morris of escapism are quite right; he does wish to escape from the world of external reality. But what they too often fail to see is that he escapes *to* a more universal internal reality. (195)

Even though the language of the poem causes confusion, Morris expresses meaning at a more primal level. The ladies clearly experience the emotional effect of their situation, as does the reader. A mysterious gloom or dread hangs over the ladies as they are confined in a state of limbo. They experience profound isolation and lack all hope. Some readers view the ladies' deaths at the end of the poem as a positive occurrence. In death, the ladies may finally find peace or at least achieve an escape from their current miserable state. Many students will portray the group crossing the bridge to death in the poem's conclusion with smiles on their faces, or they will portray the lovers reunited in an embrace and kiss.

I repeat this storyboard exercise with "The Tune of Seven Towers," but because the poem lacks much real-time action, I take a slightly different approach. After reading the poem, I ask students to consider what may have led up to the scene Morris portrays, and what will happen after it. The scene of the poem presents Yoland of the flowers describing a desolate and haunted place, probably the castle of Seven Towers. She then seductively urges Oliver to return there for her things—a mission that we sense will not end well for him. Again, much of the story is elided or left unclear. "The Tune of Seven Towers" invites the reader to create a past story, and to speculate about the future. For the first two frames on their storyboards, students create images portraying what may have happened before the scene in the poem. In the next two frames, they portray the action of the poem itself. Then, in the final two frames, they portray what they think will happen after the scene of the poem.

Most readers can agree that some major catastrophic event has occurred at the castle to leave it empty and haunted. Morris leaves the reader to imagine what that past disaster may have been. In the "before" frames, many students will portray a war, probably suggested by the mention of "battlements," in which the inhabitants of the castle were defeated and massacred. Others imagine that a plague has occurred, or a fire. Readers are also invited to speculate about the pasts of the poem's two characters.

Perhaps they fled before the catastrophe. Perhaps Yoland was a queen having an illicit affair with the knight Oliver. Perhaps they were a king and queen who left their people to die. Perhaps Yoland is making the whole thing up, and has a very different past.

Students' representations for the frames portraying what is presented during the poem tend to vary less, though the poem does leave itself open to a variety of visual interpretations by leaving out much in the way of specific detail. In contrast to Rossetti's richly colored and minutely detailed painting, David Staines points out, "[I]n this poem, remarkable for the comparative absence of concretely visualized details, Morris curiously refrains from borrowing any details from the painting" (460). Students will, however, often use one frame to portray a scene with Yoland speaking to Oliver, similar to the scene portrayed in Rossetti's painting. Most will also use at least one frame to portray the inhabitants of the castle described by Yoland in their ghostly forms.

In the final frames, most will follow the poem's ominous tone and portray Oliver coming to some harm in the castle. While most imagine Oliver's doom in the end, there is some debate over the portrayal of Yoland. Some see Yoland as troubled by losing Oliver, portraying her in tears or even dying from grief. Others, however, see her as a femme fatale. Critics have held a similar debate over the character of Yoland. David Latham makes the argument for her as femme fatale, seeing Oliver as only one in a long string of her victims (51). He suggests that she was not even a castle maiden at all, but a sinister imposter in the castle (52). However, Oberg and Silver take more sympathetic approaches to her. To Oberg, Yoland is a victim of fate who does not desire Oliver's death (134). Silver similarly describes her as "simply fated to be fatal, she is as much a victim as her lover" (*Romance* 42). "The Tune of Seven Towers," like the other dream poems from Morris's *The Defence*, opens up the reader to multiple possibilities for interpretation and imagination.

Imaginative Reading

Peter Faulkner describes Morris's poem "The Wind" as "a nightmare poem which we can hardly explain but which imposes its strange vision upon the reader" (22). In the poem, an old Norseman appears haunted by some unnamed dread. He views his surroundings with delusions reflecting fear and anxiety. Early in the poem, he slips into a strange dream that begins with his amorous pursuit of Margaret, and ends in his discovering her dead body. He awakes only to have a final haunting vision of "the ghosts of those that had gone to the war" (81). The poem provides for multiple possibilities and forces readers to imagine what has happened and what its contexts may be. What exactly happens in the dream? What is the relationship between the speaker and Margaret? Do they have sex? Why and how does she die? What significance is the war? What might have motivated the dream? Along with these unanswered questions, the poem provides a number of symbols and metaphors that call for exploration.

Many of the details in the poem are obscure, but the refrain contains a number of images that set a clear tone. Repeated 11 times throughout the fairly short poem, it reads, *"Wind, wind! thou art sad, art thou kind? / Wind, wind, unhappy! thou art blind, / Yet still thou wanderest the lily-seed to find"* (4–6). Oberg regards the wind as a metaphor for the speaker's ever-wandering memory. David Bentley emphasizes the disruption of the natural cycle with the image of the wind seeking the lily-seed, which suggests "that the wind, like the dawn, has failed to discover new life in the speaker" (33). The wind also reflects chaos and the potential cruelty of fate, a theme powerfully evoked in the speaker's dream where he feels helpless and confused by Margaret's death. Because the action of the dream is portrayed so vaguely, the reader shares in his emotional experience of helpless confusion in the face of tragedy. We feel strong emotions over Margaret's death, even though, or perhaps even more so because, we cannot understand what exactly happened or why.

The action of the dream opens itself up to multiple interpretations. I use this poem to engage my students' imaginations, asking them to try, creatively and logically, to fill the gaps in the text. One ambiguity in the poem leaves us wondering what exactly occurred between the two characters in the dream. Bentley and Oberg offer nearly opposite interpretations of this aspect of the text, which cause them to read Margaret's death and the significance of the poem very differently. Bentley argues that Margaret and the speaker do not have sex, that the speaker appears to have propensity for inaction, and that "Margaret's death has been caused, not by any identifiable act on the part of the speaker, herself, or persons unknown, but that it is to be seen as the result of the speaker's *failure to act*, his failure to confront her sexuality" (35). Oberg, however, argues that Margaret and the speaker do have sex. Far from inactive, the speaker ravishes Margaret then perhaps murders her, or she commits suicide because of lost honor (150). The key lines, in terms of how one reads the action of the dream, come after the speaker has pursued her amorously and she appears to have given in. These suggestive lines read, "I kiss'd her hard by the ear, and she kiss'd me on the brow, / And then lay down on the grass, where the mark on the moss is now, / And spread her arms out wide while I went down below" (49–51). These lines are immediately followed by the refrain. Then the speaker says, "And then I walk'd for a space to and fro on the side of the hill, / Till I gather'd and held in my arms great sheaves of the daffodil" (55–56). Has the sexual act simply been implied but elided, or was it interrupted by his going "down below" on the side of the hill to gather flowers?

We can also consider other possibilities for what exactly happens to Margaret. How we interpret the scene where "her head fell back on a tree, / And a spasm caught her mouth" (41–42), dictates our reading of the sequence that follows. When the speaker describes her at this point as "fearful for me to see" (42), he may indicate that she is afraid of him or that she is attempting to hide something from him. Perhaps she is sick here, having a seizure, and attempting to hide her illness. Later, this illness that the speaker fails to notice kills her. Or, perhaps she has accidentally hit her head during their flirtation and is simply trying to hide it out of embarrassment. It is also possible that the injury sustained in this moment is what kills her. If we read the following lines, she remains mostly inactive other than, according to the speaker, returning a kiss. Perhaps she tries to conceal the severity of the injury, or perhaps the speaker leaves out some crucial information here that would implicate him in the injury and in her death. The aggressive descriptions of his pursuit of her may imply that he actually rapes her before covering her with flowers. The speaker certainly betrays some delusional perceptions at other points in the poem, so we may not want to take his version of the dream at face value.

Along with what happens in the dream, the reader is also invited to speculate about the motivation behind the dream. Bentley sees Margaret as an old love. He argues that the speaker relives a repressed scene in his dream (35). Ekbert Faas also sees Margaret as a former love, but is less sure about whether the dream reflects a real occurrence. He writes, "One wonders whether the speaker is relating actual events or merely articulating homicidal fantasies" (182). The dream, Faas suggests, may be motivated by hurt or angry emotions toward the former love object. Morris draws us into the speaker's emotional experience, without defining it specifically. We only sense that he appears haunted and deeply disturbed by something that becomes manifest in his delusions and in his dream. Faas writes that "'The Wind,' like other of Morris's poems, somehow embodies unconscious emotions more directly, prompting the reader to assume and reenact them in the process" (183).

Another possibility for the speaker's powerful affective experience reflected in the dream could be that he is living, or has lived, in a state of war, witnessing its destructiveness. Armstrong brings up this possibility, seeing the wind as an "indifferent" and "predatory force" (249). She reads Morris's poetry as socially resistant in general and speculates that "The

Wind" is Morris's Crimean-war poem (250). The dream of Margaret's death could reflect the general destruction and confusion of war displaced into the dream situation. Or, perhaps Margaret was a former love who was actually killed in a war. This reading would make the connection more clear between the dream of Margaret and the ghost soldiers who march in afterwards in the poem.

While details of the poem remain ambiguous and allow for imaginative reading, the tone is fairly clear. We can use this intensely emotional poem to encourage students to explore their own response to it, while also encouraging them to empathize with the characters and their affective states. I have students choose which stanza they feel most intensely, without defining it. While some students will choose the climatic moment where the speaker discovers Margaret, others feel the speaker's loneliness at the beginning more intensely. Others will choose the more erotic moments in the poem, while some will feel fear in the moments leading up to the climax. After students have focused in on a particular stanza, they then try to describe what feelings that stanza evokes in them. Students will come to see the difficulty of translating a feeling into language. I encourage them to create their own metaphors, or to follow a chain of associations, to express their emotions. Finally, to get them even further into the experience, and to encourage empathy with the characters in the poem, students create their own fictional first-person narrative where they imagine that they are one of the characters in the poem experiencing the deeply felt scene first hand. This allows students to explore the depth of an emotion, while also offering some distance.

The poem "Golden Wings" functions through a similar ambiguity in action, while establishing a clear emotional tone. Faulkner writes of the poem, "'Golden Wings,' like many other of these poems, is atmospheric and suggestive rather than very clear in the narrative, but in most cases this increases the reader's involvement" (22). The poem achieves its emotional power through its extremes. It begins with a description of Ladies' Castle, a paradise where flora and fauna flourish, peace abounds, and ladies and knights live and love in happiness. But Morris soon undercuts this Edenic vision by introducing Jehane who can feel no happiness in paradise because her love is not with her. Her love is not anyone in particular, but an ideal that she hopes will appear someday. In the end, she goes out to seek him and is later discovered slain. After her death, the early, happy imagery of paradise is reversed and the landscape becomes a cruel, ravished wasteland. In the poem's final lines, we discover another dead body, this time of a man.

The poem leaves us with one major question, which I focus on in class discussions. Did Jehane make the right decision in leaving the castle?

The obvious or immediate answer may tend to be "no." since it led to her death and to the destruction of her homeland paradise. Yet, we may admire Jehane for her independence or for her fearless quest for what is most important to her—love. Amanda Hodgson argues that Jehane desires action in the real world as opposed to the futility of the enclosed castle—but leaving leads to her death and the destruction of the "beautiful place." Hodgson explains, "[T]his extremely complex poem is concerned with the problem of a good which is incapable of development opposed to an evil which is destructive but contains elements of life-giving force" (48). Life in the castle seems like paradise initially, but perhaps it is inevitably doomed as it does not allow for growth or development.

I encourage my students to engage with the figure of Jehane by responding to this creative work through their own creativity. Jehane's story is told mostly from a third-person perspective, with the exception of the scene where she decides she must leave the castle. When Jehane does have a voice, she expresses her passionate yearning for love. I have my students write a monologue from Jehane's point of view while she is living in the castle. This encourages empathy with her so that students may try to understand why she makes her fatal decision to leave. After this, they do a second writing exercise where they imagine Jehane after she has left the castle, a scene not portrayed in the poem. This second part of the activity puts Jehane in a position where she may reflect on her decision. Students may also use this part of the activity to provide an explanation of what causes her death.

Personalizing Metaphors

By reflecting universal emotions linked to frustration, loss, and failure, "Spell-bound" offers readers the opportunity to consider their own experiences as analogous to, though distinct from, those of the poem's speaker. The speaker is a knight trapped in a desolate landscape and separated from his love by a wizard's spell. In his isolation, the knight envisions his love as she suffers for him. Silver explains that the knight's reverie "projects the prisoner's desires onto his lady and reveals his frustrated sexuality rather than hers" ("Dreamers" 31). As a dramatic monologue, the poem enables us to focus on the knight's perspective, which is one of desperate yearning.

The poem's rich metaphoric imagery adds to the tone of hopeless desperation. I use the poem to allow my students to explore the effects of metaphoric language as a particularly powerful means of emotional expression, and to apply the metaphors of the poem to their lives. The landscape in which the knight is trapped becomes one of the central metaphors. The speaker describes the unreaped corn that makes up his surroundings: "The year wears round to autumn-tide, / Yet comes no reaper to the corn" (5–6). This central metaphor reflects the theme of the poem: unfulfilled potential—specifically, in the knight's case, the unfulfilled potential for love. Students will freewrite on what this metaphor means to them—what is the unreaped corn in their lives? This brings students in contact with their own associations with the poetic metaphor, which allows for self-exploration and also enables them to better understand how the poem achieves its particular emotional power through metaphor. Many college students, particularly freshmen, relate this central metaphor of the poem to being away from home, often for the first time, separated from friends, family, and significant others. Others see the metaphor in terms of their unrealized potential as they seek to find their place in the world.

Following up on the unreaped-corn metaphor, I then ask students to think of the wizard's spell in these terms. As a metaphor, the wizard's spell becomes the barrier to whatever the reader is trying to accomplish or realize. I ask students to consider what they wrote about the unreaped-corn metaphor, and then write about what the wizard's spell would be in their lives. It may be the circumstances that separate them from important relationships, or the thing that keeps them from doing their best in college. The wizard may be an external or possibly even an internal force. Tomkins writes, "[T]he power that inhibits action seems intimately close, also part of [the speaker] himself"—an "uncomprehended psychological hindrance" (66–67). Reading the wizard metaphorically as a cause of the lack of fulfillment, or an obstacle, allows readers to consider the barriers that keep them from achieving their goals or realizing their desires.

Finally, I ask students to think about defeating the wizard. In the poem, the knight's sword appears to represent the means through which he could do this. At the poem's conclusion, the knight imagines his love coming to him with his sword wherein he says, "My heart upswells and I grow bold" (80). He recalls how it has served him well in the past when he first won her. "And you have brought me my good sword, / Wherewith in happy days of old / I won you well from knight and lord" (77–79). The sword represents safety, power, and joy, all associated with the success of winning his love initially. It is the object that could help him realize his potential. Like the spell, this object could be external or internal. In considering the sword as a metaphor and relating it to their situations, students examine what might give them confidence or what would perhaps enable them to achieve their potential—to reap their corn.

Many of Morris's poems allow us to imagine more detail, to expand on and explore various meanings, and to feel the emotions expressed by their speakers and characters. Like dreams, these poems function less through logic than through more primary processes of expression, and thus, we experience them on a primal level. As we struggle to make meaning of these texts, they give rise to affective responses, as well as mental visualizations, that we may explore. While the stories portrayed in these poems are idiosyncratic, readers relate to them emotionally because they express universal desires for love and happiness in the face of an often cruel and senseless reality. They also encourage the imaginative capacities of readers by leaving out information that would lead to easy or "obvious" interpretations. The ability of these poems to thwart understanding calls on readers to imaginatively create some kind of comprehensibility or meaning by adding missing details themselves. These characteristics of Morris's dream poems allow for a classroom approach that focuses less on settled meanings, and more on affect and image. Through these poems, we can instill in our students a more relativistic and broader appreciation of poetic texts, while also allowing them to explore their emotional, expressive, and creative capacities.

Chapter Nine
Desire and Reparation: Rossetti's *Goblin Market* and Other Poems

Despite Christina Rossetti's ties with the Pre-Raphaelite movement,[1] her aesthetic owes more to the principles of nineteenth-century Tractarian writers like John Keble, Isaac Williams, and John Henry Newman. One might worry that a devotional poet like Rossetti would alienate some students and limit possibilities for finding meaning. After all, a strictly Christian belief system tends to close off meaning and desire as it envisions a concrete object in Christ who would provide ultimate fulfillment through spiritual union after death. Because this union is the ultimate goal of life to Christians, Rossetti's poetry often implies a renunciation of the world. These traits of absolutism and renunciation would stand in direct opposition to an approach to poetry that stresses an opening up of meaning and encourages active participation in the object world that would lead to social change.

However, it is actually Rossetti's Tractarian aesthetics that make her poetry ideal for a therapeutic pedagogy. The Tractarian concepts of reserve and analogy are of particular importance for understanding Rossetti's work. Her use of reserve leads her to value contemplation over absolute meaning. This contemplation requires alertness and engagement with the world. Reserve is practiced through analogy where elements of the world, especially the natural world, are contemplated in order to achieve a better understanding of the spiritual world. Many of Rossetti's analogies follow reparative, or redemptive, structures that acknowledge suffering while maintaining hope. Rossetti's poetry frequently operates through open-ended allegory and vague symbolism. Often the exact object and nature of the desires of her speakers are left unclear, and thus many readers can relate to her portrayals of yearning and despair. Rossetti's poetry is primarily contemplative and expressive, which makes it valuable for raising self-awareness and offering recognition in the classroom. Many readers also find solace in her transcendence of the negative aspects of life that is as much a poetic transcendence as a theological one. The hopeful elements of her poetry arise from the hope that religion provided her, though they are typically presented through symbolism rather than dogmatism.

Rossetti's poetry ultimately reflects an active engagement in the external world that brings both personal and social implications with it. She does not reject the world, but renounces worldly things that lead to the kind of vanity and narcissism that would impede prosocial attitudes and behavior. Instead, what we find in her poetry is contemplation and enjoyment of the world where the self is linked to the external in potentially positive ways. In my classes, I consider how Rossetti's poems open themselves to readers' interpretations and contemplations, how they keep desire in play, and how they offer reparation. Dinah Roe, in her book on Rossetti's "devotional imagination," allows that "Rossetti's own insistence, stylistically and theologically, on the slipperiness of meaning, the pitfalls of translation and interpretation, and the shortcomings of human understanding, encourages her readers to think and feel for themselves" (7). In Rossetti, we find a poet of contradiction and great emotional and imaginative complexity. Rossetti is a devout Christian who, in many instances, writes open-ended poems that actually encourage more relativistic thinking and a more personal approach to reading poetry. She is a poet of deep despair and worldly renunciation who often writes life-affirming poetry expressing images of profound joy. Rossetti achieves reparative moments through her poetry, just as she expresses moments of pain and longing. Desire comes through in her language, often accompanied by anger, debilitating fear, or overwhelming depression. But, as a poet, Rossetti finds reparation to both internal and external worlds through fantasy, image, and language. Because Rossetti's poems often follow a reparative structure that offers emotional support, and because they use vital but ultimately ambiguous images and symbols, much of her poetry carries potential for encouraging personal exploration, making it a valuable tool both within and outside of the classroom. Below, I explore a number of poems from Rossetti's most famous and most frequently anthologized volume, *Goblin Market and Other Poems*. As with Tennyson's *In Memoriam*, I often use this volume with the metaphor and experiential exercises described in chapter five.

Contemplating Desire

To illustrate the concept of reserve, I introduce Rossetti's poem "A Pause of Thought." This poem provides a clear example of the complexity of desire in Rossetti and portrays desire as essentially aimless. The speaker of the poem "looked for that which is not, nor can be" (1). By leaving the object of desire nameless, students are able to project their own desires into the poem. As Constance Hassett writes, "Desire in its many varieties and gradations was regarded by Rossetti as absolutely central to poetry. It is more than a theme, however; the finest Rossettian poem itself stirs desire" (*Christina* 11). Because of its reserve in locating an absolute object of desire, "A Pause of Thought" becomes, instead, a contemplation of desire itself. The speaker recognizes that her desire is objectless and unappeasable, and even contemplates giving it up, but she never can. The poem ends, like many of Rossetti's poems, with a tone of regret. Hassett writes that in this poem "Rossetti's speaker regrets the emptiness of her chosen pursuits" (*Christina* 74). But, in spite of herself and knowing there is no chance for success, the speaker will "again / Turnest to follow it [the object of desire]" (19–20).

Rossetti shows an awareness that desire never ends; it is only endlessly displaced. The speaker cannot, even with age, escape the drive to pursue the elusive object of desire, nor can she will herself to give it up. She recognizes that the lack she experiences is a source of pain, but she cannot avoid it as long as she lives. As students contemplate their goals, desires, and identities, they will also come to recognize that nothing will provide them with absolute fulfillment. Yet, this poem of depression and lack also has an affirmative quality. The final lines show that she will continue in her pursuit. This is the jouissance of desire. Desire shows us that we are alive. Students will often read this in a positive way when they come to understand both the limits of desire and the vitality that comes with it. The way Rossetti continues to seek, at least in part, is through producing poetry that seeks reparation in language. This poem is reparative to readers because it offers realistic recognition of the nature of desire and the human drive to struggle with it. Some students use the poem in order to reflect on the value of failure and the courage of perseverance when pursuing goals. Students can also come to recognize that throughout their lives, they will always have new goals and that their identities need not remain fixed. Through the contemplation of desire in poetry, they can come to embrace themselves as subjects-in-process and find joy and exhilaration in it.

To illustrate analogy, I turn to Rossetti's devotional poem "'Consider the Lilies of the Field,'" where she explains that "[f]lowers preach to us if we will hear" (1).[2] This method of reading nature through analogy appears throughout Rossetti's writing. The first verse catalogues several different flowers and offers descriptions of each that become analogies. The rose, for example, is "most fair" (3), but all of its "loveliness is born / Upon a thorn" (4–5). As an analogy, this image might reflect the good and bad found in everything or the misleading nature of outward appearances. But Rossetti uses reserve in her presentation of the flowers. As Roe writes of the poem, "Rossetti gives the reader certain images and voices, but she leaves it up to the reader to make associations and connections" (17). The second verse moves away from flowers to lower forms of plant life like grass and moss. These too, Rossetti insists, "Tell of His love who sends the dew" (22). The message here becomes more specifically spiritual as the theme of God's provision for all things emerges. Of course, those familiar with the Bible will recognize the allusion to Matthew 6:28 in the poem's title, a passage where Christ teaches of God's provision. My Christian students who are already predisposed to finding comfort in this idea will often respond positively to this poem. Many people use spiritual beliefs as a way of coping with the difficulties of life. This poem is also valuable for reinforcing self-worth, since it shows God's love as universal.

"May (I cannot tell you how it was)" is another excellent poem to use when introducing Rossetti's aesthetics as it provides a succinct example of analogy and reserve. It is also an emotionally powerful poem that uses rich, striking imagery. McGann uses "May" to exemplify the way Rossetti's poems "test and trouble the reader by manipulating sets of ambiguous symbols and linguistic structures" (*Beauty* 215). The poem begins with the secrecy, or reserve, that we often see in Rossetti's poetry when she writes, "I cannot tell you how it was" (1). Readers immediately want to know what "it" is, but the speaker cannot, or will not, tell us. The ambiguous pronoun, McGann writes, "pushes the work into a terrifying level of generality" (216). McGann explores several possibilities, while Alison Chapman argues that "his interpretation does not account for the poem's ambiguity and withdrawal of meaning, nor its curiously haunting effect on the reader" (25). In the classroom, I encourage students to explore the poem for possibility while maintaining that any specific meaning is unknowable. If one were insisting on finding specific meaning in this poem, this could be a source of frustration. However, if we learn to read for emotional experience, we can find much here to relate to. Hassett writes about the poem, "Sometimes, a poem confesses that feeling exceeds lyric formation, admits its own inarticulateness, and proceeds as it must" (*Christina* 55).

The poem's first stanza presents images that bring up positive feelings and positive associations with the month of May, showing potential and fertility in the natural world. These symbols from nature come to represent the idea of potential in general to readers. The second stanza, however, takes on a more negative tone. We find out that whatever "it" is, "it did but pass" (10). We learn that all of the potentials in nature that we saw in the first stanza were only temporary and went unrealized. The poem concludes, "With all sweet things it passed away, / And left me old, and cold, and grey" (12–13). Hassett writes, "When 'May' comes to an end, the lines are still reluctant to specify the loss they regret...No particular loss, but rather the enigma of loss, remains the poem's undiminished concern"

(*Christina* 57). With the ambiguity of "it" throughout, the poem becomes more universal. Students will project their own experiences with loss and disappointment into it. Everyone has had "sweet things" pass away in their life, whether loved ones, or childhood, or simply happy times from the past. The poem does not capture a specific set of circumstances, but through the analogy of time and seasons passing, and the elements of the natural world that pass with them, it captures an affective state that nearly anyone can relate to. Students will use the poem not only to reflect on past losses, but also to learn from them and look to the future in a reparative way.

The poem "Shut Out" brings up similar emotions and responses. The poem's original title was "What happened to me?" the answer to which the reader never completely finds out.[3] The poem opens with the speaker looking through "iron bars" (2) at a garden that had been hers, but now was lost. She describes a "shadowless spirit" (9) who builds a wall so that she cannot even see her garden. In the end, she describes herself in a pleasant outdoor setting, but cannot be happy since her "delightful land is gone" (24). The poem's imagery, of course, echoes that of Genesis or *Paradise Lost*. What the speaker has done to be shut out, or what the poem symbolizes exactly, remains a mystery. But what the poem expresses is a deep regret for becoming detached from a place that one holds dear, and a feeling of being trapped. Students will respond to the poem by reflecting on feelings of hopelessness attached to various kinds of losses. Or, frequently, they will relate to the suffocating feeling of being trapped where they do not want to be—perhaps stuck at work or stuck inside when they would rather be outside. Students also respond to the connection with nature established in the poem. They will write about their desire to be out in nature in general, or about their connection to a specific, special place.

Rossetti uses nature analogies to express regrets again in the poems "An Apple-Gathering" and "Another Spring." These two poems work well together to encourage students to contemplate the value and potential danger of both renunciation and engagement in their own lives, and get them to think about finding a balance. This is an especially appropriate issue for traditional college-aged students who often seek new pleasures and new forms of identity, but tend to be prone to excess. "An Apple-Gathering" portrays a speaker who explains that she "plucked pink blossoms from mine apple tree / And wore them all that evening in my hair" (1–2). But upon returning "in due season" (3) the speaker finds "no apples there" (4). Her neighbors who all now have full baskets of apples see her empty-handed and mock her as they pass. She becomes filled with regret when she sees their joy in the harvest. Her thoughts of regret then turn to Willie, a former love. She asks, "Ah Willie, Willie, was my love less worth / Than apples with their green leaves piled above?" (17–18). Apparently, Willie does value the apples that are now in season over the love that they once had. The speaker, however, had put more value on their relationship. She says, "I counted rosiest apples on the earth / Of far less worth than love" (19–20). But what they had shared is now gone. In the end, she is left to sit alone in the cold night.

The implication here is that the speaker chose the immediate gratification of wearing the pretty blossoms so that when the time came to harvest the apples, she had none. Her neighbors, who showed greater restraint, were rewarded in the end and able to enjoy the fruits of the harvest. Students will often relate to the speaker themselves, or they may write about others they have known who resemble the speaker. Either way, they assign a personal meaning to the symbolic blossoms and apples. Mary Arseneau writes that "in a poem such as 'An Apple-Gathering' the literal and natural details are as true as the sexual, moral, or religious readings interpretable in those details" (39). One may read the poem through Christianity where renouncing the gratifications that the world offers, with the blossoms being gratifications that are seen as sinful, will allow one to attain greater rewards later on in Heaven (apples). But Rossetti also brings up the human relationship with the speaker and Willie, and students may focus more on this. Nearly everyone has had the experience of rushing into a relationship and regretting it later for any number of reasons. Relationships may bring joys or even physical pleasures, but with a lack of restraint one often becomes hurt or humiliated like the speaker of the poem. Students will use the poem to consider a number of other forms of regret due to excess, for example, not studying enough in high school because of a too active social life. Some students will write about poor financial decisions. Others will write about various types of impulsive behavior that they recognize in themselves such as impulsive eating and making impulse purchases. The allegory remains open for students to read themselves or others into it, but again, the emotion of loss and regret is captured through analogy.

Rossetti's poem "Another Spring," however, offers a very different perspective. Diane D'Amico explains that "Another Spring," among other poems written in the late 1850s, "suggest[s] that Rossetti began during those years to reconsider her earlier negative vision of the world" (63). While many of Rossetti's poems appear to favor restraint in life or even the renunciation of the material world for the greater rewards of the spiritual, "Another Spring" stands out as an antirenunciation poem with its carpe diem theme. Here the speaker, who is perhaps dying, tells of all the ways she would embrace life if she might only "see another Spring" (1). As in "An Apple-Gathering," Rossetti uses the imagery of plucking flowers. Now, however, the speaker says that she will have her flowers "at once not late" (8). In contrast to "An Apple-Gathering," this having of flowers is now something to celebrate, not regret. Rossetti's speaker "would not wait for anything" (22). She clings to life and all of the potential joy of the natural world including flowers, animals, and weather.

The speaker in this poem wants to live without the regrets that one who renounces life would have. She will seek joy in life, and her desire is firmly and lovingly connected with the object world. She does not split the evil world from a loving Heaven, but finds positive images in worldly things. In "Another Spring," we may say that life itself is, broadly, the object of desire. Rossetti recognizes the nature of desire, however, as always fleeting, hence the underlying tone of desperate yearning throughout even a poem that looks favorably on life. As a contrast to "An Apple-Gathering," "Another Spring" encourages fortitude in students and encourages them to think about the need to embrace life and to live without regrets that come with inaction—a very different form of regret than we see in "An Apple-Gathering." Students will use the poem to write about what they would like to do in life given the opportunity, or what they would regret not doing. Such contemplations could even lead students to take positive personal or social actions in the real world. Taken individually, each of these poems appears to offer a moral or preference, closing off possibility or contemplation, but taken together they show the contradictions within the individual and open themselves up. Taken together, these poems offer two perspectives, both of which have value and both of which have flaws, which lead students to consider the need to find balance.

The personal and social implications of this balance are closely linked. One who is prone to excess or to seeking immediate gratifications without considering consequences, or one whose desire is bounded to the wrong types of things, can lose self-awareness and fail to realize their potentials. This could include committing crimes or acts of violence. In a college or even high school atmosphere, this often comes in the form of partying too much and neglecting doing the kinds of things that will prove personally and socially beneficial. In more extreme, but not infrequent, cases, one may develop a substance-abuse problem or may contract an STD. In less extreme cases, one can simply fail to manage time effectively, or one may lose sight of one's true desire or one's priorities and goals. Excess often leads to a form of social apathy that is as dangerous and as hopeless as renunciation. It is good to be engaged in the world, not just politically, but for your own enjoyment. Total renunciation can lead to depression and apathy where one neglects both the self and the other. With Rossetti's two poems, students can contemplate balance—seeking engagement without excess, and restraint without deprivation. Students consider the importance of not squandering their lives and their potentials. They consider their goals and desires, while remaining cautious about excess. This contemplation becomes especially important for young students in a phase of life where they are already likely trying to figure these things out.

Reparative Structures

Spring is consistently portrayed in Rossetti's poetry as a positive time of renewal and reparation. The poem "The First Spring Day" provides a representative example. It uses the season to create an analogy about faith and doubt. After describing the winter, Rossetti writes, "I am sore in doubt concerning Spring" (6). Her doubt as to whether the season will actually arrive is short-lived. However, she soon relates the change of season to her own state wondering, "If heart and spirit will find out their Spring, / Or if the world alone will bud and sing" (9–10). She is concerned here with her own figurative spring, which refers to her personal or spiritual redemption. The poem concludes, however, on a reassuring, reparative note where, reassured of her own spring's arrival she writes, "Sing, voice of Spring, / Till I too blossom and rejoice and sing" (16–17). Through analogy, Rossetti is reassured of her own renewal by the ever-renewing cycles she sees in nature.

"Winter Rain" also finds pleasure and meaning in the cyclical wholeness of nature and its seasons. Rossetti reacts to the dreary winter rain by imagining the springtime life that it will give rise to. The poem is not an escapist fantasy so much as a recognition and celebration of the poet's sense of wholeness and meaning in the natural world. She comes to understand that "[w]here the kind rain sinks and sinks, / Green of Spring will follow" (3–4). The rain will feed the land and the winter provides a necessary precursor for the joyous spring. In the poem, Rossetti turns also to the animal world with images of love, procreation, and maternal nourishment. Then she looks to flora, and finally to humanity with similar types of procreative imagery associated with spring. She sees the fecundity in all of nature, and, poetically, transforms the rainy winter day. "Winter Rain" provides an example of the reparative function of Rossetti's imagination. Seeing nature as whole object, Rossetti does not react against the winter rain as bad, but repairs the whole object through poetically imagining the good that will arise.

Much of Rossetti's poetry offers recognition to negative emotions that she must find symbols and language to counter. She often finds comfort and meaning in the world through the cycles of nature. It is not surprising that poetry therapists often discuss the healing power of the natural world in similar terms. Barbara Kreisberg and Charles Rossiter explain that "the rhythms of our lives parallel life cycles found in all living things. Focusing on our connection with nature brings contentment and deepens our understanding of our selves" (173). Darline Hunter and Shannon Sanderson propose "blending the healing qualities of both nature and poetry" in therapy (211). They write, "The form, rhythm and beat of poetry echo the rhythm of nature and the rhythm of the client's life. The four seasons can be used as a metaphor for life. When the client is in tune with the seasons, the life-death-life cycles of nature, then they can recognize the ephemeral quality of life, bringing wholeness and harmony to life" (215).[4] Many people have positive memories of communing with a place in nature where they experienced a sense of mental clarity or came to sense a profound order in the world. Of course, nature also has its brutal side, and we can have students consider this as well, so that nature will be seen as a whole object and not just an idealized one.

Like Wordsworth, Rossetti's poetry contains powerful implications for environmental ethics and eco-justice. As our relationship with nature becomes an increasingly prominent and important issue in our contemporary world, I find that many students react very strongly to nature poetry. Ecocritics have extensively explored the value of such poetry and literature in these terms, and we can make use of it in the classroom to get students to consider the profound relationship that humankind has with the environment. Rossetti's poems about the cycles of nature lead students to consider how their mood is often tied to the weather and the season, which reinforces their understanding of their connection with nature. They will often discuss nature literally, looking forward to the coming of spring and the joyful associations they have with it. These poems lead students to consider and pay closer attention to nature, thus, cultivating a deeper respect for the natural world. Students will also respond to the seasonal analogies figuratively. As with the seasons, they come to understand, the things currently happening in their own lives will pass.

If "Winter Rain" provides an example of the natural word as a whole, meaningful, and ultimately good object, "Up-Hill" does the same with life. Mazza actually recommends this poem for examining belief and understanding in poetry therapy (154–155). The poem's dialogic structure provides realistic but hopeful answers to common concerns about life. The first voice asks questions like, "Does the road wind up-hill all the way?" (1). To which the second answers, "Yes, to the very end" (2). The voice that answers recognizes, honestly, that life is a difficult struggle. However, in spite of life's difficulties, the responding voice assures the questioner, and the reader, that all will be provided for. We are told that we are not alone and that others will help us on our journey. In spite of life's inevitable hardships, there will be "beds for all who come" (16).

"Up-Hill" assesses life from the depressive position by acknowledging both the good and the bad—the joy and the sorrow—that will come with life. It reacts to the bad in life by providing hope, and showing that the world and life are ultimately good objects. Students use this poem to consider both the struggles they face in life and where they find support during troubled times. Typically this support comes in the form of loving others—friends or family members. This can help to raise awareness of the importance of relationships in the difficult struggle of life. Our relationships with others can help us cope, overcome fears and doubts, and find courage to achieve what we want to in the journey of life. Love gives us confidence and an essential sense of self-worth. Students also consider that love must be returned. Just as they find support in others, they should offer support and caring to others. The poem leads students to better understand their own needs, and to see the importance of taking actions to fulfill the needs of others.

Another poem that allows students to feel positive and locate a sense of self-worth through love is "A Birthday." As a joyous celebration of love, "A Birthday" is the most purely positive poem of the *Goblin Market* volume. It typically leads students to consider the good or reparative objects in their lives. The establishment of a pure good object, though part of a paranoid/schizoid split, is essential as an early relationship prototype provided that one later comes to a more realistic assessment of it. "A Birthday" is a good poem to begin with early in a semester in order to establish poetry as a good object and to get students comfortable with exploring emotions—in this case, positive ones. The poem essentially provides a poetic monument to love. It attempts to capture the pure essences of love and joy through creativity. Rossetti creates numerous images to reflect an inner state of exultation based on strong feelings of love toward an object. The poem begins by seeking images in the natural world to capture feelings of love. It opens with two similes where the speaker's heart is like "a singing bird" (1) who is nesting, and like "an apple tree / ... with thickset fruit" (3–4). We recognize fertility in both the nest that provides a happy home for the bird and her eggs and in the fruitful tree. Hassett points out how the potential in the nest of the first simile is "realized in the ... ripeness of the second" (*Christina* 7). Both images provide positive links to the maternal object. The speaker continues, "My heart is like a rainbow shell / That paddles in a halcyon sea" (5–6). We begin to move away from the strictly natural world toward a more imaginative one as the shell becomes personified by paddling in the sea. A shell, like the earlier nest, provides a home for living organisms. It becomes a safe womb image able to, and enabling one to, explore the calm, comfortable seas of the external object world. But even these images, the speaker feels, fall short of her inner state. She says, "My heart is gladder than all these / Because my love is come to me" (7–8). We discover the root of all of her happiness as object love. The poem begins by offering loving, joyful images that one may associate with the nourishing maternal body—the essential, primary good object—but the speaker ultimately finds greater happiness in the external world of object love. Still, the maintenance of this primary loving image proves essential; the image of the loving object must be repaired and preserved for the possibility of object love. The first stanza of "A Birthday" offers the reader an array of such strong, loving images.

The second, and final, stanza of the poem moves away from the natural world toward the world of artistic creation. The speaker commands that a dais be erected as a man-made monument to her love—what Lynda Palazzo describes as "a temple...to the beauty of a human emotion" (95). While nature supplies certain images of joy, safety, and love that may prove reparative, the speaker recognizes that capturing the image of love must be a creative act. Like the subject performing reparation, one must actively create the adequate image of the pure, loving object. Rossetti engages in this creative act through the poem, as the speaker of the poem engages in it during the second stanza by ordering her monument. Both succeed in creating such an object for the reader to enjoy, adapt, and find comfort in. The poem ends, as James Doubleday points out, with the discovery of the "birthday" as the final adequate image emerging where all others fall short (30). Hassett writes that the imagery of the second stanza "provides the objective correlative to the self-centered gloriousness of new love" (*Christina* 8). As the love object in the poem brings about "the birthday," or the feeling of rebirth, the reader experiences the same feeling of renewal that comes with reparation and with object love.

With "A Birthday," students will typically reflect on the positive emotions that the poem is designed to evoke. However, we must be somewhat careful here. While nearly everyone will have some experience of love that the poem brings up, students who are suffering from a want of love or lost love may find the poem too hopeful. Because the portrayal of good is so pure in "A Birthday," it lacks realistic recognition of negative emotions and may alienate some students, potentially bringing about a negative response. Typically, however, students will write about how their loving relationships bring them happiness and help them to cope. They will sometimes discuss a new love they have found, or their dreams of an ideal future love. The poem allows students to explore the joy associated with love. Love makes them feel special as individuals and increases their sense of self-worth. Rosalie Brown, Arleen Hynes, and Deborah Langosch discuss using poetry therapy to help "clients discover their own strengths and healthy aspects of the self" (149). "A Birthday" allows students to explore these aspects and perhaps locate new potentials. Along with evoking positive feelings, the poem also shows how love can provide inspiration. After their written responses, we can follow up by having students create their own monument to love or to their love object(s)—whether lovers, friends, or family members—through poetry or another artistic medium. Here students experience firsthand the connection between love and creative inspiration, and also the reparative aspects of creativity.

"If I Had Words"

I end here with Rossetti's poem "If I Had Words," which captures the essence of poetic renewal and reparation that I stress in this book. This is an unpublished poem that was composed in 1864, two years after the *Goblin Market* volume. "If I Had Words" may be introduced at the beginning of a semester or section to discuss of the value of language and self-exploration, or at the end to provide closure and perspective. Suzanne Waldman in her psychoanalytic (Lacanian) treatment of Dante Gabriel and Christina Rossetti cites the poem as "quest for sublimation" (24). The poem "explicitly portrays language as a route beyond the confines of the self" (23). In Lacan's terms, the poem achieves "a state of desire freed from the ego's libidinal attachments" (23). The poem begins with the speaker regretting her lack of words. She says, "I have no voice wherewith to cry" (4). Rossetti shows us the importance of language and the necessity of expression. The speaker feels an obscure sense of longing and misery, common to human experience. Without language, she is unable to integrate and own her experience. It remains out of the reach of her creative, imaginative, and reparative function. She links language to life itself, and its lack to hopelessness and death. Without words she lacks "strength" (5) and "heart" (6). Her "soul is bound" (7) and "crushed" (8). Her thoughts are fragmented and can only "wander here and there" (9). They offer her nothing that she "may live thereby" (12). Not integrated into language, her feelings only cause suffering.

The second part of the poem echoes the first. Instead of "If I Had words," she muses, "If I had wings as hath a dove" (17). With such wings, she "would seek the land of love" (19). Language here is linked with the transcendental image of a soaring dove, but, more significantly, it is linked to love, which one can only realize in the symbolic, object world, the world of communication and relationships. In the closing stanza of the poem, Rossetti continues to link words, more explicitly, with reparative love. If she had wings, she "would make haste to find out love" (27). Reminiscent of the speaker of "Another Spring," she imagines a life lived without regret.

The poem ends, "Then if I lived it might be best, / Or if I died I could but die" (31–32). These closing lines echo those of *In Memoriam* Lyric VIII, where the poet offers the "flower of poesy" in the elegy to his lost friend: "That if it can it there may bloom, / Or dying, there at least may die" (23–24). Tennyson, in this lyric, finds comfort in the act of poetic creation as it links him to his object of both love and despair. Rossetti treats love and language in a similar way. With words and love, she could find peace one way or another. Without them, there is only confusion and regret. Rossetti's poem succeeds in expressing her vague longing even as it argues it cannot. It captures an emotional state in language even as it realizes language's limitations. It also argues for the value—the necessity—of language. Through poetic language, we renew ourselves by integrating our fragmented experience and gaining deeper self-awareness. Language links us to others who provide loving recognition for our experiences, and to whom we may offer our own empathetic recognition. Poetic language also engages and enables our creativity through which we can constantly renew ourselves and perform reparation. As Rossetti describes, poetic language can provide the wings that revive us and reconnect us to the world. This is where the value of poetry lies, and this is what we can offer our students.

NOTES

Introduction: The Therapeutic Value of Poetry

1. Excepting the work of a few notable scholars like Jeffrey Berman, Mark Bracher, and Norman Holland, and Murray Schwartz.
2. While originally appearing in Sigmund Freud's dream work from *The Interpretation of Dreams*, the concepts termed "the three registers of experience" are typically associated with Jacques Lacan's symbolic, imaginary, and real. My use of the three registers is rooted more in Freud, but has also been influenced by two contemporary adaptations of the concepts: Mark Bracher's identity registers (*Radical Pedagogy*), which relate them to identity, and Wilma Bucci's multiple code theory (*Psychoanalysis and Cognitive Science*), which looks at them in cognitive science terms. I discuss the three registers in detail in chapter two.
3. Kenneth Gorelick and Peggy Osna Heller write that "[r]eading, writing, and interchange help us to know our inner landscape better and to right-size our connections with the world beyond our skin. All poetry-making is about the attempt to connect these two domains" (259).
4. The Association for Poetry Therapy was founded in 1969 by Dr. Jack Leedy and others, though the therapeutic use of poetry can be traced back to ancient times. A succinct overview of the history of the field and the foundation of The National Association for Poetry Therapy can be found on the NAPT website under "History" at www.poetrytherapy.org/history.html.
5. As Kenneth Gorelick and Peggy Osna Heller figuratively put it, "[F]inding the map—choosing the correct ones and rejecting unsuitable ones—is the most important task of the voyager" (261).
6. Or, as Holland and Schwartz put it, "[W]hat does this mean to me?" (viii-ix). In their work, this involves learning about one's personality and considering how it affects the way one reads a text.
7. Kristeva's *le sujet en procès* is sometimes translated as "subject-on-trial."
8. Reparation is a prominent theme throughout Klein's work from the 1929 essay "Infantile Anxiety Situations Reflected in a Work of Art and in the Creative Impulse" forward. It is most thoroughly treated in the 1937 essay "Love, Guilt and Reparation." I discuss reparation in detail in chapter four.

1 Gaining Awareness and Overcoming Defenses

1. With the entrance into the symbolic comes a jouissance of separation. Jouissance refers to pain found in pleasure when one attempts to transgress the social prohibitions of the pleasure principle by attaining wholeness with the other. This transgression can only occur, paradoxically, once the subject has achieved separation from the maternal and entered the social realm where such prohibitions exist.
2. Cramer discounts other criteria that attempt to differentiate between these two processes, including coping as normal and defense as pathological, based on a lack of empirical evidence.
3. Of course, the use of the term "sublimation" in psychoanalysis originated with Sigmund Freud. The concept appears and develops throughout his work.

2 (Neuro) Psychoanalytic Regression and Integration

1. Several poetry therapists make this assertion. Stainbrook writes that poetry provides tools for defragmentation by "providing a wholeness of consciousness—an integration of emotion, cognition, and imagery—with which to create and maintain personal meaning" (11). One of the major benefits of poetry therapy, Stephen Rojcewicz points out, is its promotion of "an integration of basic raw emotions, freedom of expression, and a highly organized poetic structure, allowing primitive feelings and impulses to be placed in perspective, mastered, and expressed in a more constructive manner" (7). Finally, Leon explains, "The structure of the creative product promotes a sense of unity, thereby maintaining cohesion against centrifugal fragmentation" (389).
2. Both Michael Maltby (49) and Paul Christensen (88) acknowledge this "magical" quality of poetry. According to Maltby, we experience this quality "as much sensually as verbally and that moves us through the realm of words to somewhere beyond them" (49). Poetic language brings us back to a pre-symbolic state of nearly endless possibility, paradoxically, through the symbolic mode of language. Rafael Campo explains that "in poetry, the instinctual and the emotional coexist on par with the intellectual and the rational" (19). In poetry, we witness our core not only being exposed but also being put into a formal, coherent structure conducive to assessment and revision. Akhtar concurs that poetry seems to have "uncanny access" to the unconscious. "Reading poetry informs one about the inner state of affairs, [and] enhances empathy with the self" (236).
3. As Francis Henry and Phyllis Luckenbach-Sawyers explain, "Ecstasy [achieved through reading poetry], which often accompanies visualization and meditative states, is a time-honored method of transcending our ordinary consciousness and a way of helping us arrive at insights we could not attain otherwise" (28). Charles Ansell states, "Creative art is an experience of transcendence. Psychologically, art which transcends the experience witnessed by the mind presses deeper into states of feeling not immediately accessible to consciousness" (20).
4. Freud points out that the "three forms of regression [topical, temporal, and formal] are, however, basically one, and in the majority of cases they coincide,

for what is older in point of time is at the same time formally primitive and, in the psychic topography, nearer to the perception end" (*V* 548). In each of these models, the regression through which poetry operates gets us in touch with our more primal selves and enhances self-awareness.
5. In his most recent book, *Forms of Vitality*, Stern discusses vitality in relation to the arousal systems recognized by neuroscience. These systems, he explains, clearly play a large role in making the experience of vitality forms possible (57).
6. Meerloo explains: "It is sometimes a great struggle in psychotherapy to liberate a patient from such compulsive self-imitations and repetitions; and without a therapeutic regression to the origin of this ancient language of rhythms, the patient will fail in his attempt at self-recollection. For this reason poetry, as a well-chosen form of communication, is a welcome adjunct to psychotherapy" (65).
7. Ferdinand de Saussure teaches us this in his first principle of the linguistic sign (67).
8. My example recalls Andrew's explanation of his father's philosophical work to Lily in Virginia Woolf's *To the Lighthouse*: "'[T]hink of a table then,' he told her, 'when you're not there'" (23).
9. See Freud's *Interpretation of Dreams* or, for a more succinct treatment, *On Dreams*.
10. This, I admit, is a controversial assumption challenged most notably by John Allan Hobson via his activation-synthesis hypothesis of dreams. This hypothesis appears throughout his work (see, for example, *The Dreaming Brain*).
11. In recent years, we have seen the emergence of a new interdisciplinary field called neuropsychoanalysis where psychoanalytic theorists and practitioners use neurobiology to qualify, verify, and alter many of the concepts of psychoanalysis. Neurologist and Nobel laureate Eric Kandel has said that "psychoanalysis still represents the most coherent and intellectually satisfying view of the mind" (64). But he stresses the need for continued collaborations between the fields of neurobiology and psychoanalysis. Psychoanalysis, Kandel says, "can define for biology the mental functions that need to be studied for a meaningful and sophisticated understanding of the biology of the human mind" (38). Kandel also suggests that psychoanalysis may need neurobiology in order to remain relevant. "Psychoanalysis," he writes, "might reenergize itself...by developing a closer relationship with biology in general and with cognitive neuroscience in particular" (64).
12. While there are a number of sources on the biology of the brain and its relation to the mind, I have found Jeanette Norden's lecture series *Understanding the Brain* to be the most clear and thorough.
13. Named for their discoverers Paul Broca and Carl Wernicke, respectively.
14. See also pp. 201–208 of *Literature and the Brain*.
15. Norden discusses this widely accepted biological speculation in Lecture 30.
16. I revisit this in chapter six in relation to politics and pedagogy. Drew Westen and George Lakoff have both recently published books about liberal politicians' failure to realize Descartes' error, and it is an error that literature teachers still often make when implementing social justice pedagogy. Reason

is not enough to achieve neurological changes that alter political thought processes and opinions—emotional motivation is required.
17. Holland uses Jaak Panksepp's term for this system, the SEEKING system.
18. Neuroscience teaches us that these systems are all highly subjective.

4 The Poem as (Self-, Transformational, Transitional, and Reparative) Object

1. To Bion, thinking is an alpha-element as opposed to simply having thoughts, which is a beta-element.
2. Real knowledge is opposed to empty knowledge or a form of knowledge that avoids the attainment of the kind of emotional awareness that might induce anxiety. Bion calls this avoidance of knowledge "–K."
3. Klein differentiates between "envy" (an angry feeling toward an other who possesses something the subject desires), "jealousy" (which is felt toward two people in a relationship), and "greed" (the insatiable desire to attain another's objects) (*Envy* 181).

5 A Poetry Therapy Model for the Classroom

1. The model I am referring to here is a version of Mazza's R.E.S. (Receptive/Prescriptive, Expressive/Creative, and Symbolic/Ceremonial) integrative poetry therapy model, which was adapted by Mazza to Lewis Wolberg's eclectic brief treatment model.
2. Representing the Receptive/Prescriptive aspect of Mazza's model.
3. Acts like keeping a journal represent the Expressive/Creative aspect of Mazza's model. Choosing or adopting a poem as one's own represents the Symbolic/Ceremonial aspect of Mazza's model.
4. Examples of specific poems cited in this chapter may be found in *The Penguin Book of Romantic Poetry* edited by Jonathan and Jessica Wordsworth.
5. I tend to favor written exercises over verbal responses for this approach. Holland and Schwartz in their Delphi Seminars have also noticed how having students write their subjective responses tends to keep things more focused, as opposed to jumping around the classroom getting brief verbal responses from students, which may lack any connection (32).
6. Mahrer presents this model in several of his books. It is presented most succinctly in his book *Becoming the Person You Can Become*.

6 Cultivating Empathy: Wordsworth's *Lyrical Ballads*

1. This authority includes the authority of the free market.
2. Cognitive scientists use the term "conceptual metaphor" to refer to the way metaphors structure our thinking or structure how we conceptualize issues.
3. Lakoff explains this family/nation metaphor in chapter 3 of *The Political Mind*, "The Brain's Role in Family Values" (77–91).

4. This view is guilty of what neurologist Antonio Damasio calls Descartes' Error in his influential book of that title.
5. Bracher lists Marxist, feminist, New Historicist, queer, postcolonialist, and multiethnic pedagogies.
6. Bracher cites Batson, "Empathy, Attitudes, and Action," and Levy.
7. Batson describes no less than eight related but distinct phenomena referred to as empathy ("These Things").
8. Hatfield et al. cite Jean Decety and P. L. Jackson.
9. Cognitive scientists use the term frames (or scripts) to describe the structures that we think with. This includes sets of associations, expectations of events or institutions, analogies through which we think about certain issues, biases, etcetera.
10. I discuss this in chapter four.
11. However, Sober and Wilson assert that empathy may not be the only cause of altruism and that empathy does not necessarily lead to altruism (231–237). Still, they argue in the first part of *Unto Others* that altruism has an evolutionary value, and this would also imply the evolutionary, biological primacy of empathy if we accept the connection between the two.
12. Lakoff refers to this as "democratizing knowledge."
13. See the work of Rich Furman and Phyllis Klein and Perie Longo.
14. I typically use the Penguin Classics edition, which reproduces the original 1798 text of *Lyrical Ballads*. Quotations of poetry in the remainder of this chapter are taken from it. Though, I do rely on Michael Mason's edition for some of the notes.
15. Edward Titchener first used the English term "empathy" in 1909 translating it from the German *Einfühlung* used previously by Theodor Lipps (1913).
16. Keats criticizes Wordsworth's egotism in his 1818 letter to John Hamilton Reynolds (99). Also, later that year, Keats refers to Wordsworth's "egotistical sublime" in a letter to Richard Woodhouse (214).
17. In psychology, this bias is referred to as the "fundamental attribution error."
18. Mason points out that Wordsworth uses this as a parallel to the more current antirevolutionary action that Britain was taking against France at the time (140n). Mason cites Wordsworth's 1842 advertisement for the poem (reproduced in Mason 270–271).
19. Wordsworth's later poem "Alice Fell" uses the same kind of rescue narrative structure with the speaker in the role of altruistic hero.
20. Dorothy was actually only about a year-and-a-half younger than William.
21. The story originally comes from Erasmus Darwin's *Zoonomia*. The anecdote from Darwin's book is reproduced in the Mason edition of *Lyrical Ballads*. Mason also points out that Wordsworth saw Gill's unending coldness as a psychological symptom rather than the result of a supernatural curse (103), citing Wordsworth's 1802 preface.

7 A Reparative Text: Tennyson's *In Memoriam*

1. Queen Victoria found comfort in the poem after the death of her husband Prince Albert in 1861.

2. On the musical elements of the poem, see the prosodic explorations of Gates and Gigante.
3. David Kennedy has recently demonstrated how Peter Sacks made "Mourning and Melancholia" the dominant model for looking at elegy for the past 30 years with his influential book *The English Elegy*. An overview of *In Memoriam* criticism written since Sacks largely confirms the influence of Sacks's book. However, despite the ubiquity of this approach, no critic, including Sacks, has found the application of Freud's economic model to *In Memoriam* entirely satisfactory (Albright, Craft, Armstrong, and Joseph). This general dissatisfaction has led several twenty-first-century critics of the poem to abandon a psychoanalytic approach to the poem's mourning altogether (Noble, Douglas-Fairhurst, Gold, and Krasner).
4. Tammy Clewell points out that, despite its flaws, "literary critics... have persisted in using the Freudian model... to evaluate narrative representations of death, loss, and bereavement" (48). Clewell also argues that Freud, himself, eventually abandoned the model he had put forth in "Mourning and Melancholia."
5. These include the stages of denial, anger, bargaining, depression, and acceptance.
6. Bell writes, "[B]y including all which is experienced in a particular moment, it becomes possible for a person to observe not only *what* is being dealt with, but *how* the interactions of thoughts are taking place." He continues, "The goal is to include everything just as it is experienced so that one can say, in reflection, this was what it was like for me to be alive at that moment. With the recording of many moments, self understanding is gained" (179).
7. Tennyson is quoted as referring to the poem as "too hopeful... more than I am myself" (Ray 41).
8. Because it is so rich in metaphors and images, and because it is so emotionally intense, I often use Lyric L to introduce the concepts of the three registers of experience and to show students how they will begin to use these concepts in the metaphor and experiential exercises.
9. Critics generally cite Lyric LVI as the height of the poet's despair. Many see Lyric XCV as the poem's climax. Here, through a moment of epiphany, Tennyson comes to see God/nature/world as a whole and ultimately good object—important for his personal reparation.

8   Integrating Experience: Morris's *The Defence of Guenevere and Other Poems*

1. The exception to this would be Morris's later, socialist writings. Though, one could argue that they are not properly Pre-Raphaelite.
2. I cite where she first uses the term here (page 2), but Helsinger discusses this concept throughout her book *Poetry and the Pre-Raphaelite Arts*.
3. Rossetti's paintings *The Blue Closet* and *The Tune of Seven Towers* are both available on the Rossetti Archive edited by Jerome McGann: www.rossettiarchive.org/index.html.

9 Desire and Reparation: Rossetti's *Goblin Market and Other Poems*

1. Her brother, Dante Gabriel, was one of the founders of the movement. Christina also contributed to *The Germ*—the short-lived journal of Pre-Raphaelite writing.
2. The *Goblin Market* volume ends with a section of "devotional" poems.
3. See the note in Crump's edition of Rossetti's poetry (n252). The title was changed by Dante Gabriel Rossetti.
4. Geri Giebel Chavis also devotes a chapter of her book, *Poetry and Story Therapy*, to the therapeutic value of nature.

Works Cited

Adams, Kathleen and Stephen Rojcewicz. "Mindfulness on the Journey Ahead." *The Healing Fountain: Poetry Therapy for Life's Journey.* Ed. Geri Giebel Chavis and Lila Lizabeth Weisberger. St. Cloud, MN: North Star Press of St. Cloud, 2003. 7–31.

Akhtar, Salman. "Mental Pain and the Cultural Ointment of Poetry." *International Journal of Psychoanalysis* 81.2 (2000): 229–243.

Albright, David. *Tennyson: The Muses' Tug-of-War.* Charlottesville: UP of Virginia, 1986. Virginia Victorian Studies.

Ansell, Charles. "Psychoanalysis and Poetry." *Poetry in the Therapeutic Experience.* Ed. Arthur Lerner. New York: Pergamon, 1978. 12–23.

Armstrong, Isobel. *Victorian Poetry: Poetry, Poetics, and Politics.* New York: Routledge, 1993.

Arseneau, Mary. "'May My Great Love Avail Me': Christina Rossetti and Dante." *The Culture of Christina Rossetti: Female Poetics and Victorian Contexts.* Ed. Mary Arseneau, Antony H. Harrison, and Lorraine Janzen Kooistra. Athens, OH: Ohio UP, 1999. 22–45.

Bate, Jonathan. *The Song of the Earth.* Cambridge, MA: Harvard UP, 2000.

Batson, C. Daniel, "These Things Called Empathy: Eight Related But Distinct Phenomena." *The Social Neuroscience of Empathy.* Cambridge: MIT Press, 2009. 3–15.

———, Judy G. Batson, Jacqueline K. Slingsby, Kevin L. Harrell, Heli M. Peekna, and R. Matthew Todd. "Empathic Joy and the Empathy-Altruism Hypothesis." *Journal of Personality and Social Psychology* 61.3 (1991): 413–426.

———, Johee Chang, Ryan Orr, and Jennifer Rowland. "Empathy, Attitudes, and Action: Can Feeling for a Member of a Stigmatized Group Motivate One to Help the Group?" *Personality and Social Psychology Bulletin* 28.12 (December 2002): 1656–1666.

———, Marina P. Polycarpou, Eddie Harmon-Jones, Heidi J. Imhoff, Erin C. Mitchener, Lori L. Bednar, Tricia R. Klein, and Lori Highberger. "Empathy and Attitudes: Can Feeling for a Member of a Stigmatized Group Improve Feelings Toward the Group?" *Journal of Personality and Social Psychology* 72.1 (1997): 105–118.

Baumeister, Roy F., Karen Dale, and Kristin L. Sommer. "Freudian Defense Mechanisms and Empirical Findings in Modern Social Psychology: Reaction Formation, Projection, Displacement, Undoing, Isolation, Sublimation and Denial." *Journal of Personality* 66.6 (December 1988): 1081–1124.

Bell, George L. "Poetry Therapy: A Focus on Moments." *Arts in Psychotherapy* 11.3 (Fall 1984): 177–185.

Bentley, D. M. R. "William Morris' The Wind." *Trivium* 13 (1978): 31–37.
Benvenuto, Bice and Roger Kennedy. *The Works of Jacques Lacan: An Introduction.* New York: St. Martin's, 1986.
Berger, Milton M. "Poetry as Therapy—and Therapy as Poetry." *Poetry Therapy: The Use of Poetry in the Treatment of Emotional Disorders.* Ed. Jack J. Leedy. Philadelphia: Lippincott, 1969. 75–87.
Berman, Jeffrey. *Empathic Teaching: Education for Life.* Boston: U of Massachusetts P, 2004.
The Bible. Introduction and notes by Robert Carroll and Stephen Prickett. New York: Oxford UP, 2008. Oxford World's Classics. Authorized King James Vers.
Bion, Wilfred. *Seven Servants: Four Works by Wilfred R. Bion.* New York: Aronson, 1977.
Bollas, Christopher. *Being a Character: Psychoanalysis and Self Experience.* New York: Hill and Wang, 1992.
———. *The Shadow of the Object: Psychoanalysis of the Unthought Known.* New York: Columbia UP, 1987.
Bouson, J. Brooks. *The Empathic Reader: A Study of the Narcissistic Character and the Drama of the Self.* Amherst: U of Massachusetts P, 1989.
Bowlby, John. *A Secure Base: Parent-Child Attachment and Healthy Human Development.* New York: Basic Books, 1988.
Bracher, Mark. "How to Teach for Social Justice: Lessons from Uncle Tom's Cabin and Cognitive Science." *College English* 71.4 (March 2009): 363–388.
———. *Radical Pedagogy: Identity, Generativity, and Social Transformation.* New York: Palgrave Macmillan, 2006.
———. "Teaching for Social Justice: Reeducating the Emotions through Literary Study." *JAC* 26.3–4 (2006): 463–512.
———. "Rouzing the Faculties: Lacanian Psychoanalysis and the Marriage of Heaven and Hell in the Reader." *Critical Paths: Blake and the Argument of Method.* Ed. Dan Miller, Mark Bracher, and Donald Ault. Durham, NC: Duke UP, 1987. 168–203.
Bradley, A. C. *A Commentary on Tennyson's* In Memoriam. 3rd ed. Hamden, CT: Archon Books, 1966.
Brenman, Eric. *Recovery of the Lost Good Object.* Ed. Gigliola Fornari Spoto. New York: Routledge, 2006.
Britzman, Deborah P. *Novel Education: Psychoanalytic Studies of Learning and Not Learning.* New York: Peter Lang, 2006.
———. *After-Education: Anna Freud, Melanie Klein, and Psychoanalytic Histories of Learning.* Albany: SUNY Press, 2003.
Brown, Rosalie, Arleen McCarty Hynes, and Deborah Langosch. "Celebrating Self-Worth." *The Healing Fountain: Poetry Therapy for Life's Journey.* Ed. Geri Giebel Chavis and Lila Lizabeth Weisberger. St. Cloud, MN: North Star Press of St. Cloud, 2003. 149–172.
Bryden, Inga. *Reinventing King Arthur: The Arthurian Legends in Victorian Culture.* Burlington, VT: Ashgate Publishing Ltd., 2005.
Bucci, Wilma. *Psychoanalysis and Cognitive Science: A Multiple Code Theory.* New York: Guilford, 1997.
Calhoun, Blue. *The Pastoral Vision of William Morris: The Earthly Paradise.* Athens: U of Georgia P, 1975.

Campo, Rafael. *The Healing Art: A Doctor's Black Bag of Poetry.* New York: Norton, 2003.
Chapman, Alison. *The Afterlife of Christina Rossetti.* New York: St. Martin's Press, 2000.
Chavis, Geri Giebel. *Poetry and Story Therapy: The Healing Power of Creative Expression.* Philadelphia: Jessica Kingsley Publishers, 2011.
Cho, K. Daniel. *Psychopedagogy: Freud, Lacan, and the Psychoanalytic Theory of Education.* New York: Palgrave Macmillan, 2009.
Christ, Carol T. *Victorian and Modern Poetics.* Chicago: U of Chicago P, 1984.
———. *The Finer Optic: The Aesthetic of Particularity in Victorian Poetry.* New Haven: Yale UP, 1975.
Christensen, Paul. "Magical Properties of the Poem: Rhythm and Sound." *Poetry as Therapy.* Ed. Morris R. Morrison. New York: Human Sciences, 1987. 87–99.
Clewell, Tammy. "Mourning beyond Melancholia: Freud's Psychoanalysis of Loss." *Journal of the American Psychoanalytic Association* 52.1 (2002): 43–67.
Cole, Allan Hugh. "Elegiac Poetry: A Pastoral Resource with Complicated Grief." *Pastoral Psychology* 53.3 (January 2005): 189–206.
Cozolino, Louis J. *The Neuroscience of Psychotherapy: Building and Rebuilding the Human Brain.* New York: Norton, 2002.
Craft, Christopher. "'Descend, and Touch, and Enter': Tennyson's Strange Manner of Address." *Genders* 1 (1988): 83–101.
Cramer, Phebe. "Defense Mechanisms in Psychology Today" *American Psychologist* 55.6 (June 2000): 637–646.
———. "Coping and Defense Mechanisms." *Journal of Personality* 66.6 (December 1998): 335–357.
Crootof, Charles. "Poetry Therapy for Psychoneurotics in a Mental Health Center." *Poetry Therapy: The Use of Poetry in the Treatment of Emotional Disorders.* Ed. Jack J. Leedy. Philadelphia: Lippincott, 1969. 38–51.
Damasio, Antonio R. *Descartes' Error: Emotion, Reason, and the Human Brain.* New York: Avon Books, 1994.
D'Amico, Diane. *Christina Rossetti: Faith, Gender, and Time.* Baton Rouge: Louisiana State UP, 1999.
Day, Aidan. *Tennyson's Skepticism.* New York: Palgrave Macmillan, 2005.
Decety, Jean and P. L. Jackson. "The Functional Architecture of Human Empathy." *Behavioral and Cognitive Neuroscience Reviews* 3 (2004): 71–100.
Doidge, Norman. *The Brain That Changes Itself: Stories of Personal Triumph from the Frontiers of Brain Sciences.* New York: Penguin, 2007.
Doubleday, James F. "Rossetti's 'A Birthday.'" *The Explicator* 44.2 (Winter 1986): 29–30.
Douglas-Fairhurst, Robert. *Victorian Afterlives: The Shaping of Influence in Nineteenth-Century Literature.* New York: Oxford UP, 2002.
Eco, Umberto. "The Poetics of the Open Work." *The Open Work.* Trans. Anna Cancogni. Cambridge, Massachusetts: Harvard UP, 1989.
Erdelyi, Matthew Hugh. "Defense Processes Can Be Conscious or Unconscious." *American Psychologist* 56.9 (September 2001): 761–762.
Faas, Ekbert. *Retreat into the Mind: Victorian Poetry and the Rise of Psychiatry.* Princeton, NJ: Princeton UP, 1988.

Faulkner, Peter. *Against the Age: An Introduction to William Morris*. Boston: George Allen & Unwin Ltd., 1980.
Feldman, Michael and Elizabeth Bott Spillius. "General Introduction." *Psychic Equilibrium and Psychic Change: Selected Papers of Betty Joseph*. Ed. Michael Feldman and Elizabeth Bott Spillius. New York: Routledge, 1989. 1–12.
Ferenczi, Sandor. *First Contributions to Psycho-Analysis*. London: Karnac, 1980.
Fink, Bruce. *A Clinical Introduction to Lacanian Psychoanalysis*. Cambridge: Harvard UP, 1997.
Fox, William Johnson. "Tennyson—Poems, Chiefly Lyrical—1830." *Victorian Scrutinies: Reviews of Poetry 1830–1870*. Ed. Isobel Armstrong. London: Athlone, 1972. 71–83.
Freud, Anna. *The Writings of Anna Freud Volume II: Ego and the Mechanisms of Defense*. Trans. Cecil Baines. New York: International Universities, 1973.
Freud, Sigmund. *The Standard Edition of the Complete Psychological Works of Sigmund Freud*. Ed. and trans. James Strachey. 24 vols. London: Hogarth, 1981.
Friedlander, Lisa. "Reflecting on Couples Connections." *The Healing Fountain: Poetry Therapy for Life's Journey*. Ed. Geri Giebel Chavis and Lila Lizabeth Weisberger. St. Cloud, MN: North Star Press of St. Cloud, 2003. 227–254.
Furman, Rich. "Using Poetry and Written Exercises to Teach Empathy." *Journal of Poetry Therapy* 18.2 (June 2005): 103–110.
Galin, David. "Implications for Psychiatry of Left and Right Cerebral Specialization: A Neurophysiological Context for Unconscious Processes." *Archives of General Psychiatry* 31.4 (October 1974): 572–583.
Gates, Sarah. "Poetics, Metaphysics, Genre: The Stanza Form of *In Memoriam*." *Victorian Poetry* 37.4 (1999): 507–520.
Gigante, Denise. "Forming Desire: On the Eponymous *In Memoriam* Stanza." *Nineteenth-Century Literature* 53.4 (1999): 480–504.
Gold, Barri J. "The Consolation of Physics: Tennyson's Thermodynamic Solution." *PMLA* 117.3 (2002): 449–464.
Goldner, Virginia. "The Poem as a Transformational Third: Commentary on a Paper by Barbara Pizer." *Psychoanalytic Dialogues* 15.1 (2005): 105–117.
Goleman, Daniel. *Social Intelligence: The New Science of Human Relationships*. New York: Bantam, 2006.
Gorelick, Kenneth. "Poetry Therapy." *Expressive Therapies*. Ed. Cathy A. Malchiodi. New York: Guilford, 2005. 117–140.
——— and Peggy Osna Heller. "Finding a Map to Travel by." *The Healing Fountain: Poetry Therapy for Life's Journey*. Ed. Geri Giebel Chavis and Lila Lizabeth Weisberger. St. Cloud, MN: North Star Press of St. Cloud, 2003. 257–289.
Gosso, Sandra. "Introduction." *Psychoanalysis and Art: Kleinian Perspectives*. Ed. Sandra Gosso. New York: Karnac, 2004.
Grayson, Deborah Eve. "Coping with Fear and Anger." *The Healing Fountain: Poetry Therapy for Life's Journey*. Ed. Geri Giebel Chavis and Lila Lizabeth Weisberger. St. Cloud, MN: North Star Press of St. Cloud, 2003. 81–103.
Grinberg, Lebon, Dario Sor, and Elizabeth Tabak de Bianchedi. *Introduction to the Work of Bion: Groups, Knowledge, Psychosis, Thought, Transformations, Psychoanalytic Practice*. Trans. Alberto Hahn. New York: Aronson, 1977.
Hair, Donald S. *Tennyson's Language*. Buffalo: U of Toronto P, 1991.

Hallam, Arthur Henry. *The Writings of Arthur Hallam*. Ed. T. H. Vail Motter. New York: MLA, 1943.
Hamilton, James W. "'Mental Pain and the Cultural Ointment of Poetry': Comment." *International Journal of Psychoanalysis* 81.6 (2000): 1221.
Harrison, Mary-Catherine. "The Paradox of Fiction and the Ethics of Empathy: Reconceiving Dickens's Realism." *Narrative* 16.3 (October 2008): 256–278.
Hassett, Constance. *Christina Rossetti: The Patience of Style*. Charlottesville: U of Virginia P, 2005.
———. "The Style of Evasion: William Morris' *The Defence of Guenevere, and Other Poems*." *Victorian Poetry* 29.2 (1991): 99–114.
Hatfield, Elaine, Richard L. Rapson, and Yen-Chi L. Le. "Emotional Contagion and Empathy." *The Social Neuroscience of Empathy*. Cambridge: MIT Press, 2009. 19–30.
Hayward, Helen. "Tennyson's Endings: *In Memoriam* and the Art of Commemoration." *English* 47 (1998): 1–15.
Helsinger, Elizabeth K. *Poetry and the Pre-Raphaelite Arts: Dante Gabriel Rossetti and William Morris*. New Haven: Yale UP, 2008.
Henry, Frances Louise and Phyllis Luckenbach-Sawyers. "The Arts and Healing." *Poetry as Therapy*. Ed. Morris R. Morrison. New York: Human Sciences, 1987.
Hentschel, Uwe, Juris G. Draguns, Wolfram Ehlers, and Gudmund Smith. "Defense Mechanisms: Current Approaches to Research and Measurement." *Defense Mechanisms: Theoretical, Research and Clinical Perspectives*. Boston: Elsevier, 2004. 3–41.
Hitchcock, Jan L. and Sally Bowden-Schaible. "Is It Time for Poetry Now? Therapeutic Potentials—Individual and Collective." *Journal of Poetry Therapy* 20.3 (September 2007): 129–140.
Hobson, J. Allan. *The Dreaming Brain*. New York: Basic Books, 1989.
Hodgson, Amanda. *The Romances of William Morris*. New York: Cambridge UP, 1987.
Holland, Norman N. *Literature and the Brain*. Gainesville, FL: The PsyArt Foundation, 2009.
———. *The Dynamics of Literary Response*. New York: Columbia UP, 1989.
——— and Murray M. Schwartz. *Know Thyself: Delphi Seminars*. Gainesville, FL: The PsyArt Foundation, 2008.
Holmes, Jeremy. *The Search for the Secure Base: Attachment Theory and Psychotherapy*. New York: Brunner Routledge, 2001.
Hood, James W. *Divining Desire: Tennyson and the Poetics of Transcendence*. Burlington: Ashgate, 2000.
Hunter, Darline and Shannon Sanderson. "Let Mother Earth Wrap Her Arms Around You: The Use of Poetry and Nature for Emotional Healing." *Journal of Poetry Therapy* 20.4 (December 2007): 211–218.
Hymer, Sharon M. "The Therapeutic Nature of Art in Self Reparation." *Psychoanalytic Review* 70.1 (Spring 1983): 57–68.
Hynes, Arleen McCarthy and Mary Hynes-Berry. *Bibliotherapy—The Interactive Process: A Handbook*. Boulder, CO: Westview, 1986.
Iacoboni, Marco. *Mirroring People: The New Science of How We Connect with Others*. New York: Farrar, Straus and Giroux, 2008.

Jones, Alice A. "The Experiencing Language: Some Thoughts on Poetry and Psychoanalysis." *Psychoanalytic Quarterly* 66.4 (October 1997): 683–700.
Joseph, Betty. *Psychic Equilibrium and Psychic Change: Selected Papers of Betty Joseph.* Ed. Michael Feldman and Elizabeth Bott Spillius. New York: Routledge, 1989.
Joseph, Gerhard. "Producing the 'Far-Off Interest of Tears': Tennyson, Freud, and the Economics of Mourning." *Victorian Poetry* 36.2 (1998): 123–133.
Kandel, Eric R. *Psychiatry, Psychoanalysis, and the New Biology of the Mind.* Washington, DC: American Psychiatric Publishing, 2005.
Kavaler-Adler, Susan. *Mourning, Spirituality and Psychic Change: A New Object Relations View of Psychoanalysis.* New York: Brunner-Routledge, 2003.
Keats, John. *John Keats.* Ed. Susan J. Wolfson. New York: Longman, 2007. Longman Cultural Edition.
Keen, Suzanne. "A Theory of Narrative Empathy." *Narrative* 14.3 (October 2006): 207–236.
Kennedy, David. *Elegy.* New York: Routledge, 2007. The New Critical Idiom.
Kirchhoff, Frederick. *William Morris.* Boston: Twayne Publishers, 1979.
Klein, Melanie. *The Selected Melanie Klein.* Ed. Juliet Mitchell. New York: Free, 1987.
———. *Envy and Gratitude & Other Works: 1946–1963.* n.p.: Delacorte Press, 1975.
———. "Love, Guilt and Reparation." *Love, Hate and Reparation: Two Lectures by Melanie Klein & Joan Riviere.* London: Hogarth, 1937. 57–119.
Klein, Phyllis and Perie Longo. "Therapeutic Implications of Poetic Conversation." *Journal of Poetry Therapy* 19.3 (September 2006): 115–125.
Kohut, Heinz. *How Does Analysis Cure?* Chicago: U of Chicago P, 1984.
———. "The Future of Psychoanalysis." *The Search for the Self.* Ed. Paul H. Ornstein. Vol. 2. New York: International UP, 1978. 663–684. 4 vols.
———. *The Restoration of the Self.* New York: International UP, 1977.
Kopp, Richard R. *Metaphor Therapy: Using Client-Generated Metaphors in Psychotherapy.* New York: Brunner/Mazel, 1995.
Krasner, James. "Doubtful Arms and Phantom Limbs: Literary Portrayals of Embodied Grief." *PMLA* 119.2 (2004): 218–232.
Kreisberg, Barbara and Charles Rossiter. "Being with Nature." *The Healing Fountain: Poetry Therapy for Life's Journey.* Ed. Geri Giebel Chavis and Lila Lizabeth Weisberger. St. Cloud, MN: North Star Press of St. Cloud, 2003. 173–196.
Kristeva, Julia. *Colette.* Trans. Jane Marie Todd. New York: Columbia UP, 2004.
———. *Black Sun: Depression and Melancholia.* Trans. Leon S. Roudiez. New York: Columbia UP, 1989.
———. *Tales of Love.* Trans. Leon S. Roudiez. New York: Columbia UP, 1987.
———. *Revolution in Poetic Language.* Trans. Margaret Waller. New York: Columbia UP, 1984.
———. *Desire in Language: A Semiotic Approach to Literature and Art.* Ed. Leon S. Roudiez. Trans. Thomas Gora, Alice Jardine, and Leon S. Roudiez. New York: Columbia UP, 1980.
Kübler-Ross, Elizabeth. *Death: The Final Stage of Growth.* Englewood Cliffs, NJ: Prentice-Hall, 1975.

Lacan, Jacques. *Écrits*. Trans. Bruce Fink. New York: Norton, 2002.

———. *The Seminar of Jacques Lacan: Book XI: The Four Fundamental Concepts of Psychoanalysis*. Ed. Jacques-Alain Miller. Trans. Alan Sheridan. New York: Norton, 1998.

———. *The Seminar of Jacques Lacan: Book VII: The Ethics of Psychoanalysis, 1959–1960*. Ed. Jacques-Alain Miller. Trans. Dennis Porter. New York: Norton, 1997.

———. *The Seminar of Jacques Lacan: Book III: The Psychoses, 1955–1956*. Ed. Jacques-Alain Miller. Trans. Russell Grigg. New York: Norton, 1993.

———. *The Seminar of Jacques Lacan: Book I Freud's Papers on Technique, 1953–1954*. Ed. Jacques-Alain Miller. Trans. John Forrester. New York: Norton, 1991.

———. *The Seminar of Jacques Lacan: Book II: The Ego in Freud's Theory and in the Technique of Psychoanalysis, 1954–1955*. Ed. Jacques-Alain Miller. Trans. Sylvana Tomaselli. New York: Norton, 1991.

Lakoff, George. *The Political Mind: Why You Can't Understand 21st-Century American Politics with an 18th-Century Brain*. New York: Viking, 2008.

Latham, David. "Gothic Architectonics: Morris's 'Tune of Seven Towers.'" *The Pre-Raphaelite Review* 2.2 (1979): 49–58.

LeDoux, Joseph. *The Synaptic Self: How Our Brains Become Who We Are*. New York: Penguin, 2003.

Leedy, Jack J. "Principles of Poetry Therapy." *Poetry Therapy: The Use of Poetry in the Treatment of Emotional Disorders*. Ed. Jack J. Leedy. Philadelphia: Lippincott, 1969. 67–74.

Leon, Irving G. "Bereavement and Repair of the Self: Poetic Confrontations with Death." *Psychoanalytic Review* 86.3 (1999): 383–401.

Levine, Stephen K. *Poiesis: The Language of Psychology and the Speech of the Soul*. Bristol, PA: Kingsley, 1992.

Levy, Sheri R. "Reducing Prejudice: Lessons from Social-Cognitive Factors Underlying Perceiver Differences in Prejudice." *Journal of Social Issues* 55 (1999): 745–765.

Lipps, Theodor. *Zur Einfühlung*. Leipzig: Engleman, 1913.

Longo, Perie J. and Alma Maria Rolfs. "Encountering Change and Life's Transitions." *The Healing Fountain: Poetry Therapy for Life's Journey*. Ed. Geri Giebel Chavis and Lila Lizabeth Weisberger. St. Cloud, MN: North Star Press of St. Cloud, 2003. 39–58.

Lourie, Margaret A. "The Embodiment of Dreams: William Morris's 'Blue Closet' Group." *Victorian Poetry* 15 (1977): 193–206.

Mahrer, Alvin R. *Becoming the Person You Can Become*. Boulder, CO: Bull, 2002.

Maltby, Michael. "Wordless Words: Poetry and the Symmetry of Being." *Acquainted with the Night: Psychoanalysis and the Poetic Imagination*. Ed. Hamish Canham and Carole Satyamurti. New York: Karnac, 2003. 49–70.

Mazza, Nicholas. *Poetry Therapy: Theory and Practice*. New York: Brunner-Routledge, 2003.

McGann, Jerome J. *Dante Gabriel Rossetti and the Game That Must Be Lost*. New Haven: Yale UP, 2000.

———. *The Beauty of Inflections: Literary Investigations in Historical Method and Theory*. New York: Oxford UP, 1985.

Meerloo, Joost A. M. "The Universal Language of Rhythm." *Poetry Therapy: The Use of Poetry in the Treatment of Emotional Disorders.* Ed. Jack J. Leedy. Philadelphia: Lippincott, 1969. 52–66.

Miceli, Maria and Cristiano Castelfranchi. "Further Distinctions between Coping and Defense Mechanisms?" *Journal of Personality* 69.2 (April 2001): 287–296.

Morris, William. *The Collected Works of William Morris.* Ed. May Morris. 24 vols. New York: Russell & Russell, 1966.

Morrison, Morris Robert. "Poetry Therapy with Disturbed Adolescents." *Poetry Therapy: The Use of Poetry in the Treatment of Emotional Disorders.* Ed. Jack J. Leedy. Philadelphia: Lippincott, 1969. 88–103.

Newman, Leonard S. "Coping and Defense: No Clear Distinction." *American Psychologist* 56.9 (September 2001): 760–761.

Noble, Christopher Stephen. "Behind a Black Veil: Bodies in Mourning, the Rhetoric of Dread, and the Nineteenth Century British Elegy." Diss. University of California, Irvine. 2000.

Norden, Jeanette. *Understanding the Brain.* Dir. Jon Leven. Perf. Jeanette Norden. 6 DVDs. Teaching Company, 2007.

Oberg, Charlotte H. *A Pagan Prophet: William Morris.* Charlottesville, VA: UP of Virginia, 1978.

O'Neill, Michael. *Romanticism and the Self-Conscious Poem.* Oxford: Clarendon Press, 1997.

Palazzo, Lynda. "Christina Rossetti's 'A Birthday': Representations of the 'Poetic.'" *The Journal of Pre-Raphaelite Studies* 7.2 (May 1987): 94–96.

Panksepp, Jaak. *Affective Neuroscience: The Foundations of Human and Animal Emotions.* New York: Oxford UP, 1998.

Pater, Walter. *Walter Pater: Three Major Texts (The Renaissance, Appreciations, and Imaginary Portraits).* Ed. William E. Buckler. New York: New York UP, 1986.

Patston, Lucy L. M., Ian J. Kirk, Mei Hsin S. Rolfe, Michael C. Corballis, and Lynette J. Tippett. "The Unusual Symmetry of Musicians: Musicians Have Equilateral Interhemispheric Transfer for Visual Information." *Neuropsychologia* 45.9 (2007): 2059–2065.

Peltason, Timothy. *Reading* In Memoriam. Princeton, NJ: Princeton UP, 1985.

Ray, Gordon. *Tennyson Reads 'Maud.'* Vancouver: Publications Centre, U of British Columbia, 1968.

Reiter, Sherry and Lila Lizabeth Weisberger. "Coping with Grief and Loss." *The Healing Fountain: Poetry Therapy for Life's Journey.* Ed. Geri Giebel Chavis and Lila Lizabeth Weisberger. St. Cloud, MN: North Star Press of St. Cloud, 2003. 110–146.

Riesenberg-Malcolm, Ruth. "Bion's Theory of Containment." *Kleinian Theory: A Contemporary Perspective.* Ed. Catalina Bronstein. New York: Brunner-Routledge, 2001. 165–180.

Roe, Dinah. *Christina Rossetti's Faithful Imagination: The Devotional Poetry and Prose.* New York: Palgrave Macmillan, 2006.

Rojcewicz, Stephen. "Medicine and Poetry: The State of the Art of Poetry Therapy." *International Journal of Arts Medicine* 6.2 (1999): 4–10.

Rossetti, Christina. *The Complete Poems of Christina Rossetti.* Ed. R. W. Crump. Baton Rouge: Louisiana State UP, 1979.

Rossetti, Dante Gabriel. *Dante Gabriel Rossetti: Collected Writings*. Ed. Jan Marsh. Chicago: New Amsterdam, 2000.
Rossiter, Charles, Rosalie Brown, and Samuel T. Gladding. "A New Criterion for Selecting Poems for Use in Poetry Therapy." *Journal of Poetry Therapy* 4.1 (Fall 1990): 5–11.
Rudnytsky, Peter L. "Introduction." *Transitional Objects and Potential Spaces: Literary Uses of D. W. Winnicott*. Ed. Peter L. Rudnytsky. New York: Columbia UP, 1993. xi–xxi.
Sacks, Peter M. *The English Elegy: Studies in the Genre from Spenser to Yeats*. Baltimore: Johns Hopkins UP, 1987.
Saussure, Ferdinand. *Course in General Linguistics*. Ed. Charles Bally and Albert Reidlinger. Trans. Wade Baskin. New York: Fontana/Collins, 1974.
Schwartz, Sophie. "What Dreaming Can Reveal about Cognitive and Brain Functions during Sleep? A Lexico-Statistical Analysis of Dream Reports." *Psychologica Belgica* 44.1–2 (2004): 5–42.
Segal, Hanna. *The Work of Hanna Segal: A Kleinian Approach to Clinical Practice*. Northvale, NJ: Aronson, 1990.
Shelley, Percy Bysshe. *Percy Bysshe Shelley*. Ed. Stephen C. Behrendt. New York: Longman, 2010. Longman Cultural Edition.
Shloss, Gilbert A. *Psychopoetry*. New York: Grossett, 1976.
Silver, Carole. "Dreamers of Dreams: Toward a Definition of Literary Pre-Raphaelitism." *The Golden Chain: Essays on William Morris and Pre-Raphaelitism*. Ed. Carole G. Silver. New York: William Morris Soc., 1982. 5–52.
———. *The Romance of William Morris*. Athens, OH: Ohio UP, 1982.
Silverman, Hirsch L. "Creativeness and Creativity in Poetry as a Therapeutic Process." *Art Psychotherapy* 4.1 (1977): 19–28.
Sober, Elliott and David Sloan Wilson. *Unto Others: The Evolution and Psychology of Unselfish Behavior*. Cambridge, MA: Harvard UP, 1998.
Solms, Mark and Oliver Turnbull. *The Brain and the Inner World: An Introduction to the Neuroscience of Subjective Experience*. New York: Other, 2002.
Solomon, Irving. *A Primer of Kleinian Therapy*. Northvale, NJ: Aronson, 1995.
Stainbrook, Edward. "Poetry and Behavior in the Psychotherapeutic Experience." *Poetry in the Therapeutic Experience*. Ed. Arthur Lerner. New York: Pergamon, 1978. 1–11.
Staines, David. "Morris' Treatment of His Medieval Sources in *The Defense of Guenevere and Other Poems*." *Studies in Philology* 70 (1973): 439–464.
Stern, Daniel N. *Forms of Vitality: Exploring Dynamic Experience in Psychology, the Arts, Psychotherapy, and Development*. New York: Oxford UP, 2010.
———. *The Interpersonal World of the Infant*. New York: Basic, 1984.
Sullivan, Harry Stack. *The Interpersonal Theory of Psychiatry*. Ed. Helen Swick Perry and Mary Ladd Gawel. New York: Norton, 1953.
Tennyson, Alfred. *In Memoriam*. Ed. Susan Shatto and Marion Shaw. Oxford: Oxford UP, 1982.
Titchener, E. B. *Experimental Psychology of the Thought Processes*. London: Macmillan, 1909.
Tompkins, J. M. S. *William Morris: An Approach to the Poetry*. London: Cecil Woolf, 1988.
Trout, J. D. *Why Empathy Matters: The Science and Psychology of Better Judgement*. New York: Penguin, 2009.

Tucker, Herbert F. *Tennyson and the Doom of Romanticism*. Cambridge: Harvard UP, 1988.
Turley, Richard Marggraf. *The Politics of Language in Romantic Literature*. New York: Palgrave Macmillan, 2002.
Vaillant, George E. *The Wisdom of the Ego*. Cambridge: Harvard UP, 1993.
Vaughan, Susan C. *The Talking Cure: The Science Behind Psychotherapy*. New York: Owl, 1998.
Waldman, Suzanne M. *The Demon and the Damozel: Dynamics of Desire in the Works of Christina Rossetti and Dante Gabriel Rossetti*. Athens, OH: Ohio UP, 2008.
Warren, Robert Penn. "A Poem of Pure Imagination: An Experiment in Reading." *Selected Essays*. New York: Random, 1958. 198–305.
Waska, Robert. *Projective Identification in the Clinical Setting: The Kleinian Interpretation*. New York: Brunner-Routledge, 2004.
Westen, Drew. *The Political Brain: The Role of Emotion in Deciding the Fate of the Nation*. New York: Public Affairs, 2007.
Wilde, Oscar. *The Major Works*. New York: Oxford UP, 2008. Oxford World's Classics.
Winnicott, D. W. *Playing and Reality*. New York: Tavistock, 1982.
Woolf, Virginia. *To the Lighthouse*. San Diego: Harcourt, 1927.
Wordsworth, Jonathan and Jessica. Eds. *The Penguin Book of Romantic Poetry*. New York: Penguin, 2005.
Wordsworth, William. *Wordsworth's Literary Criticism*. Ed. W. J. B. Owen. Boston: Routledge, 1974.
—— and Samuel Taylor Coleridge. *Lyrical Ballads*. 2nd Edition. Ed. Michael Mason. New York: Pearson Longman, 2007. Longman Annotated Texts.
—— and Samuel Taylor Coleridge. *Lyrical Ballads*. New York: Penguin, 2006.

Index

action/application phase, 84–91
Armstrong, Isobel, 113, 123–4, 132, n156

Batson, C. Daniel, 94–5, 97–8, n155
  empathy-altruism hypothesis, 94
Berman, Jeffrey, 46, n151
Bible, 140
Bion, Wilfred
  alpha-elements, 56–7, n154
  beta-elements, 56, n154
  contact-barrier, 56
  container, 45–6, 55–7
Bollas, Christopher, 62–3
  transformational object, 59–60
Bowlby, John, *see* secure base
Bracher, Mark, 6, 43–4, 50, 94, n151, n155
Britzman, Deborah, 44, 45, 48
Broca's area, 31, n153
Browning, Robert
  "Caliban upon Setebos," 80
Bucci, Wilma, 24–5, 27, n151
  multiple code theory, 27
  referential process, 24–5

Christ, Carol, 124
Clewell, Tammy, n156
Coleridge, Samuel Taylor
  "Pains of Sleep," 79
coping, *see* Cramer, Phebe: coping versus defense
countertransference, 42, 53, 55
Cozolino, Louis, 30–1, 32

Cramer, Phebe, 8, n152
  coping versus defense, 11–12
  creative phase, 91–2

Damasio, Antonio, 33, n155
defense mechanisms, xviii–xx, 8–15
  denial, 9
  reaction formation, 9, 64
  sublimation, 12, n152
  see also projective identification
Descartes, René, 33

Eco, Umberto, 82
ego, xviii, 1–8, 14–15, 32–4
ego psychology, 8, 30, 33
empathy, xxii–xxiii, 45–7, 62–3, 78–80, 98–105, n155
  see also Klein, Melanie; Kohut, Heinz
endemic reward system, 34
experiential therapy, 78, 84–8, 92, n154

Ferenczi, Sandor, 19
Freud, Anna, 8–12
  Ego and the Mechanisms of Defense, 8
Freud, Sigmund, 48, 108, n152
  Condensation, 18, 23–4
  "Creative Writers and Day-Dreaming," 20
  dream work, 18, 26–7, n151
  fantasy, 12–13
  "Formulation on the Two Principles of Mental Functioning," 20

Freud, Sigmund—*Continued*
  Interpretation of Dreams, 18, 124, n151, n153
  "Mourning and Melancholia," 110–11, n156
  primary and secondary processes, 18, 20–4, 32
  see also regression: formal, temporal, topical
Furman, Richard, 79, n155

Galin, David, 30
Goleman, Daniel, 42, 46–7

Hallam, Arthur, 107–8, 111–13, 116, 120
Harrison, Mary-Catherine, 95
Hassett, Constance, 125, 139–40, 146–7
Helsinger, Elizabeth, 123, n156
Hemans, Felicia
  "The Dreaming Child," 81
Hobson, John Allan, n153
Holland, Norman, xx, 13, 32, 34, n151, n153–4
  and Murray Schwartz, xiv, 81, n151, n154
Hynes, Arleen McCarthy and Mary Hynes-Berry, xiv, xvi, xxi–xxiii, 13–14, 47, 75, 77, 92

Integration, 24–35

Joseph, Betty, 41, 47–53, 57
  manipulation, 48, 52
  "Patient Who is Difficult to Reach, The," 48
  placation, 48–52
  rejection, 48–9

Kandel, Eric, 30, n153
Kavaler-Adler, Susan, 114
Keats, John, 83, 98, n155

"On First Looking into Chapman's Homer," 67
Keen, Suzanne, 95
Klein, Melanie
  "A Contribution to the Psychogenesis of Manic-Depressive States," 64
  depressive position, 39–41, 64–5, 67–73, 112–13, 115, 121, 146
  empathy, 65
  envy, 48, 68–9, n154
  "Infantile Anxiety Situations Reflected in a Work of Art and in the Creative Impulse," 63, n151
  "Love, Guilt, and Reparation," 65, n151
  "Mourning and its Relation to Manic-Depressive States," 108–11
  paranoid/schizoid position, 38–40, 48, 64–5, 69–73, 112–13, 146
  transference, 55, 57
  whole object, 39–45
  see also projective identification; reparation
Kohut, Heinz
  empathy, 60–1, 96
  selfobject transference, 58
Kopp, Richard, *see* metaphor therapy
Kristeva, Julia, 63, 71–3
  imaginary father, 73
  semiotic chora, 6–8, 22, 32
  subject-in-process, xix, n151
  symbolic, 7–8, 32
  thetic, 7
Kübler-Ross, Elizabeth, 111

Lacan, Jacques, 1–6, 8, 33–4, 148, n151
  desire, 4–6
  imaginary ego, xviii, 1–3
  lack, 4–6
  metaphor, 18, 23–4
  mirror stage, 2, 3
  object a, 4

Lakoff, George, 93–4, 96–7, n153–4
left/right brain model, 30–2
limbic system, 34

Mahrer, Alvin, *see* experiential therapy
Mazza, Nicholas, xv, xx, 75–9, 81,
    84, 145, n154
McGann, Jerome, 127, 140, n156
metaphor therapy, 78, 84, 88–92
mirror neurons, 97
Morris, William
    "Blue Closet, The," 126–9
    Defence of Guenevere and Other
        Poems, 123–36
    "Golden Wings," 133–4
    "How I Became a Socialist," 125
    "Spell-bound," 134–5
    "Tune of Seven Towers, The," 126–30
    "Wind, The," 130–3
mourning, 59, 107–22, n156

nature poetry, 83–4, 103–4, 144–5
Neurons, 28–9
neuroplasticity, 29–30
neuropsychoanalysis, 28–35
neuroscience (neurology), 19
    see also neuropsychoanalysis
Norton, Caroline
    "Be Frank with Me," 81
    "Recollections," 81

Pater, Walter, 124–5
poetry therapy, xiii–xvi, 55, 75–85,
    91–2, 111, 125, 145,
    147, n151
Pre-Raphaelite aesthetics, 123–6
projective identification, 37–46, 48–53

regression, 6, 9, 17–24, n152–3
    formal, 20–4
    temporal, 19–20
    topical, 18–19
renewal, xi–xii, xvi–xx, xxiii–xxv,
    14–15, 17, 24, 56, 62–3

reparation, xi–xii, xx–xxv, 39–41,
    56, 61–73, 107–22, 137–41,
    144–9, n151, n156
response/examination phase, 81–4
Roe, Dinah, 138–9
Rossetti, Christina, 137–49
    "Another Spring," 141–3
    "Apple-Gathering, An," 141–3
    "Birthday, A," 146–8
    "Consider the Lilies of the Field,"
        139–40
    "First Spring Day, The," 144
    Goblin Market and Other Poems,
        138–48, n157
    "If I Had Words," 148–9
    "May," 140–1
    "Pause of Thought, A," 138–9
    "Shut Out," 141
    "Up-Hill," 145–6
    "Winter Rain," 144–5
Rossetti, Dante Gabriel, 124, 126,
    148, n156–7

Sacks, Peter, 113, n156
secure base, 46–7
Segal, Hanna, 108, 110
self-awareness, 43
    see also renewal
self-system, *see* Sullivan,
    Harry Stack
Shelley, Percy Bysshe, 83
    "Defense of Poetry, The," 98
    "To Harriet," 81
Smith, Charlotte, 79
    "Beachy Head," 83
social change, 72, 123, 137
social justice, 79, 94–5, 98–9,
    104, n153
Solms, Mark and Oliver Turnbull,
    19, 31–3
Stern, Daniel
    Forms of Vitality, n153
    Internal World of the Infant, 20
    vitality affects, 20–1

Sullivan, Harry Stack, 9–10
Superego, 8, 11, 13, 40–3, 70
supportive/emphatic phase, 78–81

Tennyson, Alfred, 107–8, 111–22, n156
 "Break, break, break," 59
 In Memoriam, 107–8, 111–22, 138, n155–6
  Prologue, 113
  I, 115–16
  V, 116
  VIII, 149
  XVI, 117–18
  XXI, 113
  L, 118–20, n156
  LVI, 113, n156
  XCV, n156
  XCVI, 120
  C, 120–1
  CVIII, 121
  CXXII, 121
  CXXIII, 121
  CXXIX, 121
 Mariana poems, 80
 Poems, Chiefly Lyrical, 107
third object, 62, 82
three registers, xii, xvi–xviii, 24–8, 34–5, n151
 affective register, 26
 imaginary register, 25–6

linguistic register, 25
top/down brain model, 30, 32–3
Tractarianism, 137
Trout, J. D., 96

Vaillant, George, 11

Warren, Robert Penn, 3
Wernicke's area, 31, n153
Westen, Drew, 93–4, 96–7, n153
Wilde, Oscar, 125
Winnicott, D. W.
 object permanence, 45
 potential space, 61
 relating versus using, 44–5
 transitional object, 61–2
Woolf, Virginia, n153
Wordsworth, William
 "Alice Fell," n155
 "Convict, The," 102–3
 "Daffodils," 83
 "Female Vagrant, The," 100–1
 "Goody Blake and Harry Gill," 104–5
 "Lines Left upon a Seat in a Yew-Tree," 99–100
 Lyrical Ballads, 98–105, n155
 Preface to *Lyrical Ballads*, 107
 Prelude, The, 83
 "Simon Lee," 101–2
 "Tintern Abbey," 83, 103–4

GPSR Compliance

The European Union's (EU) General Product Safety Regulation (GPSR) is a set of rules that requires consumer products to be safe and our obligations to ensure this.

If you have any concerns about our products, you can contact us on

ProductSafety@springernature.com

In case Publisher is established outside the EU, the EU authorized representative is:

Springer Nature Customer Service Center GmbH
Europaplatz 3
69115 Heidelberg, Germany

"In *A Therapeutic Approach to Teaching Poetry*, the journey from theory to text in both literary criticism and psychology has been gracefully extended to personal and social development. As an educator and therapist, I have found that whether the poetic is experienced in the classroom or clinic, whether it is written or read alone or with others, it can serve in growth and healing capacities. Todd O. Williams, in this scholarly and practical book, is in effect making a compelling offer to writers, educators, therapists, and others to continue a dialogue to advance the common ground in literary, therapeutic, educational, and community-building studies."
— Nicholas Mazza, Dean and professor, College of Social Work, Florida State University; author of *Poetry Therapy: Theory and Practice*

"Drawing on the work of Freud, Klein, Lacan, Kristeva, cognitive psychoanalysis, neuropsychoanalysis, and poetry therapy, Williams offers a theoretically sophisticated and classroom-tested strategy for teaching poetry in a way that promotes cognitive and emotional developments that contribute both to students' greater personal well-being and to social justice. This is a brilliant and ground-breaking book that will be indispensable to anyone who cares about the personal or social benefits of reading and studying poetry."
— Mark Bracher, Kent State University; author of *Radical Pedagogy: Identity, Generativity, and Social Transformation*

"This is a valuable book for teachers who want their practice to be truly useful to students. The argument is eminently practical, and the writing is lucid, well-organized, and conceptually shrewd."
— Marshall Alcorn, George Washington University; author of *Changing the Subject in English Class: Discourse and the Constructions of Desire*

A Therapeutic Approach to Teaching Poetry develops a poetry pedagogy that offers significant benefits to students by helping them to achieve a sense of renewal (a deeper awareness of self and potentials) and reparation (a realistic, but positive and proactive world view). Todd O. Williams offers a thorough examination of the therapeutic potential of poetry, explaining its personal and social benefits, and providing unique pedagogical strategies derived from poetry therapy and other therapeutic models. In taking this approach, Williams also enlarges the range of interpretive possibilities for the nineteenth-century poetry he treats.

Todd O. Williams is an assistant professor of English at Kutztown University of Pennsylvania. His primary research interests are in nineteenth-century British poetry and psychological approaches to literature and pedagogy. His work has been published in several journals including *Prose Studies*, *Journal of William Morris Studies*, *Evolutionary Review*, *Reader*, and *Journal of Poetry Therapy*.

palgrave
macmillan

Cover Image: Photography by Audrey Rose Photography
Cover design by: Oscar Spigolon

ISBN 978-1-349-34298-3

www.palgrave.com

Uncovering the Traits of Successful Environmental Leaders

ECO WINNERS

KATYA PRONICHENKO